THE REVELS PLAYS

Founder Editor

Clifford Leech 1958–71

General Editors

F. David Hoeniger, E. A. J. Honigmann and J. R. Mulryne

WOMEN BEWARE WOMEN

Women Beware Women

THOMAS MIDDLETON

EDITED BY

J. R. MULRYNE

THE REVELS PLAYS

MANCHESTER
UNIVERSITY PRESS

This edition first published by Methuen & Co. 1975

Reprinted 1981, 1983, 1986
by
Manchester University Press
Oxford Road, Manchester MI3 9PL

ISBN 0 7190 1614 2

ERRATA

p. xiii, l. 22: *for* C.P. *read* C.J.
p. xvi, l. 22: *for* Phillips *read* Phillipps
p. xxviii, l. 11: *for* idiosyncracies *read* idiosyncrasies
p. xliv, fn. 1, l. 4: *for* 79 *read* 70
p. xlv, l. 21, *for* wordly-wise *read* worldly-wise
p. lxiv, l. 9, *for* (80–3) *read* (80–3),
p. lxv, fn. 4, *for The Moral Vision of Jacobean Tragedy read Jacobean Tragedy: The Quest for Moral Order*
p. 14, l. 5, *for* yet. *read* yet?
p. 22, l. 13, *after* SORDIDO *add and* Servant
p. 73, l. 27, *for* headache *read* headache,
p. 116, l. 16, *for* the *read* the wriggling; *for* he *read* he wrigling

Printed and bound in Great Britain by
Biddles Ltd, Guildford and King's Lynn

In memory of T.W.M.

General Editors' Preface

The series known as the Revels Plays was conceived by Clifford Leech. The idea for the series emerged in his mind, as he explained in his preface to the first of the Revels Plays in 1958, from the success of the New Arden Shakespeare. The aim of the new group of texts was 'to apply to Shakespeare's predecessors, contemporaries and successors the methods that are now used in Shakespeare editing'. The plays chosen were to include well known works from the early Tudor period to about 1700, as well as others less familiar but of literary and theatrical merit: 'the plays included,' Leech wrote, 'should be such as to deserve and indeed demand performance.' We owe it to Clifford Leech that the idea became reality. He set the high standards of the series, ensuring that editors of individual volumes produced work of lasting merit, equally useful for teachers and students, theatre directors and actors. Clifford Leech remained General Editor until 1971, supervising the first seventeen volumes to be published.

The Revels Plays are now under the direction of four General Editors, E. A. J. Honigmann, J. R. Mulryne, David Bevington and E. M. Waith. The publishers, originally Methuen, are now Manchester University Press. Despite these changes, the format and essential character of the series will continue, and it is hoped that its editorial standards will be maintained. Except for some work in progress, the General Editors intend, in expanding the series, to concentrate for the immediate future on plays from the period 1558–1642, and may include a small number of non-dramatic works of interest to students of drama. Some slight changes have been forced by considerations of cost. For example, in editions from 1978, notes to the introduction are placed together at the end, not at the foot of the page. Collation and commentary notes will continue, however, to appear on the relevant pages.

The text of each Revels play, in accordance with established practice in the series, is edited afresh from the original text of best authority (in a few instances, texts), but spelling and punctuation are modernised and speech headings are silently made consistent. Elisions in the original are also silently regularised, except where metre would be affected by the change; since 1968 the '-ed' form is used for non-syllabic terminations in past tenses and past participles ('-'d' earlier), and '-èd' for syllabic ('-ed' earlier). The editor emends, as distinct from modernises, his original only in instances where error is patent, or at least very probable, and correction persuasive. Act divisions are given only if they appear in the original or if the structure of the play clearly points to them. Those act and scene divisions not found in the original are provided unobtrusively in small type and in square brackets. Square brackets are also used for any other additions to or changes in the stage directions of the original.

Revels Plays do not provide a variorum collation, but only those variants which require the critical attention of serious textual students. All departures of substance from 'copy-text' are listed, including any relineation and those changes in punctuation which involve to any degree a decision between alternative interpretations; but not such accidentals as turned letters, nor necessarily additions to stage directions whose editorial nature is already made clear by the use of brackets. Press corrections in the 'copy-text' are likewise included. Of later emendations of the text, only those are given which as alternative readings still deserve attention.

One of the hallmarks of the Revels Plays is the thoroughness of their annotations. Besides explaining the meaning of difficult words and passages, the editor provides comments on customs or usage, text or stage-business – indeed, on anything he judges pertinent and helpful. Each volume contains a Glossarial Index to the Commentary, in which particular attention is drawn to meanings for words not listed in *O.E.D.*

The Introduction to a Revels play assesses the authority of the 'copy-text' on which it is based, and discusses the editorial methods employed in dealing with it; the editor also considers his play's date and (where relevant) sources, together with its place in the work of the author and in the theatre of its time. Stage history is offered, and in the case of a play by an author not previously represented in the series a brief biography is given.

It is our hope that plays edited in this fashion will promote further scholarly and theatrical investigation of one of the richest periods in theatrical history.

E. A. J. HONIGMANN
J. R. MULRYNE
DAVID BEVINGTON
EUGENE M. WAITH

Contents

Preface

This edition aims to present an accurate modernized text of *Women Beware Women*, based on the 1657 octavo. An Introduction and Commentary deal with problems of a textual and bibliographical kind, discuss the play's date and sources, and offer a critical approach to a play recognized as a major tragedy of the period. One appendix carries extended translation of possible sources in Italian, printed and manuscript, as well as transcription from a source in English. This is the first time these have been made available in an edited text.

My work on Middleton began at Cambridge under the direction and with the encouragement of Professor M. C. Bradbrook and the late Mr F. L. Lucas. Since then I have imposed upon the interest and patience of students and colleagues at the Shakespeare Institute, University of Birmingham, the University of Edinburgh and the University of California at San Diego and Berkeley: to all of them I am grateful. I am grateful also for critical discussion to Professor Christopher Ricks, then of Worcester College, Oxford; to Professor R. B. Parker of the University of Toronto for comments on the sources; to Wendy Butler and Brian Meeson for information about the staging of the play by the Alumnae Club at Toronto; to the late Professor C. P. Sisson for expert commentary on handwriting; and to Terry Hands of the Royal Shakespeare Company for the opportunity to discuss and help with the Stratford production. I have been greatly assisted by permission to work in the libraries of the University of Cambridge, the British Museum, the Victoria and Albert Museum, Worcester College, Oxford, Trinity College, Cambridge, and the University of Edinburgh; and in the Bodleian Library, the National Library of Scotland, the Bibliothèque de l'Arsenal, Paris, and the Biblioteca Nazionale and the Biblioteca Riccardiana e Moreniana in Florence. Numerous librarians and their staffs in Britain and America have generously answered my queries about copies of the 1657 octavo in their possession. I am especially indebted to Professor Arthur Brown of the University of London for a prolonged loan of his copy of *Two New Playes*. Thanks are also due for research grants to the Universities of Edinburgh, Birmingham and Cambridge. My wife, Eithne, has assisted me greatly with some of the chores of editing. My heaviest debts are however owed to the two General Editors under whom I have worked: to Professor Clifford Leech for his zealous and inspiriting interest and encouragement, and for his scrupulous and unsparing commentary over a number of years, and to Professor David Hoeniger for hastening completion of the work with equally generous and perceptive assistance.

J. R. MULRYNE

University of Edinburgh
September 1973

Abbreviations

(For abbreviations of previous editions of *Women Beware Women* see Intro., pp. xx–xxi)

Abbott	E. A. Abbott, *A Shakespearian Grammar* (new ed. 1878).
Bald	T. Middleton, *A Game at Chesse*, ed. R. C. Bald (Cambridge, 1929).
Beaumont and Fletcher, *Wks*	*Beaumont and Fletcher*, ed. A. R. Waller and Arnold Glover (Cambridge, 1905–12), 10 vols.
Bentley	G. E. Bentley, *The Jacobean and Caroline Stage* (1941–68), 7 vols.
C.B.E.L.	*Cambridge Bibliography of English Literature.*
Chambers, *E.S.*	E. K. Chambers, *The Elizabethan Stage* (1923), 4 vols.
Chapman, *Wks*, *Comedies* Chapman, *Wks*, *Tragedies*	*The Plays and Poems of George Chapman*, ed. Thomas Marc Parrott (1914), 2 vols.
Dekker, *Wks*	*The Dramatic Works of Thomas Dekker*, ed. Fredson Bowers (Cambridge, 1953–61), 4 vols.
Dolmetsch	M. Dolmetsch, *Dances of England and France 1450–1600* (1949).
Ford, *Wks*	*The Dramatic Works of John Ford*, ed. W. Gifford, new ed. A. Dyce (1869), 3 vols.
Greg, *Bibliography*	W. W. Greg, *A Bibliography of the English*

	Printed Drama to the Restoration (1939–59), 4 vols.
Jonson, *Wks*	*Ben Jonson*, ed. C. H. Herford and Percy and Evelyn Simpson (Oxford, 1925–52), 11 vols.
Linthicum	M. Channing Linthicum, *Costume in the Drama of Shakespeare and his Contemporaries* (Oxford, 1936).
Lyly, *Wks*	*The Complete Works of John Lyly*, ed. R. Warwick Bond (Oxford, 1902), 3 vols.
Middleton, *Wks*	*The Works of Thomas Middleton*, ed. A. H. Bullen (1885–7), 8 vols.
M.L.R.	*Modern Language Review.*
Moryson	Fynes Moryson, *Shakespeare's Europe; unpublished chapters of Fynes Moryson's 'Itinerary'*, ed. Charles Hughes (1903).
Moryson, *Itinerary*	Fynes Moryson, *An Itinerary containing his ten yeeres travell* (Glasgow, 1907), 4 vols.
Mulryne	J. R. Mulryne, *A Critical Edition of Thomas Middleton's 'Women Beware Women'*, unpubl. thesis (Cambridge, 1962).
Nares	Robert Nares, *A Glossary . . . of English Authors*, ed. J. O. Halliwell [-Phillips] and T. Wright (1888), 2 vols.
Nashe, *Wks*	*The Works of Thomas Nashe*, ed. R. B. McKerrow (1905–10), 5 vols.
O.E.D.	*Oxford English Dictionary.*
Partridge	Eric Partridge, *Shakespeare's Bawdy* (1947).
P.M.L.A.	*Publications of the Modern Language Association of America.*
P.Q.	*Philological Quarterly.*
R.E.S.	*Review of English Studies.*
S.T.C.	A. W. Pollard, G. R. Redgrave *et al.*, *A Short-Title Catalogue of Books Printed in*

	England, Scotland and Ireland . . . 1475–1640 (1950).
Sugden	E. H. Sugden, *A Topographical Dictionary to the Works of Shakespeare and his Fellow Dramatists* (Manchester, 1925).
Swetnam	Joseph Swetnam, *The araignment of lewde, idle, froward and unconstant women* (1622 ed.).
T.H.	*The True History of the Tragicke Loves of Hipolito and Isabella Neapolitans. Englished* [tr. Alexander Hart ?] (1628).
WBW	*Women Beware Women.*
Webster, *Wks*	*The Complete Works of John Webster*, ed. F. L. Lucas (1927), 4 vols.
Wing, *S.T.C.*	Donald G. Wing, *Short-Title Catalogue of Books Printed in England . . . 1641–1700* (New York, 1945–56), 3 vols.

The titles of Shakespeare's plays are abbreviated as in C. T. Onions' *A Shakespeare Glossary* (ed. 1953); line-numbering and quotations are taken from the Globe Shakespeare (ed. 1864). References to Middleton's other works are from A. H. Bullen, *The Works of Thomas Middleton*, 8 vols. (London, 1885–7). Quotations from plays already published in this series are indicated by 'Revels ed.'.

Introduction

I. THE TEXT

Editions

Women Beware Women survives in a single early text, printed thirty years or more after the play's composition, and thirty years after the death of its author. The octavo *Two New Playes by Thomas Middleton*, published in 1657 by Humphrey Moseley, includes, in addition to the tragedy, Middleton's *More Dissemblers Besides Women.* No further edition appeared until the nineteenth century.

A block entry by Moseley in the Stationers' Register for 9 September 1653 includes the first recorded reference to the play. The relevant portion runs as follows:[1]

> Mr. Moseley Entered also for his Copies the severall Playes following ——— s XX d VI
> [fourteen plays by various authors]
> More Dissemblers besides Women
> A right Woman, or Women beware of Women
> No Witt, no helpe like a Woman—
> The Puritan Maid, modest Wife & Wanton Widdow by ——— Mr. Tho: Midleton

Moseley's entry may indicate that he envisaged a series of Middleton plays on subjects connected with women. It also constitutes sharp practice, for 'A right Woman' has been made to look like an alternative title for *Women Beware Women*, while in fact referring to an entirely different play. Moseley thus secured printing rights in two plays for a single fee.

In preparing the present edition I have collated, at first hand or on microfilm, the following twenty recorded and unrecorded

[1] Transcript from a microfilm of the Stationers' Register, Liber E.

copies of the octavo.[1] (The abbreviations used are in the left-hand column.)

BM 1	British Museum, *643.b.37.*
BM 2	British Museum, King's Library, *162.d.28.*
D 1	Victoria and Albert Museum, Dyce Collection, *D.17.P.28.*
D 2	Victoria and Albert Museum, Dyce Collection, *D.17.P.29.*
Bod 1	Bodleian Library, *Art 8°C.19.BS.*
Bod 2	Bodleian Library, Malone Collection, *Malone 247.*
W	Worcester College, Oxford.
C	Copy owned by the late Colonel Wilkinson, Worcester College, Oxford; sold at Sotheby's on 28 March 1961, to H. M. Fletcher.
Tr	Trinity College, Cambridge, *H.7.65.* (Lacks the O gathering.)
Br	Copy owned by Professor Arthur Brown, University of London. (Lacks everything after N6v.)
Con	Library of Congress, Washington, D.C.
F	Folger Shakespeare Library, Washington, D.C.
Hunt	Henry E. Huntington Library, San Marino, California.
H	Harvard University Library.
Y	Yale University Library.
Pr	Princeton University Library.
T	Texas University Library.
N	Newberry Library, Chicago.
Ch	Chapin Library, Williams College, Williamstown, Mass.
B	Boston Public Library, Massachusetts.

The following later editions have also been collated:

Dilke	*Old English Plays* [ed. C. W. Dilke], Vol. V (London, 1815).[2]
White	*Old English Drama* [ed. T. White], Vol. III (London, 1830).[3]
Dyce	Alexander Dyce, *The Works of Thomas Middleton*, Vol. IV (London, 1840).
Bullen	A. H. Bullen, *The Works of Thomas Middleton*, Vol. VI (London, 1885–7).

[1]Professor Thomas A. Lytle has drawn to my attention a further unrecorded copy of the octavo, now in the library of Massey College, University of Toronto.

[2]No editor's name is given in the original; the ascription here is from Samuel A. Tannenbaum, *Thomas Middleton: A Concise Bibliography*, Elizabethan Bibliographies, 13 (New York, 1940) p. 8.

[3]The ascription is again from Tannenbaum, p. 8. *C.B.E.L.*, I, 488 says that White was 'perhaps' the editor.

Ellis Havelock Ellis, *The Best Plays of the Old Dramatists: Thomas Middleton*, Vol. I (Mermaid series, London, 1887).

Jacobs Elizabeth R. Jacobs, *A Critical Edition of Thomas Middleton's 'Women Beware Women'* (Ph.D. thesis, University of Wisconsin, 1941).

Oliphant E. H. C. Oliphant, *Shakespeare and His Fellow Dramatists*, Vol. II (New York, 1929).

Parker R. Brian Parker, *A Critical Edition of Thomas Middleton's 'Women Beware Women'* (M.A. thesis, University of Liverpool, 1957).

Reference is made in the collation (under 'Lamb') to the extracts from *Women Beware Women* among Charles Lamb's *Specimens*, but only when Lamb's emendations are of special interest.[1] I have also used Charles Barber's edition (Fountainwell Drama Texts, Edinburgh, 1969), and Roma Gill's (The New Mermaids, London, 1968). The play appears in *Jacobean Tragedies* edited by A. H. Gomme (Oxford Paperbacks, London, 1969). Middleton quotations in my Introduction and Commentary are from Bullen, since his is the only complete edition that includes line-numbering; most of the important corrections to *Women Beware Women* were however made by Dilke and some years later by Dyce.

The publisher and the manuscript

No good reason has been uncovered for the more than thirty-year delay between the composition of *Women Beware Women* and its publication. It is tempting to guess that the players were unwilling to allow into print one of their best properties.[2] Yet, apart from Nathaniel Richards's assurance of the play's popularity, in his commendatory verses, we have no evidence that it was played at

[1]Charles Lamb, *Specimens of English Dramatic Poets*, London Library edition, n.d. pp. 125–9.

[2]When Middleton as a professional playwright submitted his manuscript to the company, the company gained full rights. As was often the case, they may not have wished to have the play published and thus made available to rival companies. In this connection it is relevant to note that of Middleton's later plays only *A Game at Chess* was published during his life-time. Several other plays, including *The Changeling*, were first printed between 1653 and 1662.

this time. *Women Beware Women* may have been disliked, the players may have lost the prompt copy, the piece may have run into political trouble;[1] we have no way of knowing.

How Moseley acquired the manuscript along with other Middleton items, we again cannot be certain. He may however have obtained it from Nathaniel Richards. The evidence is slender but appealing. First, while Moseley issued more than thirty dramatic items, only five of these, including the Middleton octavo, carry any kind of introductory or commendatory verses.[2] Each of the other four was a special publication, calling for specially-commissioned verses, and not a run-of-the-mill volume like the Middleton octavo. To ask Richards to introduce this volume may therefore imply that he had a special connection with it. Moreover, Richards writes of one only of the two plays in the volume; though his verses immediately precede *More Dissemblers Besides Women* he makes no reference to the comedy. Add to this that Richards seems to be quoting from *Women Beware Women* at four widely-scattered points in his published works,[3] and it begins to look as though he may have owned a manuscript of the play which he now sold to Moseley. The facts will bear other interpretations, but given Middleton's known willingness, in the case of *The Witch* and *A Game At Chess* at least, to copy his plays for his friends, or to have them copied, we may think the same happened here.

[1]This possibility is discussed below, p. xxxvii.

[2]See Greg, *Bibliography*, III, 1530 and the discussions of the thirty-three plays and collections in Bentley and in Chambers, *E.S.* Only extant plays are counted and collections are regarded as one item each; the Beaumont and Fletcher folio, an altogether larger undertaking, is not included. The four exceptional productions are: *Medea*, translated by 'E.S.' [Sir Edward Sherburne, according to John Curtis Reed, 'Humphrey Moseley, Publisher', *The Oxford Bibliographical Society: Proceedings and Papers*, II (1927–30), 57–142.]; *The Wild Goose Chase*, with five sets of verses celebrating the recovery of the long-lost manuscript; Brome's *Five New Playes*, a fairly substantial undertaking with three sets of verses; *Mirza* 'A Tragedie, Really acted in Persia in the last age' with five sets of verses.

[3]The reminiscences, which are all close, come in the preface to *Messalina* and in *Poems sacred and satyricall* (1641) pp. 37, 111 and 149. Details in Mulryne, I, ii–iv.

The printer and his copy

Two New Playes was published without a printer's name, but it can readily be shown that the printer was Thomas Newcomb.[1] Newcomb's ornament stock has been studied in detail by C. William Miller,[2] and it is Miller's 'Ornament 15' that appears on both the *More Dissemblers* and *Women Beware Women* title-pages. A precisely similar horizontal flaw proves that the ornament used in the Middleton octavo is that employed in at least seven other Newcomb-printed books between 1650 and 1666, three of them (1655–7) published by Moseley.[3]

The relatively sophisticated printing-techniques of the later seventeenth century, especially in a large shop like Newcomb's, make it difficult to detect the nature of underlying copy. *Women Beware Women* is, however, an especially 'clean' text, pointing to a legible, well-organized manuscript.[4] And there is evidence that the manuscript was not thoroughly readied for performance. In the printed text, Isabella is designated '*Neece*' in speech-prefixes throughout I.ii., though she is thereafter consistently given '*Isab.*': we might expect a stage manuscript to avoid this sort of confusion. Again, stage-directions in the early scenes read like an author's attempt to indicate who exactly is who:[5]

Enter Hippolito, *and* Isabella *the Neece.* (I. ii. 69.1)
Enter the Ward with a Trap-stick, and Sordido *his man.* (I. ii. 87.1)
Enter Hippolito, *and Lady* Livia *the Widow.* (II. i. 0.1)

[1]See Henry R. Plomer, *A Dictionary of the Booksellers and Printers who were at work in England, Scotland and Ireland from 1641–1667* (1907). Newcomb printed much of the Commonwealth literature and was later involved in some of the most ambitious pieces of seventeenth-century printing. In 1668 he was returned as owning three presses and a proof press, and employing seven compositors, five pressmen and one apprentice.

[2]C. William Miller, 'Thomas Newcomb: A Restoration Printer's Ornament Stock', *SB*, III (1950–51), 155–70.

[3]The seven titles are those listed in Wing, *STC* under numbers L129, D325, H360, C581, B3334, M1985, H2631.

[4]There is only one possible area of serious textual confusion, at II.ii. 404–9; see commentary.

[5]These directions are quoted in the form in which they appear in the octavo, except for typographical lay-out.

Neither of these features is decisive against underlying copy being a stage-manuscript; more telling are the directions that fail to be specific about the action for which they call:

> *Enter two or three Boys, and a Citizen or two, with an Apprentice.* (I. iii. 72.1)
> *Enter in great state the Duke and* Brancha, *richly attir'd, with Lords, Cardinals, Ladies, and other Attendants.* (IV. iii. 0.1–3)
> *Enter above . . . other Cardinals, Lords and Ladies in State.* (V. ii. 0.1–2)

A producer would require to know exactly *how many* boys, citizens, cardinals and attendants to have on stage. He would also expect more exact directions than this text gives for the two processions (I. iii. 101.1–3 and IV. iii. 0.1–4) and for the masque. Taken together with the lack of a few necessary exits, one important entrance (at III. ii. 27.1) and directions for an essential incident in the masque (at V. ii. 117.1–2), these features argue against copy originating in the theatre.

Newcomb therefore probably worked either with a carefully-prepared set of foul papers,[1] or with fair copy transcribed from these. A few features indicate, however, that his manuscript may have been lightly marked by a theatre-official. Some stage-directions in the octavo stand out from the rest by virtue of their phrasing and typographical arrangement:

(a) H3v ——*Brancha* and Mother above.	(b) I5v *Table and* – – *Chess*
(c) I8r ——*Duke above*	(d) O v *Cupids* shoot:

Each of these has the curtness of notes added by prompter or book-keeper to the extant dramatic manuscripts; the directions for action 'above', for example, lack the conventional '*Enter*' prefixed to every other entrance in the play, including some 'above'. The typography of these directions is also unusual. Except for the

[1]Using Fredson Bowers' definition: 'the author's last complete draft in a shape satisfactory to him to be transferred to fair copy.' (*On Editing Shakespeare and the Elizabethan Dramatists*, U. of Pennsylvania, 1955, p. 13.)

mistaken setting of two character-names in italic,[1] and one exit in roman,[2] the octavo's absolute consistency in using correct-fount type for stage-directions is broken twice only: in directions (a) and (d) cited above. Both completely reverse normal practice, setting roman for italic and vice-versa. This break with established working may be due to a compositor's attempt to reproduce manuscript characteristics: to copy, perhaps, italic insertions in Middleton's secretary-script text. Further, the dashes preceding directions (a) and (c), and the double hyphen incorporated in (b), are also unique in the volume: they might, conceivably, represent the strokes sometimes found before prompter's stage-directions in the extant manuscripts.[3] Direction (b), finally, reads very like a prompter's note of required properties;[4] it may anticipate the appearance of the 'Table and Chess' by seventy-five lines, and may have served as warning to have these properties ready.

Some of the play's directions for music may lend support to this theory. Most requests for music figure as part of longer stage-directions, presumably Middleton's, but three of the more laconic requests may derive from manuscript insertions:

(a) L1v *Cornets ?*

(b) N4v *Hoboys.*
Scaen 3. *Enter . . .*

(c) N6v *Florish:*
Scaen 2. *Enter . . .*

Both (b) and (c) are set above the direction for the opening of a new scene, at the left-hand margin. Although the musical effects certainly relate to the coming entrances, neither direction is placed as if this were the case, (c) in particular being situated far above the following group-entrance. Presumably Newcomb's compositor is here reproducing the lay-out of his copy, suggesting that these music-directions have been written-in after the main

1On H6v (II.i.62.1) and K2r (II.ii.419.1).

2On H5r (I.iii.101.3).

3In, for example, *Sir John Van Olden Barnavelt*; see Greg, *Documents*, I, 229 and the illustration in the second volume, specimen pages of prompt books, number 5.

4Compare Greg's discussion of *Believe as You List* and especially of the book-keeper's insertions in *The Captives* (Greg, *Sh. First Folio*, 133–4 and 141).

text. Direction (a) is unusual not only because of its abruptness (elsewhere directions read '*Cornets flourish*'), but also because of the question mark; conceivably this may represent an annotator's way of calling attention to one of his insertions.[1]

A Middleton holograph, lightly marked for performance, seems, then, a plausible hypothesis. Yet it may be that Newcomb worked with a scribal transcript from such a manuscript. A few features of Newcomb's text recall the work of the scrivener Ralph Crane.[2] Crane's favourite punctuation, the round bracket, occurs fifty-three times in *Women Beware Women*, but far less often in the other Middleton plays Newcomb printed for Moseley: thirteen times in *The Changeling*, ten times in *No Wit, No Help*, and thirteen times in *More Dissemblers Besides Women*. Also, a number of the octavo's spellings, where they depart from standard practice, look more like Crane's idiosyncrasies than Middleton's,[3] and a number of the play's typographical oddities compare interestingly with Crane's practice. In his *Game at Chess* manuscripts, Crane twice places directions for '— Musick' above and to the left of a main entrance direction, and he frequently prefixes a dash to entrances and exits, two peculiarities just noted in Newcomb's printed text.[4] On two other occasions Crane has 'reades' above and to the left of matter read aloud, using both times (contrary to his usual italic practice) a secretary script matching that of the main text;[5] on N7v the octavo prints 'Reads', using a roman fount, at the left-hand margin above the 'Argument' read out by the Duke. All of these are mere hints that Crane may have transcribed Middleton's manuscript, but then one would not expect to find clearer indications in a text so much given to tidying-up as New-

[1]Middleton himself, however, closes one of the directions in the holograph *Game at Chess* with an exclamation mark. See '*A Game at Chesse*' *by Thomas Middleton* ed. R. C. Bald (Cambridge, 1929) p. 73.

[2]For Crane, see F. P. Wilson, 'Ralph Crane, Scrivener to the King's Players', *The Library*, Fourth Series, September 1926, pp. 194–215.

[3]A comparison of distinctive Middleton and Crane spellings is given in Mulryne, II, 249–54.

[4]The Crane manuscripts are MS. Lansdowne 690 in the British Museum and MS. Malone 25 in the Bodleian.

[5]On one of these occasions the holograph has '*the Letter*', and on the other no direction.

comb's. Remembering that Crane prepared transcripts of Middleton's *Game at Chess* and *The Witch*, an editor will allow for the possibility that his familiar sophistications underlie the printed text.[1]

To sum up: the textual authority of the 1657 *Women Beware Women* may derive immediately from Middleton's autograph, with, perhaps, some slight attention from a theatre-official; equally, such a manuscript may have been copied by a professional scribe before reaching Newcomb's shop. Either inference would accord with the theory that Moseley received the manuscript from Nathaniel Richards, who in turn had it from Middleton.

The printing process

Two New Playes was printed in a shop just becoming one of the most important in London, and its typographical features reflect this situation. There are no signs of shortages of type or attempts to save paper, and the lay-out is efficient if not handsome.[2] Presswork is generally good, though there are cases of double-impression or slurring, and inking is sometimes uneven. Overall, the octavo is a good example of the carefully-produced cheaper book of the 1650's.

Newcomb's compositors worked to a standard of consistency in spelling and presentation that makes it difficult to apply the usual techniques of compositor analysis. Inference suggests, however, that as many as four compositors worked on the *Women Beware Women* gatherings. For example, gatherings I and K have a large number of round brackets (thirty-one as compared with

[1]Charles Barber (Fountainwell Drama Texts edition pp. 12–15) shows that the octavo's spellings are not Middleton's; but one would expect this, given the compositors' habit of 'modernizing' their copy. Barber's 'working hypothesis' is that 'the printer's copy was a scribal transcription made specially for the purpose in the 1650's.' I can find no evidence that any transcription belongs to the 1650's. For a full discussion of Middleton's manuscript practices see Bald.

[2]The double-column printing of song and dialogue on L4 and L4v (III. iii. 143–56) is better explained as a literal-minded attempt to reproduce copy, than as an effort to save paper: the song may have been written or pasted into the manuscript after the main body of the text.

twenty-two in the other five-and-a-half gatherings),[1] and entirely lack irregular and redundant apostrophes, a feature of the rest of the text. Gatherings L and N, in contrast, have eighteen of these apostrophes, out of twenty-four in the whole play. Spelling tests, though of limited usefulness, confirm the I/K and L/N groupings. The M gathering is distinguished by two punctuation-practices difficult to quantify but obvious to an eye accustomed to Newcomb's text: the workman here sets a comma where others use a semicolon, and he sets an unusually high proportion of illogical full stops; his is perhaps the most distinctive 'style'. Gatherings G and H show few of the idiosyncracies of the other gatherings and may have been set by another and careful workman. A tentative division of work would be: GH; IK; LNO; M. The breakdown into gatherings, the absence of any evidence to suggest cast-off copy, and the possible use of four compositors would all be consistent with the setting of an unimportant volume in a large shop; the compositors might be employed on *Women Beware Women* when they could be spared from more prestigious or urgent tasks.

Analysis of *Women Beware Women* running-titles confirms that work on the volume was leisurely.[2] The press (or presses) stood idle, for a short time at least, after the H gathering was wrought off, since both formes of I use titles from both formes of H. In the L, M and N gatherings work proceeded more deliberately still, on a single press, with titles transferred between the two formes of a single gathering. Delays occurred, that is, between the printing of one *forme* and the next. Any errors in the octavo text probably arose therefore from causes other than hasty workmanship.

Collation of twenty copies shows that press-correction took place on the inner formes of the H, I and M gatherings, and, just

[1]The uneven distribution may indicate that even more of Crane's favourite brackets appeared in the copy, and that some compositors edited them out. The opposite possibility, that the compositor of I and K added brackets to copy is less likely; I have found few uses of this device in the other Newcomb-printed plays.

[2]For detailed evidence see Mulryne, 'Half-sheet Imposition and Running-title Transfer in *Two New Playes by Thomas Middleton*, 1657', *The Library*, xxx (1975).

possibly, on inner G.[1] Of the sixty-two corrections, over three-quarters deal with punctuation, two with capitalization, three with spelling and one with word-division. Three changes only affect meaning: 'Simplicities' becomes 'Simplicitie', 'honor' becomes 'honor's', 'If' becomes 'Of'. Clearly the press-corrector saw his task as having as much to do with typographical correctness as with correct meaning. There is no evidence that he consulted copy.

This Edition

The text of this edition is based on the octavo of 1657. I have been conservative over substantive readings, for it seems clear that the octavo prints in substantive matters very much what Middleton wrote. I have therefore sometimes rejected emendations by previous editors.[2] I have emended, however, where I thought suspect readings can be explained by compositor error: the octavo shows all the familiar types of error arising from omission, anticipation, substitution, foul case, and context-influence. While it was not possible to construct a detailed profile of individual compositors, I have been able to use in a general way my knowledge of these compositors' practices. I have also brought to bear a knowledge of Middleton's writing habits, and where it seemed warranted, of Crane's, whenever an error might be explained as misreading of copy. Emendations are recorded in the collation, and the more important discussed in the commentary; the more defensible emendations by previous editors are also recorded and sometimes discussed.

Spelling has been silently modernized, following the practice of this series, with only rare exception. I have departed liberally from the octavo's punctuation, aiming at a modern pointing suitably light for a text composed for acting rather than reading. Such departure is justified, for the octavo's punctuation is patently not Middleton's. Middleton prefers commas and semi-colons (even ending a scene in *A Game at Chess* with a semi-colon)[3] while

[1]A list of press-variants appears in Appendix III.
[2]See collation at e.g. I. ii. 56; II. i. 60; III. iii. 304; V. ii. 215.
[3]See *Game at Chesse*, ed. R. C. Bald, p. 172.

the octavo freely uses the heavier stops; and in general the punctuation-practices are rather unlike Middleton's, and, for that matter, rather unlike Crane's, except in regard to the brackets. In all probability, the punctuation is largely that of Newcomb's compositors. Sometimes an editor can plainly detect the compositors at work re-punctuating their copy. In at least fifteen instances they can be seen punctuating evidently for the sake of making sense of the line or two in hand, without paying attention to, and sometimes making nonsense of, the larger context.[1] Middleton's own punctuation is of course irrecoverable, and since his syntax is frequently difficult, even untidy, I have given the reader the assistance of a familiar modern punctuation.

The stage-directions of the 1657 text, on the other hand, seem likely to preserve Middleton's intentions well, and they have thus been followed in this edition except for normalizing typography and except for placing them according to the conventions of the Revels series. The octavo hardly does justice however to Middleton's intentions for the masque in Act V. Here the directions are extremely sparse, and I have added a number of important directions, including one derived from a seventeenth-century annotation in the Yale copy of the octavo.[2] All editorial additions to the stage-directions are enclosed in square brackets, and are usually not collated; changes in the stage directions are collated. Speech-headings are silently normalized.

Lineation poses a special problem in Middleton. Following the practice of the Revels editions of *The Changeling* and *A Chaste Maid in Cheapside*, I have avoided silting up the collation of this edition with numerous lineation-changes. They are instead brought together in Appendix II. The octavo's errors arise, probably, from the compositor's inability (or the scribe's) to follow Middleton's puzzling manuscript practice, especially his

[1]See, for example, I. iii. 37–9n. Newcomb's men may have used a 'visorum', a double piece of card or light wood clasping the copy and moved down it a line or a few lines at a time as an aid to place-finding. The compositor would punctuate without knowing what was in the lines to come.

[2]See V. ii. 117.1–2n., and Mulryne, 'Annotations in Some Copies of *Two New Playes by Thomas Middleton*, 1657', *The Library*, xxx (1975).

habit of beginning a verse-line with a lower-case letter.[1] While correcting obvious errors, however, I have thought it wrong to normalize on every occasion on which the octavo prints irregular verse. Sometimes one finds a line of fourteen or more syllables, sometimes a short passage in verse or prose within a scene predominantly in the opposite medium. On the face of it, these look like compositor, or scribal, error. Bullen and Dyce, and often later editors, print the extra-long line as a line-and-a-half. But this seems to me misleading, for the reader expects some emotional or theatrical sense in the heavy pause that follows the broken line; and is disappointed. Even more, I think it wrong to bring isolated outcrops of verse or prose into conformity with the usual practice of the scene in hand, as previous editors usually do.[2] Middleton appears to have aimed at a kind of 'continuous decorum' in his handling of dramatic speech, tightening and relaxing the movement of his language as the dramatic situation directed. These outcrops of verse or prose are often anticipated by an appropriate shift towards formality or relaxation in the preceding speech or speeches. It seems reasonable therefore to preserve in a modern text what look like intentional characteristics. Occasionally the movement between verse and prose occurs *within* a single speech, and I have wherever possible preserved this unusual feature, even at the cost of rather odd-looking typography.[3] I have not, however, adopted these practices rigidly, accepting sometimes the lineation of the octavo, itself an edited text, or of Dyce, when a good case could have been made for a less orthodox typographical arrangement. In every instance I had in mind the convenience of a reader accustomed to modern editions of Jacobean plays: where I thought I could easily bring out Middleton's skilled attention to the rhythms of the theatre, I have done so; but where I thought this

[1]See Bald, *op. cit.* p. 35.

[2]This kind of editing began early. At *Game at Chess* V. iii. 205 ff. Middleton arranges the text as prose in both Trinity and Huntington manuscripts; Crane alters to verse (Lansdowne manuscript) as, with a different lineation, does the second 'good' quarto. Bald also prefers verse: using yet another line-arrangement.

[3]See, for example, II. ii. 86–92, and other editors' arrangements in Appendix II.

would merely puzzle the reader I have set the speech regularly.

2. DATE

A date for *Women Beware Women* has never been firmly established. The task is made difficult by uncertainties over the chronology of Middleton's work as a whole—which makes metrical tests virtually unusable—by the absence of a clear pattern of development in Middleton's dramaturgy, and by the self-contained nature of *Women Beware Women*, with no indisputable reference to contemporary events. The result has been informed argument for dates ranging from 1613 to 1627, with a balance in favour of the early 1620's.

F. G. Fleay first suggested an early date, placing the tragedy

> provisionally in 1613 on account of the devil with one eye and fireworks at his tail in 'the last Triumph', V. i.[1], which seems to allude to Envy and the fireworks in Dekker's *London Triumphing*, the pageant of 1612. The Ward has a part in the Mask, and plays Slander. Dekker's *Triumph* has Calumny in it.[2]

Fleay had in mind *Troia-Nova Triumphans*, or *London Triumphing*, Dekker's pageant published in 1612. The 'third device' of this involves a 'Forlorne Castle', over which Envy presides as 'chiefe Commandresse'; at the gates stand Riot and Calumny 'in the shape of Gyants, with clubs'.[3] Envy's attack on the passing chariot of Virtue brings about some use of fireworks. It is true therefore that play and masque employ similar emblematic figures; Fleay's point might even be strengthened by noticing that Bianca refers (V. ii. 45–7) not only to 'slander' (the Ward's part) but also to 'envy' in a way that suggests she may have had pageant figures in mind. It is true also that fireworks are common to both Middleton and Dekker. But Dekker has no hint of the grotesque figure—with one eye and with fireworks at his tail—nor of the stage-business—involving this figure rising from a trap-door—which alone would suggest a probable connection between the two

[1] The reference is to V. i. 7–9.
[2] *A Biographical Chronicle of the English Drama* (1891), II, 97.
[3] Quotations are from Dekker, *Wks*, III, 229–47.

works. And even if we did want to believe that Middleton was influenced by Dekker, we could reconcile our belief to a date in the 1620's by supposing that after appointment as Chronologer for the City of London in September 1620 Middleton spent a little time reviewing City pageants then in print, and felt attracted and impressed by a piece of work published in 1612 by his former collaborator.[1]

Fleay's date was accepted by Schelling[2] and more recently by Jackson I. Cope ('1613 or 1614'), who finds parallels between *Women Beware Women* and a Middleton masque of 1613, *The Triumphs of Truth.*[3] Cope's parallels centre on references in play and masque to the blinding mists of error and ignorance. He cites from the masque about a dozen instances of mists-concealing-truth, with the mists sometimes described as 'poisonous' or 'infectious'; he also cites a stage-direction describing the entry of Error with 'his head rolled in a cloud, over which stands an owl, a mole on one shoulder, a bat on the other, all symbols of blind ignorance and darkness, mists hanging at his eyes.'[4] Among the few passages from *Women Beware Women* using a similar language-pattern the closest parallel comes at II. ii. 420–3:

> Now bless me from a blasting; I saw that now
> Fearful for any woman's eye to look on.
> Infectious mists and mildews hang at 's eyes,
> The weather of a doomsday dwells upon him.

Relying on this and other (less striking) parallels, Cope maintains that 'it is hardly credible he [Middleton] would have deliberately looked back in order to adapt a minor masque he had composed some ten to fifteen years before undertaking his great tragedy. The only reasonable inference that remains to be drawn . . . is that *Women Beware Women* was written a short time after or before

[1] Middleton seems to have taken the position seriously, at least to begin with. See R. C. Bald, 'Middleton's Civic Employments' *M.P.* XXXI (1933), 65–78.

[2] Felix E. Schelling, *Elizabethan Drama 1558–1642* (New York 1959), I, 586.

[3] 'The Date of Middleton's *Women Beware Women*', *M.L.N.* LXXVI (1961), 295–300.

[4] Middleton, *Wks*, VII, 241.

The Triumphs of Truth.' But Cope's inference is at the least debatable, and rests on a supposition about Middleton's writing habits that is far from proven. The most one can say is that Middleton was twice thinking along similar lines, but whether within a short space of time or at widely separated dates remains an open question.[1]

The evidence for a date in the 1620's is almost equally slight, but does coincide with most critics' view that *Women Beware Women* comes late in Middleton's work, an opinion confirmed in a general way by metrical tests, so far as these can be applied.[2]

Baldwin Maxwell has offered what he takes to be two clear allusions to people and events outside the play; 'allusions which, if they do not argue for the year 1621, would at least seem to permit no greater extension beyond late 1620 and early 1622'.[3] One of these is mistaken. Maxwell associates I. ii. 59–61 with the Virginia Company's despatch of sixty young women to the New World between July and November 1621, as wives for the colonists. But, as Elizabeth R. Jacobs points out, similar voyages had been made previously; and Middleton speaks of hasty marriage *before* setting out for the New World, not of young women going there to be married.[4] Maxwell's other allusion deserves more notice. King James was fifty-five on 19 June 1621; Maxwell thinks Middleton refers to the king at I. iii. 89–93:

[1]Cope notices, but does not develop, a number of parallels between *Women Beware Women* and Jonson's *Masque of Hymen.* See notes at IV. ii. 219, V. ii. 50.1, 70, 97.1, 117.1–2 and 138.

[2]A comparison of the metrical characteristics of *Women Beware Women*, *The Changeling* and *A Game at Chess* appears in Mulryne, II, xviii.

[3]'The Date of Middleton's *Women Beware Women*', *P.Q.*, XXII (1943), 338–42.

[4]'A Critical Edition of Thomas Middleton's *Women Beware Women*' unpubl. diss. (Wisconsin, 1941) p. lxxv. Miss Jacobs refers to an entry in Susan Kingsbury, *Records of the Virginia Company of London* (Washington, 1934), III, 115 recording the sending of ninety 'young maids' to Virginia in 1619. Maxwell himself (*Studies in Beaumont, Fletcher and Massinger*, Chapel Hill, 1939, p. 158) refers to a 1618 project by a 'scoundrel named Robinson' to send (or be paid for not sending) rich yeomen's daughters as marriage partners to Virginia. A close parallel to the *Women Beware Women* passage comes in *The Roaring Girl* (dated by Bald 1607 or 1608) III. iii. 71; Middleton, *Wks*, IV, 52.

Moth. . . . now you shall see
Our Duke, a goodly gentleman of his years.
Bian. Is he old then?
Moth. About some fifty-five.
Bian. That's no great age in man, he's then at best
For wisdom, and for judgement.

Certainly it would be characteristic of Middleton to flatter James: his 1618 pamphlet *The Peace-Maker Or Great Britain's Blessing*[1] is conceived in this spirit. A few lines earlier (I. iii. 47–8) James's reputation as a peace-maker may well be glanced at. It is not, I think, a valid argument to say that James would resent being compared to the libertine Duke, for the lines in question come when all is pageantry and praise—the Mother heaps further compliment on the Duke a little later (ll. 108–11). Maxwell pursues his argument by saying that while Middleton cites a correct age for Bianca ('about sixteen'), the Duke of history was twenty-three when he met her and was dead at forty-six; Middleton must therefore have altered history to compliment the fifty-five year-old James. But none of the possible sources I have seen (see below) indicates the Duke's age, and one of them, Fynes Moryson's *Itinerary*, suggests a man in his middle or late years.[2] Yet, even if Middleton did not alter his sources in the way Maxwell presumes, the allusion to fifty-five is very specific and the connection with James remains a plausible one.[3]

Several references in the text suggest that Middleton may be glancing at the controversy over women that went on between the

[1]The pamphlet was first attributed to Middleton by Bullen (in Middleton, *Wks*, I, xlv–xlvi); the attribution is confirmed, but with a few passages assigned to Bacon, in Rhodes Dunlap, 'James I, Bacon, Middleton and the making of *The Peace-Maker*', *Studies in the English Renaissance Drama*, ed. Josephine W. Bennett *et al.* (New York, 1959), pp. 82–94.

[2]A careful reader of some of the manuscripts might, it is true, work out the Duke's age from the non-Malespini part of the story. But neither Maxwell nor I have clear proof that Middleton saw such a manuscript.

[3]Maxwell's case may be slightly strengthened by a somewhat similar allusion, this time to a fifty-year-old, in Middleton's *No Wit, No Help like a Woman's*, dated by Bald 'c. 1615': 'What's fifty years? 'tis man's best time and season' (II. i. 412, Middleton, *Wks*. IV, 337).

Overbury scandal in 1613 and the years 1620–21.[1] The play's title is easily explained in terms of its plot, but just possibly it derives its exact form from a popular literary skirmish within the general women-controversy. At the climax of this, one Joseph Swetnam, the author in 1615 of a pamphlet attacking 'lewd, idle, froward and unconstant women', was taken to task on the stage in a romantic tragi-comedy called *Swetnam the woman-hater arraigned by women.* Middleton's title is just conceivably indebted to a line in this play. At a highpoint of the action, the closing lines of Act three, scene one, Misogynous declares:

And Fortune, if thou be'st a deitie,
Give me but opportunity, that I
May all the follies of your Sex declare,
That henceforth Men of Women may beware.[2]

The Swetnam play was first performed, so far as we know, in 1617 or 1618, and was published in 1620.[3] If Middleton is in fact adapting one of its more memorable lines, he would be more likely to do so close upon the date of performance and publication than in later years.

Several scholars prefer a date later than Maxwell's 1621/2. L. L. Brodwin believes her critical analysis of Middleton's late plays shows that *Women Beware Women* belongs to 1623.[4] Oliphant, Bentley and, with more hesitation Miss Jacobs, think the tragedy may have been Middleton's last play, coming after *The Changeling* (1622) and *A Game at Chess* (1624).[5] Both Miss Jacobs

[1]See for example notes at III. iv. 27–9, III. iv. 67 and IV. i. 207–14. F. L. Lucas (Webster, *Wks*, II. 215–16) quotes a letter from Chamberlain to Carleton, 12 February 1620: 'our Pulpits ring continually of the insolence and impudence of Women; and to help forward, the Players have likewise taken them to task.' Louis B. Wright, *Middle-Class Culture in Elizabethan England* (Ithaca, N.Y., 1958) p. 492, says that the controversy over women, dormant for a time, broke out 'with increased fury in 1620'.

[2]Ed. Alexander B. Grosart (Blackburn, 1880) pp. 37–8.

[3]Wright (*Middle-Class Culture*, p. 492) dates the play 1620; the dates of performance are given in Bentley, V, 1416–18.

[4]See L. L. Brodwin, *Elizabethan Love Tragedy 1587–1625* (London and New York, 1972) p. 392.

[5]See E. H. C. Oliphant, ed., *Shakespeare and His Fellow Dramatists* (New York, 1929) II, 948; Bentley IV, 906; Elizabeth R. Jacobs, *op. cit.* in note 4, p. xxxiv.

and Bald[1] argue *against* such a view that, since no record of the play's licensing has been preserved, it probably antedates the first entries in Sir Henry Herbert's office-book in 1622. But this is false, for Malone and Chalmers reproduced only a selection of Herbert's entries, and 'not even all these got into print in the *Variorum* or in Chalmers's *Apology*';[2] the licensing entry could very well have since disappeared. A further argument against a late date is somewhat difficult to assess. Miss Jacobs and R. B. Parker[3] suggest that *Women Beware Women* would have been politically incautious after 1624, when negotiations began for a marriage between Henrietta Maria, a granddaughter of Francesco de' Medici, and the future Charles I of England. Certainly if an audience, or the Master of the Revels, were to realize that Middleton's Duke and Charles's prospective bride were, in history, blood-relations, it might be indiscreet to put the play before them during or just after 1624. But Middleton does not name his Duke, and only rather conscientious enquiry would first establish the Duke's identity and then link him with Henrietta Maria. Further, we have no record of *Women Beware Women* in performance at this date, perhaps for the very reason that it was found unwelcome: Middleton might have written the play after 1624 and had it disallowed. On the whole, however, it seems reasonable to suppose, as Parker does, that after the row over the *Game at Chess* Middleton would not again risk the anger of his superiors, particularly as this time he would offend his own patrons, and not only a rather widely-disliked foreign ambassador.

On balance, the few years before 1624 offer a more probable date than those after. Accordingly, Maxwell's identification of the

[1]R. C. Bald, 'The Chronology of Middleton's Plays,' *M.L.R.*, XXXII (1937), 33–43.

[2]Bentley, IV, 906. Bald recognizes that entries are selective but 'cannot help believing that if the play had been mentioned in Herbert's Office Book . . . Malone would have preserved some record of the fact.' This, however, presumes Malone, like Bald, cared about *Women Beware Women*, even though the play seems not to be mentioned between Langbaine and Lamb.

[3]R. Brian Parker, 'A Critical Edition of Thomas Middleton's *Women Beware Women*', unpubl. diss. (Liverpool, 1957).

reference to James may well be correct, and 1621 the actual date of composition or performance.

3. SOURCES

Women Beware Women draws on continental-European rather than English sources. The main plot derives from semi-fictionalized Italian history of the sort which provided Webster with material for *The White Devil*. The sub-plot comes from a French romance. Middleton's technical skill shows in the neatness with which he dovetails the two narratives; his preoccupations as a moralist show in his transforming the sensationalism of the Italian story, and the sentimentalism of the French, into an analysis of a corrupt society.

(*i*) *The Sources of the Main Plot*

The main plot is based on fact. Middleton's Duke is Francesco de' Medici (1541–87), second Grand Duke of Tuscany;[1] Bianca is Bianca Cappello, Francesco's mistress and, in time, consort. The Cardinal is Ferdinand de' Medici, Francesco's brother and successor. Leantio, Guardiano, the Mother, Livia and Hippolito are all identifiable men and women of late sixteenth-century Florence. The plot too corresponds to history, at least in a general way. Yet the people of *Women Beware Women* and their affairs differ from those of history, as a brief summary of the real Francesco and Bianca shows.

Bianca was born in Venice in 1548, daughter of a rich patrician, Bartolommeo Cappello. In the summer of 1563 she met a young Florentine named Pietro Buonaventura. The two eloped on the night of 28 November, 1563, making for Florence, and were married there on 12 December. A decree of the Venetian Council of Ten (10 December, 1563), secured by Bartolommeo, placed a price on their heads.[2] They appealed to the Florentine authorities for protection.

[1]Also the Duke in Webster's *The White Devil*.

[2]Pietro was to be brought back to Venice and executed. A translation of the decree is printed in T. A. Trollope, *A Decade of Italian Women* (1859), II, 221.

Francesco, eldest son of Cosimo de' Medici, first Grand Duke of Tuscany, was born in 1541. He was thus seven years older than Bianca. Educated in the court of Spain, he returned to Florence in September 1563, a few months before the arrival of Bianca and Pietro. His father resigned most of his powers to Francesco in June 1564, and in the same year, the young Duke met Bianca. She became his mistress. In January 1566, Francesco married Giovanna, daughter of Ferdinand I of Austria. For twelve years wife and mistress plotted and quarrelled, until in April 1578 Giovanna died. Six years earlier, in August 1572, Pietro had been assassinated. Francesco and Bianca married secretly in June 1578, and publicly on 12 October, 1579. In October 1587, at the ducal villa of Poggio a Caiano, Francesco and Bianca fell ill and died, within a short time of each other. Among the guests at the villa was Bianca's bitterest enemy, the Cardinal Ferdinand de' Medici, Francesco's younger brother. Ferdinand succeeded to the title.

Bianca's story is, from any point of view, a dramatic one. Its main difficulty is that it is dramatic on too generous a scale. There are at least four separate stories, each with its separate group of characters and each with its potential for dramatic treatment: the elopement, the seduction, the wife-and-mistress quarrel and the double death. And the time-scale is also too generous: twenty-four years between Bianca's meeting with Pietro and her death, including twelve years of friction with Giovanna and eight or nine years of rule. But history—official history at least—was also too niggardly. A dramatist would need to know or to invent how Francesco and Bianca met, how she yielded to him, and the circumstances of their deaths and Pietro's. To write a tragedy on the Francesco and Bianca theme Middleton would have to compress history in some directions and embellish it in others.

He probably found most of what he wanted ready-made in two loosely-written stories among Celio Malespini's *Ducento Novelle* (Venice, 1609).[1] Malespini improved on history, from Middleton's

[1]Malespini was first suggested as the source in Karl Christ, *Quellenstudien zu den Dramen Thomas Middletons* (Borna-Leipzig, 1905). For details of Malespini's life and work see Emil Misteli, *Celio Malespini und seine Novellen* (Wohlen, 1902). For extracts from *Ducento Novelle*, in translation, see Appendix I, Part A.

point of view, both by omission and extension. His *novelle* tell how Pietro, an impoverished bank-employee, loved a rich girl, Bianca, and how she yielded to him. One disastrous night, believing their love was about to be discovered, they fled from Venice to Florence. There they lived in poverty at Pietro's home. One day, the Grand Duke Francesco drove by in his carriage, caught a glimpse of the beautiful girl, and asked a gentleman of his court, Mondragone by name, to arrange a meeting. This Mondragone did by inviting Bianca to visit him. The arrangement was made through Mondragone's wife and with the reluctant agreement of Bianca's mother-in-law. Pietro too agreed, for he hoped the influential Signor Mondragone would bring them official shelter in Florence. At Mondragone's house, Bianca went on a tour of inspection with the Signor's wife, who contrived to leave her alone in a bedroom. The Duke appeared; Bianca pleaded for her honour; the Duke withdrew. Signora Mondragone returned to impress on Bianca the advantages of winning the Duke's favour. Bianca consented and became his mistress. Pietro soon accepted Bianca's new position, with the riches it brought himself, including a lucrative appointment as chamberlain (*guardarobbiere*). But he impudently began an affair with a rich widow, Cassandra Buongiani. Bianca tried to reason him into more prudent behaviour, but he met her with rage and insults. His public manner became ever more offensive and Roberto de' Ricci, one of Cassandra's family, decided, with the Duke's connivance, to take revenge. Pietro was killed in an ambush as he returned home from the widow's house; the next night the widow too was killed.

No verbal reminiscences of the *Ducento Novelle* in *Women Beware Women*, nor any other point of detail, makes a connection between the two beyond argument.[1] Yet it is improbable that no relationship, whether immediate or remote, exists. For Malespini coincides with Middleton to a remarkable degree. For example, he entirely omits Giovanna of Austria and Cosimo de' Medici; and he so concentrates attention on the Francesco-Bianca-Pietro triangle, as Middleton also does, as to make this and not other dimensions of the Duke's life his sole concern. Equally, he gives

[1]Karl Christ, *op. cit.*, suggests some parallels, but none is convincing.

plausible stories, very much like Middleton's, for the critical turning-points of the narrative: the Duke's first glimpse of Bianca, her seduction while being shown over an aristocratic house, Pietro's consoling himself with a rich widow, and the revenge-killing of Pietro by the widow's relative. Even in incidentals, the two accounts sometimes tally remarkably: the appointment of Pietro as *guardarobbiere* parallels the appointment of Leantio as 'captain of our fort at Rouans'; Middleton's Duke mentions that 'We have . . . provided [Bianca's] lodging near us now', in parallel with Malespini's Duke giving Bianca a fine house in the Via Maggio; Bianca's heated interview with Pietro over his behaviour with the widow finds a parallel in a scene in Middleton (IV. i. 41–104); Roberto de' Ricci planning revenge comes close to Hippolito talking with the Duke in a similar vein (IV. i. 141–76). Almost the whole configuration of Middleton's story echoes that of Malespini.

Yet differences between Middleton and Malespini, some trivial, some important, show that Malespini cannot have been the single source. For example, the *Ducento Novelle* says nothing about Bianca's attempt to poison the Cardinal, or how the scheme recoiled; the story ends with both Bianca and Francesco still alive.[1] Again, Malespini never mentions the Cardinal, though he played an important role in history, as he does in the play. Neither Malespini nor Middleton mentions Giovanna of Austria by name, but Middleton does refer to 'the first marriage of the Duke' (IV. ii. 203). In a smaller way, Pietro Buonaventura appears in Middleton as 'Leantio'; he is a 'factor' rather than a bank cashier; his acceptance of the Duke's conquest of Bianca is rewarded, not precisely with the post of *guardarobbiere*, but with the captainship of a fort. Moreover Middleton gives the Duke's age on meeting Bianca as 'about some fifty-five' (I. iii. 91), and he maintains the impression of the Duke as an experienced ruler; Malespini states no age at all. Such discrepancies might arise because Middleton altered his source deliberately; the reference to the duke's age is an obvious case in point. The material absent from Malespini might

[1]Apart, that is, from a single sentence: 'The two of them afterwards ended their days in a common and untimely death.'

have been supplied by gossip or by some general history of the Dukes of Florence; it is noticeable that the reference to Giovanna is merely a passing one, that the Cardinal is a Jacobean stage-type with no individualizing features, and that the death-scenes are treated in terms of stage-convention, with nothing to link them with the fatal events at Poggio a Caiano. A separate source may seem scarcely necessary, therefore. Yet at least two other sources of information were available and may have been used.

The first is Fynes Moryson's *Itinerary*, the manuscript section of which includes a brief account of Bianca.[1] Finished 'by 1619 or 1620 at the latest',[2] Moryson's few paragraphs[3] could not have served as a major source, since they do not describe Bianca's seduction. But Moryson does describe the deaths of Francesco and Bianca, and does bring in the Cardinal. He tells that Bianca sent the Cardinal, while he was her guest, a poisoned 'March payne', which he warily refused; that the Duke 'by ill happ meeting the messenger, did eate a peece thereof'; and that Bianca, hearing what had happened, ate some herself and died. This is quite different in setting and properties from *Women Beware Women*, but the sequence of events is closely similar. Equally, Moryson gives many small details found in *Women Beware Women*, but absent from, or different in, Malespini. For example, the Cardinal is said, rightly, to be the Duke's brother; this the play repeats (IV. i. 180). Further, he tells us that Duke 'Fraunces . . . had to wife Joane of the house of Austria'. And Moryson implies that Giovanna (Joane) was dead before Bianca and Francesco met, a distortion Middleton shares, since, though he mentions an earlier marriage for the Duke, he makes no further reference to Francesco's first wife. Moreover, Moryson, like *Women Beware Women*, presents Francesco as a middle-aged prince. In Moryson, again, Pietro is unnamed, and described as a 'marchant'; this is compatible with Middleton's change of his name to Leantio (in

[1]A large selection from the manuscript (formerly in Corpus Christi College, Oxford and now in the Bodleian) was printed in Charles Hughes' *Shakespeare's Europe: the Unpublished Chapters of Fynes Moryson's 'Itinerary'* (1903).

[2]Moryson, p. xl.

[3]See Appendix I, Part C.

no other known account is he called anything but Pietro), and with his describing him as a 'factor'.

To prove that Middleton read the *Itinerary* would require clearer evidence than this. A few general parallels between Moryson and the play will be found in the commentary. Two more specific links are intriguing if not conclusive. One explains the Mother's otherwise puzzling reference to a 'yearly custom and solemnity' which she dates precisely on 'the fifteenth of April'; Moryson describes an Italian triumphal procession which Middleton may have thought took place on that date (see I. iii. 82–4n.). The other tries to account for the mysterious 'Rouans' to which Leantio is appointed as captain of the fort; Middleton might just, it seems, be taking over the one proper name Moryson gives in connection with the Florentine forts (see III. iii. 39n.). But the debt to Moryson has to remain a matter of speculation. And this is unfortunate, for otherwise it would be attractive to find in Moryson's cool summary of the Bianca-Francesco affair the germ of Middleton's interest in it:

> . . . a Floryntine marchant intangled in his loue a Venetian gentlewoman called la Signora Bianca di Capelli, so as shee stole from her frendes, and being his Concubyne came with him to Florence, where he hauing wasted his estate in shorte tyme, shee was thought a fitt pray for a better man . . .[1]

Just such a mix of commerce and sex is found in *Women Beware Women*, within a scheme of values no less amoral.

Middleton may, then, have gleaned all he needed to know from Malespini and Moryson. The other possibility is that he read in manuscript an account of Bianca that included the Malespini version of the story but went beyond it. Since Gunnar Boklund's study of the sources of *The White Devil*, it has been apparent that Jacobean playwrights sometimes found their source-material in Italian manuscripts.[2] Many of these dealing with the Bianca story are extant in Italian and other libraries. Some merely chronicle dates and places; the majority, however, flesh out the facts as

[1] Moryson, p. 95.
[2] Gunnar Boklund, *The Sources of 'The White Devil'* (Uppsala, 1957).

Malespini does. And, surprisingly, each of those I have seen in this group distinctly recalls Malespini. Not only is the pattern of events virtually identical, but almost always there are passages, often lengthy, where the diction is word for word that of the *Ducento Novelle.* Some manuscripts add a few place-names, insert a date or two and expand or re-write a few of the speeches—the scribes may have found these last as clumsy and unconvincing as we do. Yet in general, as source-material, we may regard these manuscripts as unpublished Malespini; with the very important exception that in all but one case, out of fourteen manuscripts in this category, the writers go on at the end of Malespini's tale to describe the later life, and the death, of Bianca and Francesco. The additional matter varies in length from a sentence or two up to separate narratives as detailed as one of the Malespini *novelle*; all however note Giovanna of Austria's existence, all mention the Cardinal and his hostility towards Bianca, and most offer some version of the Moryson 'poisoned tart' story to account for the closeness in time of Bianca's death and Francesco's.[1] Almost all contain, that is, what Middleton needed to know but did not find in Malespini. It is possible, therefore, that the main plot of *Women Beware Women* derives from a single manuscript that includes, modifies and extends Malespini; and some allusion or form of words may turn up to clinch the matter. But setting out to prove the case would involve dealing with an almost illimitably varied mass of manuscript material, dating from the sixteenth to the eighteenth century and cross-related in an exceedingly intricate way. The reward might not repay the endeavour.

(*ii*) *The Source of the Sub-plot*

The source of the sub-plot is easier to locate. Writing in 1691, Gerard Langbaine claimed that 'the Foundation of this play, is borrow'd from a Romance called *Hyppolito and Isabella* octavo'.[2]

[1]For a translation of one such version see Appendix I, Part B. A more detailed discussion of the manuscripts will be found in Mulryne, 'Manuscript Source-Material for the Main Plot of Thomas Middleton's *Women Beware Women*', *Yearbook of English Studies*, v (1975), 79–74.

[2]*Account of the English Dramatic Poets* (1691), p. 374.

Langbaine meant by this a short novel entered to Nathan Field on 9 November 1627, and published by Field and Thomas Harper the following year under the title *The True History of the Tragicke Loves of Hipolito and Isabella Neapolitans*. The novel is translated from French; the anonymous translation has been attributed to Alexander Hart.

The *True History* is a standard example of a genre then very popular in Europe. It tells of a widowed magistrate named Fabricio[1] living in Naples with his beautiful daughter Isabella. Fabricio marries a rich gentlewoman called Livia, whose ungainly son by a former marriage, Pompeio, she keeps out of sight at a country house. Livia and Fabricio plan marriage between Isabella and Pompeio, so as to bring Isabella wealth and Pompeio a handsome bride. Isabella reluctantly accepts the prospect, until her uncle Hippolito, a good-looking and accomplished gallant, returns to Naples from abroad. The two fall in love. Fear on his part and shame of incest on hers keep them silent a long time, but eventually Hippolito tells the girl his love. Though her true feelings suggest otherwise, she repulses him. He falls ill of a fever. A letter from Isabella reveals her real state of mind. He decides to take counsel of his sister, a wordly-wise Nun, who suggests that he persuade Isabella to come and see her. When the girl arrives the Nun invents a story about a Marquis of Coria who, she says, seduced Isabella's mother while Fabricio was on business at Rome; Isabella, daughter of the Marquis, was to have on her wedding day a jewel of her father's, and this the Nun produces in confirmation of her tale. Both Hippolito and Isabella believe her, and Isabella willingly accepts Hippolito as her lover since there is now no question of incest. Fabricio soon grows suspicious, and thinking Hippolito's presence is making Isabella reluctant to marry, orders him to Padua. The Nun urges him to comply, for marriage between Isabella and Pompeio in his absence will provide excellent cover for his own relations with her. After the marriage, Hippolito returns and insinuates himself into the good

[1]This is the spelling used throughout the *True History*; Middleton spells 'Fabritio'. I have used, however, Middleton's 'Hippolito' in place of the 'Hipolito' of the original.

graces of Pompeio who often invites him to his house. An old maid-servant tells her suspicions to an uncle of Pompeio, who introduces a spy into the house, and as Hippolito and Isabella grow careless their guilt becomes apparent. Pompeio's uncle surprises Hippolito, Isabella and her maid as they plan to flee abroad. Hippolito slips away, but when the maid is forced to reveal the truth Isabella takes poison and dies. A few weeks later, the uncle too dies. Hippolito, baulked of revenge on the uncle, kills Pompeio and his servant as they travel towards Rome. He escapes into exile in Venice and to keep himself from starving marries a rich widow; but he soon wastes her fortune and in revenge she poisons him.

This, plainly, is the story with which Middleton worked. The cast of characters is virtually the same, and the salient events of the first half are reflected almost exactly in *Women Beware Women.* What Middleton has done, chiefly, is to clear away incidents and devices appropriate to the leisurely pace of the novel. For example, the long period of self-enquiry before Hippolito speaks to Isabella disappears; equally, Middleton avoids exchanges of letters, a narrative device on which the novel expends much space and a good deal of sentiment; and incidental occurrences, like Hippolito's banishment to Padua, disappear in the interests of dramatic economy. The whole of the story's second half, with its complicated incidents of spying and concealment, intrigue and revenge, Middleton sharply reduces. Again, the novelist's interest in trite love-lore, and his penchant for complacent moralizing, disappear before the altogether more abrasive note of *Women Beware Women.* Minor alterations include the reassignment of the name Livia, in the novel the name of Fabricio's second wife. But given these changes, the play's debt to the novel remains a heavy one, especially in three crucial exchanges: where Hippolito tells Isabella his love for her (I. ii. 186 ff.); where he confides in his sister (the Nun or Livia) (II. i. 1 ff.); and where Isabella is deceived by the story of the Marquis of Coria (II. i. 89 ff.). Here Middleton at times does little more than versify the prose in front of him; as the extracts from the *True History* in Appendix 1, Part D will show. Evidently, these were for Middleton the central moments in the novel: where desire and self-interest confront morality, and where cunning is allowed to outflank scruple.

Langbaine may not have known that the publication of the *True History* came in 1628, one year after Middleton's death, or that *Women Beware Women* may have been written seven or more years before. Middleton may of course have seen the *True History* in manuscript. He may however have worked with the original French published at Rouen in 1597 under the title *Histoire Veritable des Infortvnees et Tragiques Amours d'Hypolite & d'Isabella, Neapolitains.*[1] To decide which text Middleton actually used is not easy and is in any case of technical interest only, for the English is so literal a translation over the part of the story Middleton borrowed as to make it of little concern whether the French or the English lay open in front of him. The situation is further complicated because there are *two* French versions, not one: the Rouen version (from which the *True History* is certainly translated) is itself an authorized replacement of a pirated text, published, also in 1597, at Niort. The differences between the pirated and authorized versions over the first half of the story—the part Middleton used—are slight; only when the pirate comes upon the extended moralizings of the second half does he change and cut heavily—as the translator of the *True History* does also, though independently. Deciding the actual source is therefore a matter of weighing against each other possible verbal reminiscences, sometimes from texts in different languages. This nice calculus, too complicated to present here, points in the end, though marginally, to the Rouen version as the probable source.[2]

(*iii*) *Middleton's Use of his Sources*

Middleton had before him, then, two narratives quite readily adapted to the scope of a play. Malespini's story (or the similar manuscript) gives too much detail about the first meetings of Pietro and Bianca; Middleton starts in Florence, in the house of

[1]Samuel Schoenbaum dates the French version '1620' but this is an error. (See *Middleton's Tragedies*, New York, 1955, p. 112.)

[2]The detailed evidence will be found in Mulryne, 'The French Source for the Sub-Plot of Middleton's *Women Beware Women*', *R.E.S.*, XXV (1974).

Bianca's mother-in-law, and merely refers to previous happenings in Venice. Otherwise, he alters very little in the sequence of events. Similarly, the sub-plot required little tidying-up; Middleton merely left out the tangle of intrigues in the second half of the story, and some of the unnecessary complications in the first half. In terms of plot-interest the two stories form a natural pair: it might require a talent beyond the ordinary to notice the connection in the first place, but once seen the similarities present themselves quite plainly. Both stories for instance deal with a beautiful girl married to a dull husband, who then gives herself to a more exciting lover; more exciting in physique and social graces in Isabella's case and in wealth and power in Bianca's. In both stories marriage vows are set aside. In both, the intrigue pivots on the wiles of an older woman—in the Hippolito and Isabella story quite obviously, in the Bianca story, in the source, less so. Middleton had available therefore the perfect complements for a main and sub-plot: the two halves of a single statement, with a wide social range and a series of interlocking moral problems centred on money and sex.

Yet bringing the two stories together, without involving an intolerably large group of characters, needed all the skill of an experienced and deft playwright. Middleton saw that two characters were not essential to his plot: Cassandra Buongiani, the widow with whom Pietro falls in love, and Roberto de' Ricci, the avenger of her honour. In *Women Beware Women*, he simply gives these roles to Livia and to Hippolito. He saw also that the analogies between the Nun of the Hippolito and Isabella story and the Signora Mondragone of Bianca's story were so close that the two roles could be played by a single woman. So he took the name of a minor figure in the *True History*, Livia, and gave her the Nun's part and that of Signora Mondragone; to these he added that of the widow Cassandra Buongiani. In the source, Livia is the mother of Pompeio; the parallel figure to Pompeio in *Women Beware Women* is the Ward, for whom Middleton provides as guardian the simply-named Guardiano. But a substitute is needed in the play for the Signor Mondragone of the main source; and so Middleton has Guardiano play that role also. All this dexterous re-arrangement has its advantages: there results a tightly-organized dramatic narrative which allows Middleton quite naturally to bring together virtually the whole cast in scenes like the banquet scene and the masque, and to develop very economically the contrasts and parallels between the two stories. There is a price to pay too. We are never very clear, for example, about the relationship between Livia and Guardiano. They act together to secure Bianca's seduction in Act II scene ii and seem at home in the house in which the events take place: natural enough in the source for Signor Mondragone and his wife, but rather unexplained in the play.[1] Equally, Roberto de' Ricci had in the source a clear and obvious motive for killing Pietro; Hippolito's parallel killing of Leantio requires us to make rather strained inferences about Hippolito's motives and personality. The difficulties come together where one would expect, in the character of Livia. Middleton has concentrated into a single figure women who played three quite separate parts in the sources. The woman who in *Women Beware Women* cynically arranges Isabella's downfall and Bianca's, who admits to an ambiguous affection for Hippolito, and who, it seems, plunges helplessly into desire for Leantio, is, at the least, an especially complex figure. Her complexity derives in good measure from the conflation of separate source-characters. The actress who tries to build a coherent portrait on this groundwork faces a difficult challenge. Success in the theatre can vindicate Middleton's masterful way with his sources, but the risks he took are great.

Middleton's other alterations are less spectacular, yet telling. In re-making the Isabella and Hippolito story Middleton emphasizes from the beginning the human difficulties attached to marrying off Isabella to a fool; in the source these difficulties seem scarcely noticed. In the source, again, *both* Hippolito and Isabella hear and believe the Marquis of Coria story; in the play Isabella alone hears it, while Hippolito is content to accept unexplained the 'miracle' of her changed attitude. The effect is to draw our

[1]The confusion over Livia's relationship with Guardiano is nicely reflected when the *Times* critic writes of 'Livia's *three* brothers' in a review of a student production at Reading. (*Times*, March 14, 1962, p. 5.)

sympathy towards the initially less unscrupulous Isabella—bringing her into line in this respect with Bianca—and to present Hippolito as one who, like so many others, is willing lightly to disregard the moral code. A broader change of temper occurs when Middleton replaces Pompeio by the Ward. By so doing he exchanges the genteel sentiment and moralism of the romance for a whole new range of feelings and attitudes—coarse and aggressive where the source is evasive and polite—and he provides too the occasion for literary effects far beyond the source's range: effects of parody, caricature and oblique commentary. Sordido is an invented character who brings out the Ward's coarseness. Fabricio is altered from the rather neutral figure in the source to a somewhat conventionally-conceived bumbling justice; thus sharpening up the play's interest in cleverness as a form of power and a source of self-corruption. All of these changes emphasize in one way or another Middleton's prime concern with ethical problems.

In the main plot, Middleton's chief task lay in drawing more distinctly the personalities involved; in fleshing-out the tale with further incidents (the banquet scene, the scene of Leantio's return from business); and in adjusting the features of the main scenes until they focus exactly the moral commentary he wishes to transmit. Leantio comes across far more distinctly, and incomparably more opinionated, than the colourless stereotype of the source; he has been taken out of the context of Renaissance Italy and assumed into a way of feeling appropriate to seventeenth-century England. In the play Bianca too has far greater emotional depth than the rather unrealized figure who precedes her, and she shows a far more striking change from self-effacing girl to arrogant duchess. Livia is of course a much richer figure than Signora Mondragone, who in Malespini is simply part of the narrative mechanism. The Duke seems to me in both play and source a conventional character, though in Middleton he has, certainly, much greater force of personality. As to altering the moral bearings of the story, the one clear change Middleton made was to keep Leantio in ignorance of Bianca's visit to Mondragone; in Malespini he knows of the visit and approves. Thus Middleton heightens the ironies of Leantio's position as he returns to his new wife, further underlines the propensity of this society to deception, and makes Leantio an altogether lonelier and more pathetic figure.

In re-organizing his source-material, Middleton compresses a great deal, sharpening up the narrative until contrasts and parallels and ironies stand out with the greatest clarity. Yet his boldest contribution, and the most characteristic, lies in those scenes that function in the play as symbolic happenings or summaries. The best-known is the chess-game scene, but others like Hippolito's dance with Isabella or the Ward's auction-ring appraisal of her, or the final masque itself, are wholly Middleton's invention, and contribute much to the process of transformation by which he gives ethical and even tragic significance to material that had previously been no more than story-telling. At these points we can most clearly see Middleton's distinctive mind coming to bear on his sources.

4. THE PLAY

The critical response

Criticism of *Women Beware Women* has often been half-hearted. Middleton critics have thought the play second in creative power to *The Changeling*, have seen it as less inventive and remarkable than *A Game at Chess*, and have had their attention deflected by controversy over *The Revenger's Tragedy*. Some critics, too, have thought parts of *Women Beware Women* artistic failures, especially the underplot of the Ward and the masque, while others have disputed the play's moral bearings. Yet, in the main, critics have been notably consistent in drawing attention to the play's successes, of plotting and characterization and language.

This agreed response began with the play's first and only seventeenth-century critic. According to his verses, Nathaniel Richards, himself a practising dramatist, relished especially the cleverness of the intrigue; he appreciated also Middleton's psychological realism, notably in his portraits of women:

> . . . he knew the rage,
> Madness of women crossed; and for the stage

Fitted their humours—hell-bred malice, strife
Acted in state, presented to the life.

More recent critics have insisted less on rage and madness, but have shared Richards's view that Middleton knew what he was about in writing of women. One and a half centuries after Richards, Charles Lamb saw the play as wearing more homely features, yet he noted the same skilful organization and insight into character as Richards. He admired the chess-game scene especially, with its adroit plotting and its air of documentary realism, emphasizing in particular how successfully Middleton provides the illusion of fullness of character and fullness of social context.[1] Swinburne went still further than Lamb. Though he protested with characteristic vehemence about the 'underplot' and the 'upshot' of the play—'the one is repulsive beyond redemption by elegance of style, the other is preposterous beyond extenuation'—he nevertheless regarded *Women Beware Women* as deploying all the theatrical skills:

> It is full to overflowing of noble eloquence, of inventive resource and suggestive effect, of rhetorical affluence and theatrical ability.[2]

Allowing for Swinburne's habitual inflation, this emphasis on the play's exceptional skill in employing visual and verbal resources is a useful one. T. S. Eliot, while indicating that by the side of *The Changeling* he found *Women Beware Women* somewhat stilted, nonetheless shared Swinburne's pleasure in Middleton's craftsmanship—to which he paid the tribute of allusion in *The Waste Land*. He also confirmed the traditional view that Middleton possessed special insight into female psychology; Middleton, he argues, 'understood woman in tragedy better than any of the Elizabethans—save Shakespeare alone.'[3]

Subsequent writers have filled in the outline response of the critics from Richards to Eliot. They have studied in detail Bianca's

[1] *The Life, Letters and Writings of Charles Lamb*, ed. Percy Fitzgerald (1876), IV, 246.

[2] *The Best Plays of the Old English Dramatists*, The Mermaid Series, *Thomas Middleton*, I, n.d., p. xxviii.

[3] *Selected Essays* (1951) p. 166.

character and Leantio's, have surveyed the pervasive ironies and been specific about the verbal skills. They have shown that the Ward's indecencies and Sordido's can be defended as integral to the play's meaning, and have argued whether the masque-ending sums up or dissipates the play's energies. In general, recent criticism has offered increasing detail and precision, rather than radically new interpretation.

Morality

Women Beware Women contrasts in its dramatic temper with most Jacobean tragedy. Despite its Italian setting and the violence and sexual licence of the narrative, the play comes across with little glamour and little fervour. Middleton's concern with ethical and social analysis, given effect through the play's language and its tight ironic structure, ensures that an audience never loses itself in the heightened life of the stage. The play anatomizes lust and hypocrisy and moral blindness but does not indulge them. Many critics have felt this austerity: Una Ellis-Fermor has written of the play's 'grimness' and 'plainness';[1] T. B. Tomlinson of its 'deliberate flatness';[2] and Samuel Schoenbaum of its 'pitiless detachment'.[3]

Middleton's basic postulate is that this is a society where moral values are either confused or have ceased to matter. So Livia, in many ways the typifying figure, can tell Hippolito:

> if you think
> My former words too bitter, which were ministered
> By truth and zeal, 'tis but a hazarding
> Of grace and virtue, and I can bring forth
> As pleasant fruits as sensuality wishes
> In all her teeming longings. This I can do.
>
> (II. i. 27–32)

The coolness of this makes it exemplary of the moral outlook of many of the play's people; for them 'truth' and 'zeal' can always

[1] *The Jacobean Drama: An Interpretation*, 4th ed. (1958), p. 138.

[2] *A Study of Elizabethan and Jacobean Tragedy* (Cambridge and Melbourne, 1964), p. 158.

[3] *Middleton's Tragedies: A Critical Study* (New York, 1955), p. 102.

be sacrificed, without much heart-searching, to sensuality or personal gain. They are, in a precise sense, morally unscrupulous. Hippolito willingly accepts the incestuous relation with Isabella; Isabella, though she baulks at incest, has no qualms about adultery; Livia only briefly regrets the part she plays in wrecking the moral code. Leantio and Bianca are different merely in their initial resistance to this outlook, but neither has a valid alternative, and both quickly conform. Moral values are for these people replaced by surface respectability, most outrageously when the Duke seeks to repair his adulterous liaison with Bianca by having her husband murdered (IV. i. 267–74). In this instance, the ethical casuistry is blatant, but in less conspicuous forms it pervades the whole play. Leantio, for example, feels guilty at his 'theft' of Bianca (it violates his mercenary ethic) but excuses it by calling it 'noble' (I. i. 37) and by claiming, like the Duke later, that ''Tis sealed from heaven by marriage' (I. i. 45). He appeals for justification not to morality but to precedent:

> I see then 'tis my theft; w' are both betrayed.
> Well, I'm not the first has stol'n away a maid,
> My countrymen have used it. (III. ii. 219–21)

Livia, in a similar way, corrupts both Hippolito and Isabella by telling them their sin is 'the done thing' (II. i. 45–7 and 113–15). Moral duties are confused with, or dissolved in, social practice. Guardiano condenses the whole attitude by a neat confusion between the English and Latin senses of 'moral', as he screens from himself the enormity of the marriage between Isabella and the Ward:

> He has been now my ward some fifteen year,
> And 'tis my purpose, as time calls upon me,
> By custom seconded and such moral virtues,
> To tender him a wife. (I. ii. 3–6)

When the Cardinal in Act IV blames the Duke for his lack of moral responsibility, the indictment extends to almost everyone in the play. *Women Beware Women* is austere and deliberately flat in temper because these people in no way defy the moral order, and by their daring acquire some kind of stature; they are half-hearted sinners, edgily aware of and half frightened by moral sanctions, though always able to compromise with, or deflect, or gloss over, their consciences. Hippolito finds the precise description for what has happened to this social group:

> Lust and forgetfulness has been amongst us,
> And we are brought to nothing. (V. ii. 146–7)

The persons of *Women Beware Women* simply contrive to *forget* their moral obligations; and the tragedy shows, bleakly enough, how completely this brings them to nothing. To describe this as a play of people corrupted by greed for sex and greed for wealth and position is to miss the real originality of Middleton's work; for the corruption he analyses is prior to and far more insidious than this. *Women Beware Women* deals with a permissive, or at least a casual, society which falls in ruins in the last act when the weakened bonds that hold it together finally give way.

Women Beware Women analyses what happens when marriage, the representative social and moral bond, is undermined by moral blindness or lack of scruple. And it does so in the context of a whole network of family relationships that ought to guarantee social and moral order. Isabella and Hippolito violate society's order by promoting a fake marriage; in the main plot, the Duke disrupts order more openly, and so poisons (the metaphor is taken literally) his own marriage. But in each case, the morality of relationship had already been undermined. Fabritio has broken morality by forcing Isabella, his daughter, to have the grotesque Ward; their 'marriage' turns out the mockery he had made it. Livia, though Isabella's aunt and Hippolito's sister, compromises morality in forwarding their liaison, and so ensures that marriage to the Ward is the merest hypocrisy. Guardiano, though guardian to the Ward, brother to Hippolito and uncle to Isabella, nevertheless forwards the same marriage, and so grotesquely parodies the family bond. Leantio, in the main plot, undermines marriage in a more subtle yet plainly related way. For him, his characteristic language implies, his wife Bianca might merely be a treasured possession, an object won through his own cleverness and industry (see e.g. I. i. 12–15). Fearful that she will be stolen, he will 'case her up', like a jewel hidden from thieves (I. i. 165–76). Given such a disvaluing of the marriage relationship, it is no more than logic that when a stronger, wealthier man turns up, he should have the jewel; a view Leantio himself implicitly accepts in sealing his new relationship with Livia:

Liv. Do but you love enough, I'll give enough.
Lean. Troth then, I'll love enough, and take enough.
Liv. Then we are both pleased enough. (III. iii. 374–6)

A blatantly material view of relationship such as this merely crystallizes the prevailing attitudes of the main plot. Middleton shows, in both plots, how social order cannot survive the acceptance of such views of human relations.

The spokesman for morality is the Cardinal, a 'wondrous necessary man' to this society's self-understanding.[1] On his two main appearances, he asks chiefly for a sense of moral order, for the Duke to recognize the position he holds as a moral example, and for an alertness to the consequences of sin. He asks in other words for moral realism. Some have taken his fluent verse and sometimes abstract vocabulary to be Middleton's way of signalling the insincerity of what he says. This is debatable.[2] What is clear is that the views he puts forward mean nothing to his listeners. The Duke merely plunges deeper into confusion, planning to add murder to adultery, and Bianca responds by accusing the Cardinal of want of charity, by which she means indulgence. From this society's point of view all that the Cardinal says is an irrelevance.

Disaster overtakes almost all the characters in the masque; the only survivors are those who by their innocence (the Cardinal) or their stupidity (the Ward, Sordido, Fabritio) can scarcely be thought immoral. The uncertainties of life in this hypocritical, contriving time—what Guardiano means by calling it 'a witty age'—are concentrated in the masque's intricate cross-plotting as characters held together superficially by the closest family bonds contrive each other's deaths. An audience is amazed at what

[1]See Inga-Stina Ewbank, 'Realism and Morality in *Women Beware Women*', *Essays and Studies*, xxii (1969), 61.
[2]See below, pp. lxxii–lxxiii.

happens, for the scene plays itself out like a speeded-up newsreel, and produces a similar effect, at once farcical and horrible. The masque is, appropriately, a wedding-masque, presented in honour of the Duke's infamous marriage: a public celebration of an event that offends public and private morality. The masque story, ostensibly dealing with choosing-in-marriage, and with the continuance of affection for life—the subject-matter of the whole play—is in fact dedicated to self-interest and violence—in this too reflecting almost all the play. The ironies spell themselves out very plainly. Livia, who arranges marriages and wrecks marriage, is cast as Juno Pronuba, the marriage-goddess, who in the course of the masque is poisoned by her fictional votary, Isabella. Hippolito, a man misled by desire, dies of Cupid's poisoned arrows, as they pretend to 'wound' him in love. Isabella, who had acquiesced in a marriage-for-wealth with the Ward, dies in a shower of flaming gold. Guardiano, the contriver, dies in his own trap. Bianca thinks to give the Duke a cup of love, but gives him instead a cup of poison and dies of it herself. All these ironies are structural in the sense that they arise fittingly out of the moral analysis the play has already undertaken. If we think of *Women Beware Women* as initially a morality play, though one whose characterization is complex and whose action is tragic, we can accept the dramatic truthfulness of the masque and the integrity of the play as a whole.

The dramatic idiom

The austerity of the play's tone is picked up in the first instance from its characteristic language. For the most part the idiom is spare and undecorated; there are few emotionally-charged speeches, and what metaphor there is tends to be denotative rather than associative. Where the language becomes elevated or emotional, in for example Leantio's praise of marriage, and revulsion from whoredom (III. ii. 1–27), or in his desolation at the loss of Bianca (III. iii. 241–62), effects of irony or contrast are often aimed at: Leantio is soon praising whoredom, not marriage, and soon he is consoling himself with Livia's wealth in place of Bianca's affection. Normally in this play Middleton's language draws its strength not from metaphor but from a kind of wit: the manipulation of a word's meaning either through its context—so that we understand a sense other than the speaker means—or through a sort of punning that brings out hidden relationships between a word's different meanings, and so takes its place in the play's ironic structure. Partly this verbal duplicity reflects the hypocrisy of many of the play's people; partly it serves to bring out the coarsening of sexual relationships represented chiefly on the level of language by the Ward and Sordido. But the wit also serves the moral analysis more directly and more subtly. Christopher Ricks has shown how the word 'business' is frequently employed in a double sense, referring both to commerce and to sex (a common seventeenth-century use), and so helping to identify how this morally bankrupt society thinks of sexual relations as more commercial than humane.[1] Ricks cites more than a dozen instances where the double meaning is either quite explicit or just beneath the surface. Leantio, most obviously, confuses his duty to commerce with his duty to feeling, and signals his confusion by using the same word for both:

> Though my own care and my rich master's trust
> Lay their commands both on my factorship,
> This day and night I'll know no other business
> But her and her dear welcome . . . (I. i. 151–54)

(The rest of the speech develops the point.) Many other examples could be cited from Leantio; the usage concentrates his habitual frame of mind. In a coarser vein, the Ward thinks *his* occupation of playing 'shuttlecock' pretty much commensurate with choosing a wife, and so he names both activities the same way. Guardiano confirms his view:

> *Ward.* What's the next business after shuttlecock now?
> *Guard.* Tomorrow you shall see the gentlewoman
> Must be your wife.
> *Ward.* [*Aside*] There's e'en another thing too
> Must be kept up with a pair of battledores.
> (II. ii. 80–3)

Besides the pun on 'business', a similar witty confusion plays about words like 'service' (the sexual sense was then more widely

[1] 'Word-Play in *Women Beware Women*', *R.E.S.* n.s. xii (1961), 238–50.

current), and 'pride' (referring to the veneer of social esteem by which these people live as well as to lustfulness). Middleton's range in his use of this wit lies between the weak pun (appropriate to Fabritio) and what Ricks has called 'urbane obscenity':

Lean. A bow i' th' ham to your greatness;
You must have now three legs, I take it, must you not?
Bian. Then I must take another, I shall want else
The service I should have; you have but two there.
(IV. i. 47–50)

(Social and sexual service are irretrievably and for this play meaningfully conflated.) Middleton has created for the play's people a shared dialect, with a kind of characteristic language-pattern that even in their use of single words reflects their submoral habit of mind. An audience learns through repeated instances (not of the same word, but of the same pattern of usage) how as in a field of force their minds turn all one way: towards ethical casuistry and confusion.

On a larger scale, but after the same pattern, Middleton structures scenes and incidents to reflect in action, as on the verbal level, the common habit of mind. Such scenes are perhaps Middleton's most individual contribution to the seventeenth-century language of drama. This society thinks of sex relationships in terms of commercial transactions; so Middleton invents a scene (III. iv) in which Sordido and the Ward, thinking of marriage, conduct a sale-ring inspection of Isabella—she is paraded like an animal at auction. The effect is to caricature, in a kind of action-metaphor, the pervasive attitude: of Leantio to his 'jewel', of the Duke 'buying' Bianca with 'wealth and honour', of Livia buying Leantio, of Fabritio and Guardiano arranging a wealthy match for Isabella. From another angle, relationships between these people are determined by wit and cunning; in this world the cleverest player wins the prizes, until at length the formula proves inadequate, and witty players kill each other and even kill themselves in the final masque. So Middleton invents the play's most celebrated scene, the chess-game, to summarize this aspect of the play-world: Bianca, the defenceless pawn, taken by a piece of higher status, a Duke, as the witty Livia 'places her man' and outplays the less skilful Mother. In another perspective, relationships are determined not by wit but by power, as Leantio has to acquiesce in the Duke's winning of Bianca (and Bianca herself has to yield to him), and as Isabella is forced to accept her father's command to marry. This view of the life-game is emphasized through the brutal game of cat-and-trap as played by the Ward. The Ward's game—a matter of violence not skill—is rapidly and obscenely connected with the game of sex, and so caricatures the play's forced sex relationships. Middleton has other stage devices that perform a comparable function. At the banquet Hippolito dances gracefully with Isabella, and the Ward clumsily imitates him. From one point of view this reflects Hippolito's fitness to be Isabella's sexual partner and the Ward's grotesque unsuitability; from another it summarizes how in this society appearance and truth are at odds—the dance of marital union is in fact the dance of cuckoldry. In a later scene, Bianca and her ladies discuss their watches, and make the watches' behaviour stand for the ladies' own behaviour with their lovers; Bianca claims precedence because she sets her watch only by the sun (i.e. the Duke) (IV. i. 1–18). Again there are two responses: Bianca has indeed made sexual gains by her partnership with the Duke, but her liaison with the 'sun' is as irregular as the ladies' watches. The little scene leads nowhere, in terms of the play's action; its sole function is that of dramatic symbol or summary.

The tragedy's most important structural device is of course the interplay between the two plots. The Hippolito and Isabella material serves, plainly, as mirror-image for the Bianca story, reflecting in an altered way the marital irregularities of the main plot.[1] The Ward and Sordido, a third grouping, are part of that process of making conscious to which the whole play is given. Critics have sometimes been dismayed at the coarseness and indecency of the pair, and Muriel Bradbrook may be right in thinking that too much space is devoted to their obscenities.[2] Yet

[1] For further discussion, see below, p. lxxiv.

[2] *Themes and Conventions of Elizabethan Tragedy* (Cambridge, 1935), p. 234. For unfavourable opinions of Middleton's use of the Ward and Sordido see Robert Ornstein, *The Moral Vision of Jacobean Tragedy* (Madison, Wisconsin, 1960) p. 191, and Schoenbaum, *Middleton's*

in general the indecencies are calculated, not random. Situated between 'foil' and 'parody', to use Richard Levin's terms,[1] the low-life pair partly set off the well-bred and sophisticated behaviour of the Duke and Bianca, Hippolito and Isabella, partly demean it by making explicit what in the politer characters are hidden or unconscious habits of feeling. The function of contrast is obvious: by comparison with these boors the other characters are 'civilized' people. But the analogies are important too. A number of examples have already been given, from the Ward's auction-ring mentality and his games-playing. Another might be quoted from his vulgar attitude to food. Sexual feeling in this play often expresses itself in terms of food and eating;[2] the Ward elicits the debasement of human ties implicit in this kind of language by his own gross parody of it. Livia's affection for Hippolito finds expression, for example, through sensing an analogy between feeling of a sexual kind and eating:

Hip. You'll make me blush anon.
Liv. 'Tis but like saying grace before a feast then,
And that's most comely; thou art all a feast,
And she that has thee a most happy guest.

(I. ii. 147–50)

On a number of other occasions the same idiom is used. The Ward vulgarizes and caricatures it by seeing the directest physiological connection between eating and lust; only a few lines before Livia's speech the Ward muses:

I'll forswear eating eggs-in-moonshine 'nights.
There's ne'er a one I eat but turns into a cock
In four and twenty hours; if my hot blood
Be not took down in time, sure 'twill crow shortly.

(I. ii. 120–3)

Tragedies, p. 103. T. B. Tomlinson, *A Study of Elizabethan and Jacobean Tragedy*, p. 159 and David M. Holmes, *The Art of Thomas Middleton*, p. 198, disagree about the extent to which Middleton is indulgent towards the two characters, Tomlinson thinking he shows 'crushing contempt' and Holmes believing that their 'animality is extenuated by its sheer obviousness.'

[1]See Richard Levin, *The Multiple Plot in English Renaissance Drama* (Chicago and London, 1971), esp. ch. 4 'Clown Subplots: Foil, Parody, Magic'.

[2]See especially M. C. Bradbrook, *Themes and Conventions*, pp. 236–8.

Middleton here as elsewhere employs the Ward—his feeding, his games-playing, his dancing, his sexual vulgarity, his want of feeling—as a way of stating the moral truths and predicting the human outcome that lie concealed behind the plausible façade of the other characters' behaviour.

It might seem that this overt manipulation of language and action could only be achieved at the expense of realism, even in the seventeenth-century meaning of the term. Sometimes the devising hand does show itself too plainly: Leantio is clearly manipulated when his two speeches on marriage, at the beginning and near the end of III. ii., flatly and by evident contrivance contradict each other. Yet within the ordered framework, Middleton creates a kind of social realism beyond the reach of most of his contemporaries. Inga-Stina Ewbank has noticed how fully Middleton establishes the 'realistic density' of his play-world. Partly he does this by an 'almost documentary use of objects'—the characters refer repeatedly to the things they see or handle or know of, thus creating around themselves a three-dimensional 'world'—and partly by their habit of offering a kind of history for their actions.[1] This realism of *milieu* is complemented and extended by a realism of social observation that is deeply knowledgeable. By the time he wrote *Women Beware Women*, Middleton had mapped out for himself a particular dramatic territory, the world of merchant-class and lower-nobility manners, and the understanding gained in repeated fictional accounts of this world is turned to advantage here. Lamb is right to praise the chess-scene not merely for its adroit ironies, but for the deeply humorous understanding it shows of social interaction. Livia's presumption of rank, never dropped, though qualified by the assumed garrulity of 'good neighbours', has been brilliantly dramatized, as has the Mother's faintly perplexed but grateful response to such a display of social affability. In this and other scenes Middleton keeps us fully aware of the existence of a social nexus that has its own influence on attitude and behaviour. *Women Beware Women* for the most part successfully reconciles contrivance and realism, though the balance is a difficult and precarious one.

[1] 'Realism and Morality', pp. 62, 63.

The Characters

In characterization, Middleton's touch is surest in the portrait of Leantio. This is not to say that Leantio is the most intricate study in the play, but his comes across as the nature Middleton knew best. The long series of comedies provided an expert knowledge of the bourgeois mentality; and Leantio figures as a perfect stereotype—on one view at least—of the bourgeois mind. The characteristic preoccupations of the comedy figures, with sex, with commercial success, with proving their own energetic cleverness, are mixed in Leantio with an assertiveness about morality that reads like a caricature of the non-conformist conscience. So boldly has Middleton drawn his cameo that an actor must beware of presenting Leantio as a wholly satirical figure.

The clear features of the portrait begin early. We may feel that the opening scene is awkwardly written, the speeches too long, the transitions too deliberate, the views, of Leantio especially, too simple and extreme. Yet a first scene does have the function of spelling out for an audience the concerns—here the social and ethical problems—with which the play is to deal; and there is even a kind of dramatic shorthand in establishing here so fully, at the bourgeois end of the scale, that interest in money, in relationships (of marriage and kinship), and in morality, that is to dominate the play. Leantio and the Mother share the same value-structure, though she is experienced and worldly-wise, where he is young and theoretic; an age-youth contrast often repeated in the play. From the beginning, the Mother insists that girls from rich homes will not be content with poverty; in reply Leantio can offer only sententiousness and romantic cliché that plainly indicate he knows nothing of real human feeling nor of himself. His attempts at self-analysis are priggish and blind:

> But beauty able to content a conqueror,
> Whom earth could scarce content, keeps me in compass;
> I find no wish in me bent sinfully
> To this man's sister, or to that man's wife:
> In love's name let 'em keep their honesties,
> And cleave to their own husbands, 'tis their duties.
> Now when I go to church, I can pray handsomely,

Not come like gallants only to see faces,
As if lust went to market still on Sundays.
(I. i. 26–34)

The tone is self-congratulatory, the frame of reference very limited, the movement of the verse, like the view it expresses, appropriate to a mind shuttered to the real world. The portrait of a self-bounded mind continues with little touches throughout the scene: in the rather prim sexual innuendo he permits himself (80–3) in the bluff heartiness he affects (107–9), in the condescension he uses towards the Mother (117–18), and especially in the equation he accepts between sexual and commercial payment (154–61). The beginning of I. iii. is again full of shrewdly, even cruelly, perceptive touches: Leantio, worried that sex has temporarily unfitted him for business, rallies his new temptation in characteristic terms:

Oh fie, what a religion have I leaped into!
Get out again for shame. (I. iii. 21–2)

There is nothing depraved or corrupt about Leantio; he suffers from a kind of inhibiting religiosity, made up of unrealized moral precepts and an almost superstitious reverence for commercial profit, which repeatedly gets in the way of real emotion and real relationships. Even when he feels Bianca's loss most acutely, his emotion is crossed with moralistic analogies (III. iii. 246–51, 256–7), and the note is often in a petty way self-justifying. Characteristically, he salves his hurt pride by accepting Livia's wealth, and by taking an opportunity to parade his gains before Bianca and to browbeat her for her immorality (IV. i. 61–104). Leantio, in the world of this play, is a victim because his own unstable morality has no defence to offer to the more experienced, less scrupulous attitudes of the others; the portrait is keenly knowledgeable and consistent.

When Leantio 'turns his heart' to hate Bianca, readers of the play, and actors, have little difficulty in accepting his changed outlook: Middleton takes some pains to sketch his inner feelings as he confronts his loss. With Bianca, the change of heart that coincides with her seduction by the Duke is altogether more abrupt and much less obviously prepared for. At one moment she seems a self-effacing, virtuous girl, at the next a strong-minded even aggressive woman wholly adapted to the hypocrisy and compromise of Florentine society. Critics have been a good deal worried over this, and rightly, for Bianca's experience to a considerable degree shows what the play is about; finding her way from the periphery of the play-world to its centre she ought more than anyone else to clarify its nature for us. Some have seen the contrast between the two Biancas as part of the play's exploration of personality: M. C. Bradbrook, for example, writes of the play as 'a study in the progressive deterioration of character', to which Bianca's change of heart importantly contributes.[1] Others accept the consistency of the portrait, but place more emphasis on the suddenness of the *volte-face*: Una Ellis-Fermor sees in Bianca that 'hardening of the spirit under certain forms of shock or misery' which Middleton delineates with peculiar insight.[2] Such critics respond favourably to the early Bianca; others explain, or explain away, the contrast with the later woman by regarding the early Bianca as merely a façade. Samuel Schoenbaum, for instance, claims that 'Bianca is able to lose her virtue only because she never really possessed it'; the marriage with Leantio 'is based on physical appetite alone', so that her submission to the Duke follows as a perfectly natural next step.[3] Irving Ribner agrees; he calls Bianca's seduction, 'with her feeble attempts at resistance', 'an elaborate game', and draws attention to what he sees as 'the essential falseness of Bianca's protestations of chastity', protestations designed to protect 'merely the appearance of virtue'.[4] David Frost attempts a middle course; while seeing the difficulty of reading (and certainly *playing*) the early Bianca as a falsely virtuous woman, he is at the same time unwilling to accept older views of a simple deterioration of character. Frost, admitting 'the dangerously sensual basis' of the affection between Bianca and Leantio, nevertheless claims 'there is not a hint that Bianca is

[1] *Themes and Conventions*, p. 224.
[2] *The Jacobean Drama*, p. 142.
[3] *Middleton's Tragedies*, p. 111.
[4] *The Moral Vision of Jacobean Tragedy*, pp. 144–5.

morally reprehensible' in her early behaviour. Her 'virtue just collapses' before the Duke because it has been 'an emotion based largely on fear of the unknown and forbidden'.[1] William Empson adopts an altogether more radical view, rejecting continuity entirely: 'the idea of "development" is irrelevant to Bianca. Nor is this crude or even unlifelike; it is the tragic idea of the play. She had chosen love in a cottage and could stick to it, but once seduced by the Duke she was sure to become a different person; what is "developed" is a side of her that she had suppressed till then altogether'.[2] Empson confronts squarely the dilemma other critics have wished away: two Biancas, each elicited by circumstances, maintained as a single character only by the accident of sharing the same name. He weakens only when he introduces the rather notional concept of 'suppression': how could a *wholly* suppressed element of character be registered either in writing or in the theatre?[3]

The meaning of the play, its 'tragic idea', seems to me to require just that separateness between the two Biancas which Empson accepts and which in the play the Mother underlines:

> She's no more like the gentlewoman at first
> Than I am like her that never lay with man yet;
> And she's a very young thing where'er she be.
>
> (III i. 66–8)

The new Bianca is unrecognizable as the same girl who entered the play's opening scene; it is possible to infer *why* she was vulnerable to the change that has taken place in her, but such inference can lead to open disagreement between competent readers. The evidence for her attachment to Leantio being 'purely sensual' or 'based largely on fear of the unknown and forbidden' or, particularly, the evidence for her virtue being a matter of

[1] David L. Frost, *The School of Shakespeare* (Cambridge, 1968), pp. 63–5.

[2] *Some Versions of Pastoral*, (1935) p. 55.

[3] L. L. Brodwin, *Elizabethan Love Tragedy* (New York and London, 1972), pp. 320–36, considers that Bianca's seduction leads to real human gains, not the 'deterioration' others have observed; by the play's end Bianca 'has built well, converting the Duke's unholy lust into a love that desires the sanctity of marriage' (p. 331). Most will think this a special point of view.

pretence, seems to me flimsy and debatable; the attempt to con struct a coherent inner biography for her appears fraught with problems. With *Women Beware Women* it is more helpful to concentrate upon what happens to Bianca rather than how and why she develops. Part of the originality of Middleton's work is that he appreciates, far more keenly than other dramatists of his day, the moral pressure exerted by a society's habit of mind; Bianca, moving from outside the play-world into its midst, becomes—perceptively and movingly—the novice fully initiated into the corrupt society.

Bianca's experience is that of an outsider introduced to a new world, or worlds. R. B. Parker has noticed the repeated use in the text of the word 'stranger'.[1] A complex interaction is set up between this word and the opposed concepts of 'affinity' and kinship; it operates strongly in the affairs of Hippolito and Isabella, where a parallel initiation to Bianca's takes place. In a play deeply occupied with the functioning of relationships, Bianca begins as an outsider attached to her new society by the single, brittle link of marriage with Leantio. Her silence in the opening scene, often remarked, is the silence of a woman observing, cautiously, her new world. As the child of a rich house, the poverty of her surroundings (which a stage production will emphasize) is unfamiliar to her; as a Venetian she comes a stranger to the alien society of Florence. The very structure of the dialogue, beginning with a long and familiar exchange between mother and son, emphasizes Bianca's apartness in contrast to their intimacy—an intimacy quickly strengthened by Leantio's humorous knowledge of his mother's foibles, and the asides the two of them share out of Bianca's hearing. The dialogue refers frequently to Bianca's position as an emotional novice in the state of marriage, as well as a newcomer to a strange city and household. Bianca recognizes her position and underlines it:

> I have forsook friends, fortunes, and my country,
> And hourly I rejoice in 't. (I. i. 131–2)

[1] 'Middleton's Experiments with Comedy and Judgement', *Jacobean Theatre*, Stratford-upon-Avon Studies I, ed. J. R. Brown and B. A. Harris (1960), p. 194.

She fully wants to be taken into her new social group, and to create her own most intimate society in the marriage with Leantio. There can be no doubting the genuine feeling of:

here's my friends,
And few is the good number. Thy successes,
Howe'er they look, I will still name my fortunes . . .
I'll call this place the place of my birth now,
And rightly too: for here my love was born,
And that's the birth-day of a woman's joys.
[*To Leantio*] You have not bid me welcome since I came.
(I. i. 132–42)

This acts as a kind of secular repetition of her marriage vows. It may be over-interpretation to find in the references to good and ill fortune (omitted here) Bianca's nervous sense of her own insecurity, and in the repeated allusion to welcome, here and later, not just a light coquetry but a genuine need for reassurance. The verse moves rather too deliberately, and may tell us nothing of Bianca's hidden feelings; yet the actress who plays the lines this way may not be far wrong. Certainly, we sense her real isolation, not only in Leantio's inability to reach out to her through the self-bounded world of preoccupations in which he lives, but also (which comes to the same thing) in his resolve to 'case her up' like a concealed treasure. From this point much else conspires to underline Bianca's newness and vulnerability. As we saw first her welcome to a strange home, we soon see Leantio's leaving her alone with her new mother-in-law as he himself goes about the other business that competes for his attention. Whether Middleton considers excessive Leantio's preoccupation with physical sex, and Bianca's, as Schoenbaum thinks, is open to debate; yet we might agree that Leantio's prudent language about sex and responsibility is bound to seem dull and poor-spirited beside the Duke's more licentious words later. On Leantio's departure, the Duke appears. As a stranger, Bianca must be told who he is, and have explained to her the ceremony he conducts. What she sees is power and confidence and social poise wholly opposite to her own anxious and impoverished situation: a man of mature years (he is 'about some fifty-five'; she is 'about sixteen') surrounded by the signs of social pre-eminence, and with a look so commanding that she feels the need to remark on it. As the first meeting with this man approaches, Middleton again prepares the ground by re-emphasizing Bianca's exposed social position. The brilliant scene of the chess game has many uses; one is to show Bianca's defencelessness as the pawn taken by the more powerful chess-piece. Repeatedly as the scene builds up the Mother and Livia touch on matters of neighbourliness and social duty; very adroitly, Middleton invokes a whole social situation, with Livia and the Mother firmly within it and Bianca outside. Both of the older women draw attention to their social skills, and refer more than once to the long years of experience that have enabled them to build these skills up.[1] Into this setting Bianca comes a stranger and an inexperienced girl. The Duke's sudden appearance as she is shown round this unfamiliar and wealthy house—the house that ostensibly symbolizes hospitality but in fact serves the opportunism of this society's values—merely finalizes the series of unsettling new social experiences she has gone through. Her immediate response, 'Oh treachery to honour!' (II. ii. 320), before the Duke says anything to affront her points perhaps to her exaggerated nervousness. The Duke, by contrast, deals with her with splendid poise, in a superbly calculated mixture of reassurance, sexual play, flattery and threats. Totally in command of the situation, he rests his answer to her moral objections not merely on promises of wealth and honour but finally on the argument he knows will speak to her most plainly:

> Come play the wise wench, and provide for ever;
> Let storms come when they list, they find thee sheltered.
> Should any doubt arise, let nothing trouble thee;
> Put trust in our love for the managing
> Of all to thy heart's peace. (II. ii. 382–6)

Leantio had provided, he claimed, 'a shelter o'er our quiet innocent loves' (I. i. 52); Bianca had said she desired in place of riches only that 'Heaven send a quiet peace with this man's love' (I. i. 127). Her sincerity seems to me beyond doubt. Even later in the play, as trouble faces her again—in the form this time of

[1] Guardiano too is of long experience: 'I have had a lucky hand these fifteen year/At such court passage with three dice in a dish.' (II. ii. 41–2).

Leantio's threats—the Duke and she use the same language:

Duke. Do not you vex your mind, prithee to bed, go,
All shall be well and quiet.
Bian. I love peace, sir.
Duke. And so do all that love; take you no care for't,
It shall be still provided to your hand. (IV. i. 124–7)

Later still, thinking she has poisoned the Cardinal and so removed the last threat to her newly-achieved position, Bianca exclaims:

Now my peace is perfect,
Let sports come on apace. (V. ii. 70–1)

The ironies are of course trenchant; in place of sports and peace come the moral storms she and the Duke think to shelter from. Yet, and this is the main point here, Bianca's desire for peace has been consistent throughout, the need of an untried, isolated, essentially friendless girl for some sort of accommodation with a society to which she is a stranger. She falls to the Duke, and then adapts to his way of thinking and feeling, not so much because of moral shallowness, but because of the pressure exercised upon her by social circumstances and by personalities stronger—not necessarily by nature but certainly by position and experience—than her own. Middleton shows his interest in how such social and personal pressures work; in following this interest we approach the play's 'tragic idea'.

Bianca's behaviour after the seduction-scene confirms the gains and losses that fall to her through exchanging innocence for experience. She has been initiated into this devious society and quickly shows her command of its practices. She browbeats Guardiano for his part in her betrayal while maintaining the veneer of polite social behaviour; and she is sufficiently acute to be conscious of her new position:

I'm made bold now;
I thank thy treachery, sin and I'm acquainted,
No couple greater. (II. ii. 439–41)

The terms are aptly those of gaining acquaintance, entering, even, into a new kind of 'marriage', one that this time elicits not meekness but the assertion of social rights and privileges. Middleton catches brilliantly the querulous note in Bianca's voice as she demands of the Mother the material comforts to which she thinks herself by social standing entitled; in almost line-by-line parody of her acquiescent viewpoint in the opening scene (III. i. 16–60). By the scene of the banquet Bianca has so far adjusted to the habits of her society as to be able to indulge in coquettish pleasantries with the Duke and win a round of applause from his court; while in heartless self-preoccupation ignoring the existence of her husband (who is now, till Livia's intervention, the outsider in this privileged group). The last encounter between the two (IV. i. 41–104) summarizes the transformation that has taken place in their inner lives as in their worldly circumstances. The poverty of the opening scene contrasts with the opulence of this (Middleton's dialogue characteristically annotates the stage-properties required), while the give-and-take fondness of those first lines balances the angry stichomythia here. Leantio remains in many ways the same man still, blind enough to use his aggressive religiosity as a weapon without admitting that he too falls under its sanctions; but it is easy to sense and even sympathize with the hurt vanity that prompts him, and to understand his by now bewildered need to see himself still as a man of principle. The pathos is intensified by the audience's ironic knowledge that Leantio's plight grows out of incompatible elements in his original and yet undisplaced scheme of values. Bianca remains in command in his presence—she is capable by nature or upbringing of pursuing a role beyond Leantio's bourgeois experience—but the pathos of her situation too makes itself felt. She may perhaps have emerged, if we accept L. L. Brodwin's view, 'as a fully matured woman',[1] but even if so it is difficult in the soliloquy before Leantio's entry not to hear, beneath the coolly reflective surface, the admission of a wasted life. Dorothea Krook notices 'the irony of her blank unawareness'[2] as she muses how her 'fortune' has led 'so far off from my birth-place/My friends, or kindred' (IV. i. 29–30) to this privileged life, and as she plans to secure a similar life-experience for her own children by ensuring their sexual liberty. Whatever her new social poise, her moral sense still

[1] *Elizabethan Love Tragedy*, p. 326.
[2] *Elements of Tragedy* (New Haven and London, 1969), p. 176.

attaches trivial meanings to liberty and restriction. The tragic irony of Bianca's life is that by escaping from Leantio's imprisonment into the 'self-realization' of the Duke's society she has really entered a cul-de-sac: a society whose values repeatedly offer her 'heart's peace', but which in truth destroy her.

Of the other figures in the main plot, none needs extensive discussion. The Duke, if not a stereotype, is an uncomplicated figure: experienced and used to command. He is the fit centre for this morally casual society, so blind to the nature of moral law that he believes—the text gives no clue to the contrary—he can legitimately arrange murder to avoid adultery. The Cardinal, his brother, poses at least minor problems. What the Cardinal says has the air of orthodox moral authority, and the stage setting (his Cardinal's dress, candles in the midst of 'darkness') tends to underline his words. The moral structure of the play also supports him; he is, according to Inga-Stina Ewbank, an 'omniscient judge' who 'represents to the play audience, a closing-in on the characters of the moral scheme they have ignored'.[1] Others find flaws in the Cardinal's message and his character. L. L. Brodwin sees parallels between the Cardinal's habit of mind and Leantio's, telling us that his 'ideal . . . is the result of "severe learning" completely divorced from experience'.[2] David M. Holmes goes further. Recalling the Cardinal of *More Dissemblers Besides Women*, whose religious shortcomings are plain, Holmes points out how readily the Cardinal of *Women Beware Women* caves in at the beginning of the final scene, despite his previous strictures on his brother's marriage:

Duke. How perfect my desires were, might I witness
But a fair noble peace 'twixt your two spirits!
The reconcilement would be more sweet to me
Than longer life to him that fears to die.
[*To Lord Cardinal*] Good sir!
Car. I profess peace, and am content.
(V. ii. 10–14)

[1]'Realism and Morality', p. 61. And see J. B. Batchelor, 'The Pattern of *Women Beware Women*', *The Yearbook of English Studies*, II (1972), pp. 78–88.

[2]*Elizabethan Love Tragedy*, p. 330.

An audience, accustomed by now to the play's idiom, will undoubtedly hear ironically the Duke's desire for 'peace' and the Cardinal's assent: peace by now means disregard for moral law. 'Profess' may also be heard in a double sense; certainly Bianca hears it so. Even if the Cardinal is not devious, he may be accused of lack of resolve; Holmes finds him a figure of 'tractable shallowness' who 'displays a weakness of character that renders him incompetent to deal with the Duke's hardened corruption'.[1] It is difficult to know where an accurate response lies. Everyone will hear at once in the rhythms of the Cardinal's speeches a note quite different from anything else in the play, but some will detect in these rhythms Middleton's underwriting of grounded orthodoxy, while others will infer the playwright's exposure of facility and insincerity. Undoubtedly the Cardinal's language can be theoretic and generalizing; but it can also be simple and direct:

> He that taught you that craft,
> Call him not master long, he will undo you.
> Grow not too cunning for your soul, good brother.
> (IV. iii. 33–5)

What the Duke has to say is merely specious beside this. The truth about the Cardinal may be that Middleton, while needing him as a mouthpiece for morality, could not resist using him as yet another 'outsider' who in the course of the play joins the society of compromise. The two aims are not incompatible, but Middleton has not quite successfully in this case signalled his intentions.

The dramatic shorthand of the play may have been overstretched in the Mother's case as in the Cardinal's. The Mother serves as part of the milieu of disillusioned worldliness into which Bianca and Leantio are introduced; she sees from the beginning the strains in the new marriage, and if at a crucial point she is given 'blind mate' by Livia, that is because Livia is a cleverer player of the same game. Where some find the portrait overstretched is in her sudden disloyalty to her son as she decides to attend the Duke's banquet.[2] It is hard not to feel that Middleton

[1] *The Art of Thomas Middleton*, pp. 163–4 and p. 171 n. 28.

[2] David L. Frost makes this point; see *The School of Shakespeare*, pp. 68–9.

is simply manipulating his characters when the Mother rejects Leantio's wish to stay away, and agrees with Bianca:

I'm of thy mind.
I'll step but up, and fetch two handkerchiefs
To pocket up some sweetmeats, and o'ertake thee. *Exit.*
Bian. [*Aside*] Why here's an old wench would trot into a
bawd now,
For some dry sucket, or a colt in marchpane. *Exit.*
(III. ii. 185–9)

Middleton preserves the play's idiom, as greed once more equates with moral falsity; but the character-drawing suffers. After the banquet the Mother disappears, and is the only important figure not present at the masque.[1]

Of the sub-plot people, Isabella and Hippolito to some extent parallel Bianca. Isabella is young and gullible, and, though scrupulous about incest, allows a false marriage to screen her affair with Hippolito; as the play progresses she finds herself more and more involved in deceit and in situations that debase her—in the banquet, for example, and when she parades before the Ward. Hippolito, a rather indefinite figure, is always willing to compromise, until in the end he can defend even murder in the service of a corrupt propriety. Livia, as sister to one and aunt to the other, provides them with the opportunity for living out their attitudes. Livia herself, since Lamb the play's most celebrated figure, often evokes from the critics a certain affection. For Lamb she is a 'good neighbour' and a 'jolly Housewife'. T. B. Tomlinson and Robert Ornstein, though both see plainly enough the sinister side of her amorality, comment on her attractions. Tomlinson writes of 'the rather engaging Livia',[2] and Ornstein does all he can to excuse her of responsibility for Isabella's fall.[3] The critics' leniency is perhaps explained by the impression Livia conveys of human depth. Among much shallower, less flexible people Livia is gifted with imagination and the skills of an actress. In a society where 'wit' and pretence are the foundations of success, she is

[1]Except of course Leantio, who has already been killed.
[2]*Elizabethan and Jacobean Tragedy*, p. 182.
[3]*The Moral Vision of Jacobean Tragedy*, p. 193.

pre-eminent. Her skill in deluding Isabella is matched by her creative talent in faking a whole social milieu for deceiving the Mother and Bianca. But her pre-eminence lies not in skill alone, but in her position as almost the only character in an unaware society to know something of her own motives:

> Beshrew you, would I loved you not so well.
> I'll go to bed, and leave this deed undone. . . .
> I take a course to pity him so much now
> That I have none left for modesty and myself.
> This 'tis to grow so liberal.
>
> (II. i. 63–70)

This may not be the most acute self-analysis, but where moral blindness in the others is a matter of habit Livia's knowledge that she is blind is some distinction. And Livia conveys the impression that she is capable of subtle and even hidden feeling beyond the others' range. It is to this impression that Daniel Dodson testifies when he constructs an intricate little drama of relationships between Livia, Hippolito and Leantio. Dodson thinks that Livia feels 'an abnormal, potentially incestuous, attraction for her brother Hippolita [*sic*]'; she is released from this by the affair between Hippolito and Isabella; then 'in her fallow condition' she sees the 'youthful virility' of Leantio and 'an immediate and violent transference takes place'.[1] It may be difficult to accept this view as it stands, yet there is at times an awkwardness amounting almost to coyness in Livia's dealings with Hippolito that goes some way to giving substance to Dodson's argument. Livia's first words to her brother are oddly emphatic and emotional:

> My best and dearest brother, I could dwell here . . .
> thou art all a feast,
> And she that has thee a most happy guest. (I. ii. 144–50)

The equation of sex and eating is the play's familiar idiom, but the whole speech has an air of intimacy unique in the text. The Livia who falls in love with Leantio is an altogether more hard-headed woman, practical and clear-sighted in her sexual re-awakening; to that extent Dodson's theory is doubtful. None of

[1] 'Middleton's Livia', *P.Q.*, XXVII (1948) pp. 378, 380.

this should obscure Livia's central role. She prospers in this society, at least until her feelings get the better of her at Leantio's death, because she embodies so fully and manipulates so cleverly the debased values by which these people live. Dorothea Krook writes that 'what Middleton is giving us in Livia is the purest, most perfect type and exemplar of worldliness . . . compared with Livia the famous malcontents of the drama of the period—Bosola, Flamineo, Vendice—are palpitating bundles of moral sensibility; their vituperations are the proof of a capacity for moral outrage which Livia has long since lost, if she ever possessed it'.[1] This in the main is Livia's significance, and in this society the source of her strength.

5. PRODUCTIONS

No professional production of *Women Beware Women* is on record between that mentioned by Nathaniel Richards and the production by the Royal Shakespeare Company at the Arts Theatre, London, in July, 1962. This first professional revival evoked varying responses. *The Times* critic called the play the 'virile product of a rare vision', and considered it 'a classic so long kept off the stage that to see it is to be gripped from start to finish, as if much learned writing on the subject had only hinted at its theatrical quality.' The *Daily Telegraph* critic, on the contrary, wrote that 'frankly, I can see very little reason for disturbing the long repose of Thomas Middleton's *Women Beware Women*', and called the play 'a lumbering piece about dark deeds in the vicious court of an imaginary Florence.' He may not, however, have been particularly attentive, for at the end he noticed only 'a couple of murders'. Philip Hope-Wallace, for *The Manchester Guardian*, commented on 'Middleton's formidable drama of sex and sin', while finding the production 'slow and unpolished', even if after the right style: 'one of stony complicity and low speaking, so as to make the drama as little cheaply lurid as may be'. There was general agreement that Ernest Milton's Cardinal came across powerfully; his speech on sin and retribution (IV. iii. 1–24)

[1] *Elements of Tragedy*, p. 164.

earned him 'a cracking round of applause'. Bernard Bresslaw played the Ward with coarseness and vigour, and a talent for vulgar knockabout that seriously threatened the balance of every scene in which he appeared. On a tiny stage, and hampered by an awkward set 'that looked like a collection of bunks in an air-raid shelter' (*Daily Telegraph*), the cast appeared frequently ill at ease, and the play's ironic structure had little chance of expressing itself through the production's halting rhythms. Bianca was played by Jeanne Hepple, Livia by Pauline Jameson, the Duke by Geoffrey Chater and Leantio by Nicol Williamson. Direction was by Anthony Page.

The most important production of the play to date was that staged by Terry Hands and the Royal Shakespeare Company at Stratford-on-Avon in July, 1969. Set in much ampler surroundings than the Arts theatre, this revival tried to bring out especially the social and financial distance between the Duke's court and the Mother's house, as well as Middleton's acutely ironic knowledge of human behaviour in matters of sex and money. The bare, raked stage was inset with black and white tiles in a chessboard pattern, and dominated by a very large, though movable, statue modelled after the Venus de Medici. For the final act a portion of the stage was raised to represent a chessboard, and on this small platform the masque and its murders were played out. The acting-style was restrained, the props few and the general tone of the production low key in an attempt to draw attention to Middleton's manipulation of his characters in ironic patterns. Resplendent velvet costumes were used for the nobles, contrasting vividly with the dun colours and poor-quality fabrics worn by Leantio and his group. Irving Wardle in *The Times* commented on the way in which this production 'glaringly exposes a very real society whose members use sex to get money and money to get sex'; and he noticed the very marked ironic counterpointing between several scenes. Among the players, Judi Dench sensitively traced Bianca's change from girlhood to (on the surface at least) womanly confidence and composure, while Brewster Mason presented an insinuating more than a commanding Duke. Elizabeth Spriggs was Livia, Susan Fleetwood Isabella, Anne Dyson the Mother,

Richard Pasco Leantio, Nicholas Selby Hippolito and Jeffrey Dench the Cardinal.

A production in March, 1967, by the University Alumnae Club at the Coach House Theatre, Toronto, made use in the small theatre of a single, multiple-level set. The director, Brian Meeson, attempted in his own words 'a basically prosaic reading'; he responded particularly to 'the features of working-class drama' in the Leantio-Mother scenes, playing them 'with Wesker in mind'. Mr Meeson's most ambitious efforts were reserved for the last Act. Having already 'increased the formality of movement, gesture and speech in Act IV', he employed music to underline the growing regularity of the action, and shifted his lighting 'from the natural to the geometric—positioned shafts of white light'. In V. ii. all the characters involved in the wedding preparations wore white domino masks and long white kid gloves, to strengthen the sense of a nuptial dance turning to a dance of death. Music was widely used ('a triumphant march giving way to an organ pavane') and the acting keyed to it: 'apart from the first few speeches [of V. ii.] every move and word was choreographed strictly to the music, the actors taking all cues from the taped background'. The production aimed to bring out 'Middleton's theatricality, his grasp of realism, and his superb handling of plot intrigue, despite the chaos of the last Act.' Bianca was played by Barbara Collier, Livia by Davena Turvey, Leantio by Michael Tregenza and the Duke by Christian Grotrian.[1]

An adaptation of *Women Beware Women* by Philip McKie was included in Granada Television's 'Play of the Week' series in January, 1965. Heavily cut at the expense of much of the play's emphasis on morality, the adaptation, according to *The Times*, turned the play into 'a melodrama of facile vice and too easily corrupted virtue'. Diana Rigg played Bianca, Gene Anderson Livia and Clifford Evans the Duke.

Among other productions in recent years was that at the Traverse Theatre, Edinburgh, in February, 1968. The play was

[1]I am indebted to Brian Meeson for details of this production; the quotations in this paragraph are his. I am also grateful to Wendv Butler for additional information.

directed by Gordon McDougall, Bianca was played by Valerie Sarruf, Livia by Zoe Hicks, the Duke by Richard Wilson and the Cardinal by John Nettles. A student production at Reading University in March, 1962, antedated the first professional revival. *The Times* critic, while feeling that the production 'lacks Machiavellian gusto', nevertheless conceded that it 'does unfold the complex plot with commendable clarity': indicating perhaps that the student producer knew precisely what he was about. Other student productions in the United States and Canada as well as Britain in the recent past have accompanied the growth of academic interest in Middleton; *Women Beware Women* is proving itself a play of great vitality on the stage as well as in the study.

WOMEN BEWARE WOMEN

[PUBLISHER'S PREFACE]

To The Reader.

When these amongst others of Mr Thomas Middleton's excellent poems came to my hands, I was not a little confident but that his name would prove as great an inducement for thee to read, as me to print them, since those issues of his brain that have already seen the sun, have by their worth gained themselves a free entertainment amongst all that are ingenious; and I am most certain, that these will no way lessen his reputation, nor hinder his admission to any noble and recreative spirits. All that I require at thy hands is to continue the author in his deserved esteem, and to accept of my endeavours which have ever been to please thee.

Farewell.

---

8. *recreative*] disposed to recreation, pastime; not in this sense in *O.E.D.*

[COMMENDATORY VERSES]

Upon

The Tragedy of My Familiar Acquaintance, Tho. Middleton.

Women Beware Women, 'tis a true text
Never to be forgot: drabs of state, vexed,
Have plots, poisons, mischiefs that seldom miss,
To murder virtue with a venom kiss.
Witness this worthy tragedy, expressed
By him that well deserved among the best
Of poets in his time: he knew the rage,
Madness of women crossed; and for the stage
Fitted their humours—hell-bred malice, strife
Acted in state, presented to the life.
I that have seen 't can say, having just cause,
Never came tragedy off with more applause.

Nath. Richards.

---

2. *drabs of state*] high-ranking whores.
5. *expressed*] written.
10. *in state*] with great pomp and ceremony.
13. Nath. Richards] the dramatist and poet Nathaniel Richards, author of *The Celestial Publican: A Sacred Poem* (1630) and *The Tragedy of Messalina, the Roman Empress* (printed 1640). Bentley (III.1001) thinks Richards may have been connected with the King's Revels company. For a possible link between Richards and the manuscript of *WBW* see Introduction p. xxii.

[DRAMATIS PERSONAE]

DUKE OF FLORENCE.
LORD CARDINAL, *brother to the Duke.*
Two Cardinals more.
A Lord.
FABRITIO, *father to Isabella.*
HIPPOLITO, *brother to Fabritio.*
GUARDIANO, *uncle to the foolish Ward.*
WARD, *a rich young heir.*
LEANTIO, *a factor, husband to Bianca.*
SORDIDO, *the Ward's man.*

LIVIA, *sister to Fabritio.*
ISABELLA, *niece to Livia.*
BIANCA, *Leantio's wife.*
MOTHER *to Leantio.*
States of Florence; Citizens; Apprentice; Boys; Messenger; Servants.
[Lords; Ladies; Nymphs; Hebe; Hymen; Ganymede; Attendants.]

THE SCENE: *FLORENCE*

9. *Bianca*] *Dyce; Brancha O.* 13. BIANCA] *Dyce; Brancha O.* 14.] *Dilke;* Widow, his Mother. *O.*

---

9. factor] a merchant's agent or clerk.

13. *BIANCA*] The octavo spells *Brancha* throughout. This is plainly incorrect, on metrical grounds alone; see III. ii. 34, 124, 136, 167 and III. iii. 22, 45, 86 and 99. Parker attributes the mistake to a confusion between manuscript 'i' and 'r'; but study of the holograph *Game at Chess* shows that a confusion between 'e' and 'r' is much more probable. Middleton seems to have spelled 'Beancha', an acceptable Jacobean form (see Marston's *Malcontent*), pronouncing the 'ch' hard. The error may have occurred at transcription (if the octavo was set up from a transcript) and is not necessarily compositorial.

15. *States*] nobles.

19. *THE SCENE:* FLORENCE] See Introduction (p. xliii) for the suggestion that Middleton may have derived the play's 'Italian colouring' from Moryson. There is nothing to show he had first-hand experience of Italy.

Women Beware Women

Act I

[Act I. Scene I.]

Enter LEANTIO *with* BIANCA, *and* MOTHER.

Moth. Thy sight was never yet more precious to me;
Welcome with all the affection of a mother,
That comfort can express from natural love.
Since thy birth-joy, a mother's chiefest gladness,
After sh' has undergone her curse of sorrows,
Thou wast not more dear to me than this hour
Presents thee to my heart. Welcome again.
Lean. [*Aside*] 'Las poor affectionate soul, how her joys speak to me!
I have observed it often, and I know it is
The fortune commonly of knavish children
To have the loving'st mothers.
Moth. What's this gentlewoman?
Lean. Oh you have named the most unvalued'st purchase

0.1. BIANCA] *Dyce;* Brancha *O throughout.* 4. gladness,] *Dilke;* gladness. *O.*

I. i. 2. *affection*] a more temporary sense than in present use: joy, pleasure.

3. *comfort*] an occasion which comforts or gives pleasure (as often in *WBW*: compare II. i. 192).

express] the root meaning 'to press out', 'elicit'. The literal meaning of ll. 2–3 is: 'Welcome with all the joy that this happy event must call forth from a mother's natural love.'

8. *speak to me*] affect me, move me.

10. *knavish*] rascally.

12. *purchase*] that which is acquired. The idea of theft may be present here (see l. 37) as well as that of acquisition in the course of business.

That youth of man had ever knowledge of.
As often as I look upon that treasure,
And know it to be mine—there lies the blessing—
It joys me that I ever was ordained
To have a being, and to live 'mongst men;
Which is a fearful living, and a poor one,
Let a man truly think on 't.
To have the toil and griefs of fourscore years
Put up in a white sheet, tied with two knots—
Methinks it should strike earthquakes in adulterers,
When e'en the very sheets they commit sin in
May prove, for ought they know, all their last garments:
Oh what a mark were there for women then!
But beauty able to content a conqueror,
Whom earth could scarce content, keeps me in compass;
I find no wish in me bent sinfully
To this man's sister, or to that man's wife:
In love's name let 'em keep their honesties,
And cleave to their own husbands, 'tis their duties.
Now when I go to church, I can pray handsomely,
Not come like gallants only to see faces,

33. Not] *O;* Nor *Dilke.*

Characteristically, Leantio's first reference to Bianca uses mercenary terms.

21. *sheet . . . knots*] a shroud or winding-sheet. John Donne's monument in St Paul's shows him swathed in a winding-sheet 'tied with two knots' at head and feet. The bed/grave equivalence of the next lines is a commonplace of Jacobean poetry and drama.

25. *mark*] *exemplum*, something 'to be marked.'

26–7. *conqueror . . . content*] Alexander the Great wept, according to tradition, because his world did not have countries enough to conquer.

27. *in compass*] within limits, content.

32–4.] Complaints about this misuse of church-going are fairly common in the early seventeenth century. Cf. Reynolds, *God's Revenge Against Murder* (1621 ed. p. 114), a work Middleton used in writing *The Changeling* (see Revels *Changeling*, pp. xxxi–xxxv): 'It is both a griefe and a scandall to any true Christians heart, that the Church ordained for thankesgiuing and Prayer vnto God, should be made a Stewes, or at least, a place for men to meet and court Ladies.'

33. *Not*] Dilke seems to have misread the octavo's broken 't' as an 'r';

As if lust went to market still on Sundays.
I must confess I am guilty of one sin, Mother,
More than I brought into the world with me;
But that I glory in: 'tis theft, but noble
As ever greatness yet shot up withal.

Moth. How's that?

Lean. Never to be repented, Mother,
Though sin be death; I had died, if I had not sinned.
And here's my masterpiece: do you now behold her!
Look on her well, she's mine. Look on her better.
Now say, if 't be not the best piece of theft
That ever was committed; and I have my pardon for 't;
'Tis sealed from heaven by marriage.

Moth. Married to her!

Lean. You must keep counsel, Mother, I am undone else;
If it be known, I have lost her; do but think now
What that loss is—life's but a trifle to 't.
From Venice, her consent and I have brought her
From parents great in wealth, more now in rage.
But let storms spend their furies; now we have got
A shelter o'er our quiet innocent loves,

---

and other editors have followed.

35–6. *sin . . . with me*] original sin.

37. *'tis theft*] The phrase 'to steal a marriage' (perhaps of Greek origin: Theocritus 22.151 has κλέπτειν γάμον δώροις) seems to have been used until the eighteenth century, although *O.E.D.* has no seventeenth-century examples.

37–8. *'tis theft . . . withal*] 'It is admittedly theft, but theft of as noble a kind as ever great man practised in gaining his position.' The distinction between morality and social esteem is deliberately blurred. The metaphor implied by 'shot up' is clarified (and some of the disregarded moral issues made explicit) at III. iii. 47–51.

40. *Though . . . death*] Cf. *Romans*, vi. 23: 'The wages of sin is death.'

45. *sealed*] confirmed, approved.

49. *Venice*] almost synonymous with sexual licence. Cf. *Coryat's Crudities* (Glasgow, 1905, I. 401): 'I will . . . make relation of their [Venetian] Cortezans also . . . especially because the name of a Cortezan of Venice is famoused over all Christendome.'

51–2. *storms . . . shelter*] a recurrent image (see Introduction, pp. lxix–lxx).

We are contented. Little money sh' has brought me;
View but her face, you may see all her dowry,
Save that which lies locked up in hidden virtues,
Like jewels kept in cabinets.

Moth. Y' are to blame,
If your obedience will give way to a check,
To wrong such a perfection.

Lean. How?

Moth. Such a creature,
To draw her from her fortune—which no doubt,
At the full time, might have proved rich and noble—
You know not what you have done. My life can give you
But little helps, and my death lesser hopes;
And hitherto your own means has but made shift
To keep you single, and that hardly too.
What ableness have you to do her right then
In maintenance fitting her birth and virtues?
Which ev'ry woman of necessity looks for,
And most to go above it; not confined
By their conditions, virtues, bloods, or births,
But flowing to affections, wills, and humours.

Lean. Speak low, sweet Mother; you are able to spoil as many
As come within the hearing; if it be not
Your fortune to mar all, I have much marvel.
I pray do not you teach her to rebel
When she's in a good way to obedience;

---

57. *If your . . . check*] 'If you are obedient enough to take notice of a rebuke.' Middleton puns on this sense of check, and check = checkmate, in the closing lines of the prologue to *A Game at Chess* (*Wks*, VII. 7): 'But the fair'st jewel that our hopes can deck,/Is so to play our game t' avoid your check.'

64. *To keep you single*] to support you in your single (unmarried) state.

68–70. *not confined . . . humours*] 'not content with what they deserve or can expect in their own social station, but seeking to satisfy in addition the promptings of ambition and fancy.' 'Affections' here = desires, probably *unreasonable* desires; 'humours' (more usually the leading traits of character) here = whims, caprices. 'Flowing' implies the metaphor of a rising tide of 'humour' (?L. *umor*).

To rise with other women in commotion
Against their husbands, for six gowns a year,
And so maintain their cause, when they're once up,
In all things else that require cost enough.
They are all of 'em a kind of spirits soon raised,
But not so soon laid, Mother. As for example,
A woman's belly is got up in a trice—
A simple charge ere it be laid down again.
So ever in all their quarrels, and their courses.
And I'm a proud man, I hear nothing of 'em,
They're very still, I thank my happiness,
And sound asleep; pray let not your tongue wake 'em.
If you can but rest quiet, she's contented
With all conditions that my fortunes bring her to:
To keep close as a wife that loves her husband;
To go after the rate of my ability,
Not the licentious swinge of her own will,
Like some of her old school-fellows. She intends

92. will,] *Dilke;* will. *O.* 92. swinge] *Dilke;* swindg *O;* swing *Dyce and later eds.* 93. school-fellows.] *This ed.;* school-fellows, *O.*

---

76. *commotion*] rebellion.

78. *once up*] when they've gained the upper hand (through being humoured).

80–1. *spirits . . . laid*] punning on the double sense of 'spirits': 'persons, characters' and 'ghosts'. To 'raise' and to 'lay' are the technical terms for summoning and dismissing ghosts.

83. *A simple charge*] ironic: a costly business.

84. *courses*] 'personal conduct or behaviour of a reprehensible kind' (*O.E.D.*).

90. *To keep close*] to stay at home, in seclusion. (*O.E.D.*, under 'close' adj. A4. gives the definition 'shut up from observation . . . secluded'.)

91. *To go . . . ability*] to keep within my means.

92. *swinge*] 'freedom of action', 'liberty to follow one's inclinations' (pronounced 'swindge'). Compare Chapman, *The Revenge of Bussy D'Ambois* I. i. 13–15 (*Wks, Tragedies,* 81): 'so when glory,/Flattery, and smooth applauses of things ill,/Uphold th' inordinate swinge of down-right power.'

92–3] The effect of my repunctuation is to contrast Bianca with her contemporaries—and this is presumably Leantio's point.

To take out other works in a new sampler,
And frame the fashion of an honest love,
Which knows no wants, but, mocking poverty,
Brings forth more children—to make rich men wonder
At divine Providence, that feeds mouths of infants,
And sends them none to feed, but stuffs their rooms
With fruitful bags, their beds with barren wombs.
Good Mother, make not you things worse than they are,
Out of your too much openness—pray take heed on 't—
Nor imitate the envy of old people,
That strive to mar good sport, because they are perfect.
I would have you more pitiful to youth,
Especially to your own flesh and blood.
I'll prove an excellent husband, here's my hand;
Lay in provision, follow my business roundly,
And make you a grandmother in forty weeks.
Go, pray salute her, bid her welcome cheerfully.

Moth. Gentlewoman, thus much is a debt of courtesy
Which fashionable strangers pay each other
At a kind meeting [*kisses Bianca*]; then there's more than one
Due to the knowledge I have of your nearness:

94–5. *take out . . . frame*] A 'sampler' is 'a piece of embroidery serving as a pattern to be copied' (*O.E.D.*); to 'take out' is to make a copy from an original; 'frame' refers to the frame on which the cloth was stretched for embroidering, as well as having its more usual sense of 'shape', 'devise'.

95–100. *an honest love . . . barren wombs*] The infertility of the rich and the fecundity of the poor is a fairly common theme. Compare the part played by this theme in Middleton's *A Chaste Maid in Cheapside* and cf. Fletcher and Massinger's almost exactly contemporary *The Spanish Curate* I. iii: (Beaumont and Fletcher, *Wks*, II. 73): ''Tis the curse/Of great Estates to want those Pledges, which/The poor are happy in: They in a Cottage,/With joy, behold the Models of their youth,/And as their Root decaies, those budding Branches/Sprout forth and flourish, to renew their age.'

100. *bags*] money-bags.

104. *perfect*] blameless, in not being tempted by youth's follies.

108. *business*] frequently equivocal (see Introduction, pp. lviii–lix).
roundly] energetically.

111–17. *Gentlewoman . . . respect*] The Mother kisses Bianca once, as courtesy towards a stranger requires, and then again in token of their kinship ('nearness'). A further kiss may be intended after l. 114.

I am bold to come again, and now salute you
By th' name of daughter, which may challenge more
Than ordinary respect. [*Kisses her again*]
Lean. [*Aside*] Why this is well now,
And I think few mothers of threescore will mend it.
Moth. What I can bid you welcome to is mean;
But make it all your own; we are full of wants
And cannot welcome worth.
Lean. [*Aside*] Now this is scurvy
And spake as if a woman lacked her teeth.
These old folks talk of nothing but defects,
Because they grow so full of 'em themselves.
Bian. Kind Mother, there is nothing can be wanting
To her that does enjoy all her desires.
Heaven send a quiet peace with this man's love,
And I am as rich as virtue can be poor:
Which were enough after the rate of mind
To erect temples for content placed here.
I have forsook friends, fortunes, and my country,
And hourly I rejoice in 't: here's my friends,
And few is the good number. Thy successes,
Howe'er they look, I will still name my fortunes;
Hopeful or spiteful, they shall all be welcome.
Who invites many guests has of all sorts,
As he that traffics much drinks of all fortunes;

---

118. *mend*] improve on.

120. *wants*] shortcomings.

121. *scurvy*] vexatious. Perhaps also with a glance at the disease, one of the symptoms of which (see l. 122) was loss of teeth.

123. *defects*] deficiencies, lacks. The Mother talks of the wants among her household goods because, says Leantio, she has grown used to the deficiencies of her own body. Moral 'defects' are not implied.

127–30.] 'If Heaven only allows me to live undisturbed in my husband's love, I shall be rich in the way that the virtuous can sometimes be poor—and that is rich enough, reckoned in a non-material way, to allow me to build whole temples of happiness here.' 'Here' may refer to the Mother's house, or may perhaps mean 'in this breast.'

133. *successes*] fortunes, good or ill (L. *succedere*, follow after).

137. *traffics*] trades.

drinks of all fortunes] Cf. the still current 'to taste adversity.'

Yet they must all be welcome, and used well.
I'll call this place the place of my birth now,
And rightly too: for here my love was born,
And that's the birth-day of a woman's joys.
[*To Leantio*] You have not bid me welcome since I came.

Lean. That I did questionless.

Bian. No sure, how was 't?
I have quite forgot it.

Lean. Thus. [*Leantio kisses her.*]

Bian. Oh sir, 'tis true,
Now I remember well. I have done thee wrong,
Pray take 't again, sir. [*They kiss again.*]

Lean. How many of these wrongs
Could I put up in an hour. And turn up the glass
For twice as many more!

Moth. Will 't please you to walk in, daughter?

Bian. Thanks, sweet Mother;
The voice of her that bare me is not more pleasing.
Exeunt [MOTHER *and* BIANCA].

Lean. Though my own care and my rich master's trust
Lay their commands both on my factorship,
This day and night I'll know no other business
But her and her dear welcome. 'Tis a bitterness
To think upon tomorrow: that I must
Leave her still to the sweet hopes of the week's end,

149. Will 't] *Dilke;* Wilt *O.*

---

138. *used well*] referring back, by a grammatical licence, to the 'guests' of l. 136.

147. *glass*] hour-glass.

149. *Will 't*] Octavo 'Wilt' is probably an error. The compositor may have found 'Wil't', a usual Middleton spelling, and have removed, as was his habit, the apparently incorrect apostrophe.

151. *my own care*] perhaps combining 'conscientiousness' and 'self-regard, care for my own advancement.' Leantio stresses the second on his next appearance, I. iii. 1 ff.

152. *factorship*] Cf. *Dramatis Personae*, l. 9n.

155–6.] The octavo lineation, ending l. 155 with 'her' is clumsy, gives undue emphasis to 'still' and leaves the following line one syllable short.

That pleasure should be so restrained and curbed,
After the course of a rich workmaster
That never pays till Saturday night. Marry
It comes together in a round sum then,
And does more good you'll say. Oh fair-eyed Florence,
Didst thou but know what a most matchless jewel
Thou now art mistress of, a pride would take thee,
Able to shoot destruction through the bloods
Of all thy youthful sons. But 'tis great policy
To keep choice treasures in obscurest places:
Should we show thieves our wealth, 'twould make 'em bolder.
Temptation is a devil will not stick
To fasten upon a saint; take heed of that.
The jewel is cased up from all men's eyes;
Who could imagine now a gem were kept
Of that great value under this plain roof?
But how in times of absence? What assurance
Of this restraint then? Yes, yes, there's one with her:

Previous editors begin l. 156 with 'Her' but this makes for difficult speaking, if metrically an improvement.

158. *After the course of*] as is the practice of.

163–5.] 'pride' has strong sexual overtones (cf. *Oth.* III. iii. 404: 'As salt as wolves in pride'); 'blood' is frequently used to mean 'lustful desires.' The placing of 'pride' is most adroit; it allows the sentence to move economically from the commonplace that Florence should be 'proud' of the beauty of her new citizen, to the reflection that a sight of that beauty would so rouse ('a pride would take') the sexual appetites of young Florentines as to bring about their undoing. Christopher Ricks notes that Middleton customarily uses 'pride' 'to stress the inseparable links between social vanity and adultery' (*R.E.S.*, n.s. XII, 1961, p. 246).

165–6. *'tis great policy . . . obscurest places*] Middleton (and other Jacobean dramatists) linked this attitude to women with Italy. Cf. Middleton, *A Mad World, My Masters*, I. ii. 21–4, (*Wks*, III, 262–3): 'there's a gem/ I would not lose,/Kept by th' Italian under lock and key:/We Englishmen are careless creatures.'

168. *stick*] scruple. The usage must have seemed a natural one to Middleton, or he would surely have avoided the clumsy repetition of the image in 'fasten upon' in the next line.

171–2. *a gem . . . plain roof*] Beaumont employs precisely the same image in *The Woman-Hater* II. i, (Beaumont and Fletcher, *Wks*, V. 89): 'Can he be sad that hath so rich a gem under his roof, as that which I doe follow?'

Old mothers know the world, and such as these,
When sons lock chests, are good to look to keys. *Exit.*

[I. ii]

Enter GUARDIANO, FABRITIO, *and* LIVIA [*and* Servant.]

Guard. What, has your daughter seen him yet. Know you that?
Fab. No matter, she shall love him.
Guard. Nay let's have fair play:
He has been now my ward some fifteen year,
And 'tis my purpose, as time calls upon me,
By custom seconded and such moral virtues,
To tender him a wife. Now sir, this wife
I'd fain elect out of a daughter of yours:
You see my meaning's fair. If now this daughter
So tendered (let me come to your own phrase, sir)
Should offer to refuse him, I were hanselled.
[*Aside*] Thus am I fain to calculate all my words
For the meridian of a foolish old man,
To take his understanding. [*To him*] What do you answer, sir?
Fab. I say still she shall love him.
Guard. Yet again?
And shall she have no reason for this love?

0.1. I. ii] Scaen. 2. *O.*

I. ii. 5. *moral*] both 'traditional, customary' (L. *mores*) and 'proper, righteous.' A conflation typical of the play (see Introduction, p. liv).

10. *hanselled*] ironic. A 'hansel' is usually auspicious: a gift received at the outset of a new year or new enterprise. Here 'I were hanselled' means: 'That would be a fine present indeed!'

12. *meridian*] the special characteristic that distinguishes one person or group from all others; in this case Fabritio's limited intelligence. Cf. Jonson *Staple of News* 'The Prologue for the Court', 1–4, (*Wks*, VI. 283): 'A Worke not smelling of the Lampe, to night,/But fitted to your *Maiesties* disport,/And writ to the *Meridian* of your *Court*,/Wee bring.'

13. *take*] capture, match.

15–16.] A frequent matter of comment in the Jacobean literature on women. Overbury (*A Wife*, 1604) gives the ideal situation: 'of that love,

Fab. Why, do you think that women love with reason?
Guard. [*Aside*] I perceive fools are not at all hours foolish,
No more than wise men wise.
Fab. I had a wife,
She ran mad for me; she had no reason for 't
For aught I could perceive. What think you, lady sister?
Guard. [*Aside*] 'Twas a fit match that, being both out of their wits.
[*To him*] A loving wife, it seemed
She strove to come as near you as she could.
Fab. And if her daughter prove not mad for love too,
She takes not after her; nor after me,
If she prefer reason before my pleasure.
[*To Livia*] You're an experienced widow, lady sister,
I pray let your opinion come amongst us.
Liv. I must offend you then, if truth will do 't,

25. her; . . . me,] *Dilke;* her, . . . me; *O.* 26. pleasure.] *Dyce;* pleasure, *O.* 27. widow,] *Dilke;* widow. *O.*

---

let reason father be,/And passion mother; let it from the one/His being take, the other his degree.' Massinger's Antonio in *A Very Woman* (V. ii; *Wks*, IV. 331) agrees with Fabritio: 'Woman, giddy woman!/In her the blemish of your sex you prove,/There is no reason for your hate or love.' Fletcher's *Women Pleased* (I. i., Beaumont and Fletcher, *Wks*, VII. 241) says bluntly: 'Love is blind man,/And he that looks for reason there far blinder.'

21–3.] Editors usually mark the whole speech 'aside'. But Fabritio would find nothing objectionable in the second statement (by itself it sounds a compliment), and the change of person ('you' l. 23) suggests direct address. Dyce's lineation seems preferable to that in the octavo. One broken line cannot be avoided, and 'A loving . . . seemed' is rhythmically acceptable. ''Twas . . . wits' may be one of the quasi-prose interjections (especially asides or other throw-away phrases) that Middleton inserts in his verse passages, and may as such have confused scribe or compositor (see Introduction, pp. xxx–xxxi).

22. *seemed*] possibly a misreading of 'seemes', Middleton's usual spelling; a quick glance might mistake Middleton's final 's' for 'd', though the letters are normally distinct.

23. *come as near*] be as like. With a glance at physical nearness.

26. *reason . . . my pleasure*] Isabella has to choose, not between reason and pleasure, but between reason and *Fabritio's* pleasure.

And take my niece's part, and call 't injustice
To force her love to one she never saw.
Maids should both see, and like; all little enough;
If they love truly after that, 'tis well.
Counting the time, she takes one man till death,
That's a hard task, I tell you. But one may
Enquire at three years' end amongst young wives
And mark how the game goes.

Fab. Why, is not man
Tied to the same observance, lady sister,
And in one woman?

Liv. 'Tis enough for him;
Besides he tastes of many sundry dishes
That we poor wretches never lay our lips to:
As obedience forsooth, subjection, duty, and such kickshaws,
All of our making, but served in to them.
And if we lick a finger then sometimes,
We are not to blame; your best cooks use it.

Fab. Th' art a sweet lady, sister, and a witty—

Liv. A witty! Oh the bud of commendation
Fit for a girl of sixteen; I am blown, man,

44. finger] *Dyce;* finger, *O.* 44. sometimes,] *Dilke;* sometimes *O.*
45. cooks use] *O;* cooks [often] use *Dyce.*

30–1. *injustice . . . never saw*] The extent of a father's rights in arranging his children's marriages was widely debated at this date. Livia's opinion here was perhaps that generally received; Sir Thomas Overbury (*A Wife*, 1614) credits King James with the remark: 'Parents may forbid their children to an unfitt marriage, but they may not force their consciences to a fitt.'

34. *Counting*] considering.

42. *kickshaws*] a fancy dish. The word is derived from F. *quelque chose*; the contemptuous force it often bears (ironically inverted here) is due to its being a slight 'something French', not one of the 'substantial English' dishes. Compare modern 'trifle'. The image is continued in 'served in' (l. 43).

45. *your . . . use it*] They make a habit of it. In allusion to the popular proverb (Tilley, L. 636) ''tis an ill cook that cannot lick his own fingers.' Dyce's insertion 'often' after 'cooks' is unnecessary; the line is tolerable Middleton.

48. *blown*] full-blown, in bloom. In contrast to 'bud' (l. 47).

I should be wise by this time; and for instance,
I have buried my two husbands in good fashion,
And never mean more to marry.
Guard. No, why so, lady?
Liv. Because the third shall never bury me.
I think I am more than witty; how think you, sir?
Fab. I have paid often fees to a counsellor
Has had a weaker brain.
Liv. Then I must tell you,
Your money was soon parted.
Guard. [*To Fabritio*] Light her now, brother.

56. Light her now, brother] *O;* Like enow. *Ellis;* Like enow./*Liv.* Brother, *Oliphant.*

55–6. *Then . . . parted*] referring to the proverb 'a fool and his money are soon parted.' (Tilley, F. 452).

56. *Light her now, brother*] Two difficulties in this line, the meaning of 'Light' and the accuracy of 'brother', have led to widespread editorial changes. 'Light' may be equivalent to 'let her light' (Abbott, section 364, gives several parallels in Shakespeare) and 'light' can mean 'come to or arrive in a place' (*O.E.D.*, light v.[1] 10b) a sense in which Middleton uses it on two other occasions in this play (III. i. 69 and III. iii. 28). The phrase as a whole therefore could be taken as 'let her come in now, brother.' This is scarcely satisfactory, but preferable to emendations so far proposed. Percy Simpson's 'Plight' for 'Light' (*M.L.R.*, XXXIII, 1938, p. 45) supposes a complete misreading by the compositor, of a kind of which we have no other example in the play. K. Deighton's ''Slight, her own brother! (*aside*' is open to the same objection, and is in addition very unconvincing dramatically (*The Old Dramatists: Conjectural Readings* (1896) p. 177). An emendation suggested in *The Gentleman's Magazine* (n.s. XIV (1840) p. 584) involves extensive rearrangement (including the entire removal of Guardiano as a speaker) and is even less justifiable bibliographically than 'Like enow' (omitting 'brother') suggested by Bullen and adopted by Ellis and Oliphant—mishearing, the basis of this change, would assume the octavo was set from dictation, of which very unusual procedure there is no evidence.

The inaccuracy of 'brother' (Guardiano is no relation of Fabritio) need not suggest textual corruption. The term was used loosely in Jacobean England, and when Isabella and the Ward marry, Guardiano and Fabritio will be relations-by-marriage. Middleton may however have slipped up. As Parker notes, the relationship between Guardiano, Livia and Fabritio remains rather undefined in the play; in the source 'Livia' and 'Guardiano' were married, whereas Livia is here Fabritio's sister and no relative of Guardiano.

Liv. Where is my niece? Let her be sent for straight
If you have any hope 'twill prove a wedding.
'Tis fit i' faith she should have one sight of him,
And stop upon 't, and not be joined in haste,
As if they went to stock a new-found land.
Fab. Look out her uncle, and y' are sure of her. [*Exit* Servant.]
Those two are ne'er asunder; they've been heard
In argument at midnight, moonshine nights
Are noondays with them: they walk out their sleeps,
Or rather at those hours appear like those
That walk in 'em, for so they did to me.
Look you, I told you truth; they're like a chain:
Draw but one link, all follows.

Enter [Servant *with*] HIPPOLITO, *and* ISABELLA *the niece.*

Guard. Oh affinity,
What piece of excellent workmanship art thou!
'Tis work clean wrought, for there's no lust, but love in 't,
And that abundantly; when in stranger things
There is no love at all, but what lust brings.
Fab. [*To Isabella*] On with your mask, for 'tis your part to see now,
And not be seen. Go to, make use of your time;
See what you mean to like; nay, and I charge you,
Like what you see. Do you hear me? There's no dallying,

---

60. *stop*] reflect, consider.

60–1. *joined . . . land*] a glance at the hastily-arranged marriages of colonists about to set out for the new overseas territories. Middleton may have Virginia in mind in the present case (for a discussion of attempts to date the play on this premise see Introduction, p. xxxiv). Equally he may be thinking of Newfoundland which, though discovered as early as 1497, was first seriously colonized by John Guy in 1610; colonies were founded there in 1617 (Trepassey) and 1618 (Harbour Grace).

65. *walk . . . sleeps*] walk together instead of sleeping.

69. *affinity*] kinship.

69–73. *Oh affinity . . . brings*] A frequent topic with Middleton, occurring first in *The Ghost of Lucrece* (1600 ed. sig. A7) written some years before 1600.

71. *clean wrought*] done in a competent, craftsmanlike way.

72. *stranger things*] men and women not related.

The gentleman's almost twenty, and 'tis time
He were getting lawful heirs, and you a-breeding on 'em.

Isab. Good father!

Fab. Tell not me of tongues and rumours.
You'll say the gentleman is somewhat simple—
The better for a husband, were you wise,
For those that marry fools live ladies' lives.
On with the mask, I'll hear no more, he's rich;
The fool's hid under bushels.

Liv. Not so hid neither,
But here's a foul great piece of him methinks;
What will he be, when he comes altogether?

Enter the WARD *with a trap-stick, and* SORDIDO *his man.*

Ward. Beat him?
I beat him out o' th' field with his own cat-stick,
Yet gave him the first hand.

Sord. Oh strange!

Ward. I did it,
Then he set jacks on me.

Sord. What, my ladies' tailor?

80. *Isab.*] *Dilke; Neece. O throughout I. ii.* 90. ladies'] Ladies *O;* lady's *Dilke.*

---

80. *tongues*] gossip. A sense not in *O.E.D.* (but compare sense 5).

85. *bushels*] large quantities of anything, in this case money. Cf. *Matthew*, V. 15: 'A wise man does not light a candle and set it under a bushel.'

87.1. trap-stick] also called 'cat-stick' below. Dyce quotes Strutt, *Sports and Pastimes:* 'TIP-CAT, or perhaps more properly, the *game* of CAT, is a rustic pastime well known in many parts of the kingdom. Its denomination is derived from a piece of wood called a *cat*, with which it is played; the cat is about six inches in length, and an inch and a half or two inches in diameter, and diminished from the middle to both ends, in the shape of a double cone; . . . when the cat is laid upon the ground, the player with his cudgel or cat-stick strikes it smartly, it matters not at which end, and it will rise with a rotatory motion, high enough for him to beat it away as it falls, in the same manner as he would a ball.'

89. *first hand*] first strike. The 'him' of these lines (as far as l. 92) is the 'ladies' tailor'; in l. 91 the voice-stress falls on 'beat' (to give prominence to the pun; see note) and not on 'him too.'

90. *jacks*] low-bred or common fellows.

Ward. Ay, and I beat him too.
Sord. Nay, that's no wonder,
He's used to beating.
Ward. Nay, I tickled him
When I came once to my tippings.
Sord. Now you talk on 'em,
There was a poulterer's wife made a great complaint of you last night to your guardianer, that you struck a bump in her child's head, as big as an egg.

Ward. An egg may prove a chicken, then in time the poulterer's wife will get by 't. When I am in game, I am furious; came my mothers' eyes in my way, I would not lose a fair end. No, were she alive, but with one tooth in her head, I should venture the striking out of that. I think of nobody when I am in play, I am so earnest.
Coads-me, my guardianer!
Prithee lay up my cat and cat-stick safe.
Sord. Where, sir, i' th' chimney-corner?
Ward. Chimney-corner!

97. chicken,] *Dilke;* chicken *O.* 97. time] *Dilke;* time; *O.*

---

92. *beating*] punning on 'beaten' = embroidered. Compare L. Barrey, *Ram Alley* (1616. v. 452): '[clad] in beaten velvet.' (*O.E.D.*) A reference may also be intended to the tailor's reputation for dishonesty, and the 'beatings' he could therefore expect.

tickled] ironic inversion: defeated heavily, 'thrashed.'

93. *tippings*] 'a term of the game' says Dyce. Not in *O.E.D.*

93–103.] To chop this passage into verse, as earlier editors do, merely hobbles Middleton's brisk prose. 'Now you talk on 'em' completes a verse line, even though it introduces a speech in prose; a not uncommon practice in Middleton. Verse begins again with 'Prithee . . . safe.'

98. *get*] gain. A *poulterer's* wife would sell the chicken.

100. *fair end*] An 'end' is the term still used in bowls for each division of the game. *O.E.D.* says it was formerly in use in billiards and other sports. A 'fair end' must be one favourable to the speaker.

103. *Coads-me*] 'apparently an altered or "minced" adjuration.' (*O.E.D.*)

105–7. *chimney-corner . . . burn*] These lines are full of bawdy innuendo. A similar equivocation on 'chimney' (the vagina) occurs in Fletcher's *Women Pleas'd*, IV. iii. 1 (Beaumont and Fletcher, *Wks*, VII. 293). 'Cat' was a cant term for a harlot; 'safe' = free from infection; 'burn' was commonly associated with venereal disease.

Sord. Yes, sir, your cats are always safe i' th' chimney-
corner,
Unless they burn their coats.
Ward. Marry, that I am afraid on!
Sord. Why, then I will bestow your cat i' th' gutter,
And there she's safe I am sure.
Ward. If I but live
To keep a house, I'll make thee a great man,
If meat and drink can do 't. I can stoop gallantly,
And pitch out when I list; I'm dog at a hole.
I mar'l my guardianer does not seek a wife for me;
I protest I'll have a bout with the maids else,
Or contract myself at midnight to the larder-woman,
In presence of a fool, or a sack-posset.
Guard. Ward.

108–9. *Why . . . sure*] perhaps with reference to the proverb 'they agree like two cats in a gutter' (Tilley C. 185).

110. *great*] eminent; corpulent.

111–12. *I . . . hole*] introduced largely for the sake of the (not very clear) puns and innuendos. Parker explains 'stoop' and 'pitch' as hawking terms, the second referring in addition to hunting (as indeed the first might also—see *O.E.D.*) thus introducing 'dog at a hole.' But all three may have been technical terms in the game of tip-cat: 'stoop', 'pitch out' and 'hole' would all be relevant expressions, the last two particularly if the game were played, not with Strutt's 'double cone', but as it is by children today, with a short stick projecting over a hole. Each of the three expressions doubtless includes a sexual innuendo. 'Stoop gallantly', ostensibly 'bow elegantly', also glances at 'stoop-gallant' a term originally used to refer to the 'sweating sickness' and then to any disease, usually venereal, that humbled gallants. Nashe suggests (with a *double entendre*) that one could entitle a play '*Stoope Gallant*, or *The Fall of pride*' (*Have With You; Wks*, III. 114.). 'Dog at' = adept at.

114. *a bout*] 'a bout, turn, occasion of physical love' (Partridge).

116. *In presence of*] A verbal contract of marriage was binding if uttered in the presence of one witness. Compare the 'betrothal scene' (I. i) in Webster's *Duchess of Malfi*.

fool] Bullen thinks a play on 'fowl' is intended. More probable is a simple pun on the delicacy called a 'fool'. Cf. John Florio, *World of Words*, 1598: '*Mantiglia*, a kind of clouted creame called a foole or a trifle in English.' (*O.E.D.*)

sack-posset] hot milk curdled with sack, and with sugar, spices and other ingredients added.

Ward. I feel myself after any exercise
Horribly prone: let me but ride, I'm lusty;
A cock-horse straight i' faith.
Guard. Why, Ward, I say.
Ward. I'll forswear eating eggs-in-moonshine 'nights.
There's ne'er a one I eat but turns into a cock
In four and twenty hours; if my hot blood
Be not took down in time, sure 'twill crow shortly.
Guard. Do you hear, sir? Follow me, I must new school you.
Ward. School me? I scorn that now, I am past schooling.
I am not so base to learn to write and read;
I was born to better fortunes in my cradle.
Exit [GUARDIANO, *the* WARD *and* SORDIDO.]
Fab. How do you like him, girl? This is your husband.
Like him or like him not, wench, you shall have him,
And you shall love him.
Liv. Oh soft there, brother! Though you be a justice,
Your warrant cannot be served out of your liberty;
You may compel out of the power of father
Things merely harsh to a maid's flesh and blood,

120. eggs-in-moonshine 'nights] *This ed.;* Eggs in Moon-shine nights *O.*

---

118. *prone*] i.e. to venery.

119. *A cock-horse*] a hobby horse; a Jacobean cant term for a mistress or whore.

120. *eggs-in-moonshine 'nights*] 'nights' is primarily adverbial, though intended also to act punningly as the noun qualified by 'moonshine.' 'Eggs-in-moonshine' was a dish resembling poached eggs. Robert May, *The Accomplisht Cook* p. 437 (5th ed. 1685; first published 1665) gives the recipe: 'Break them [the eggs] in a dish upon some butter and oyl melted or cold, strow on them a little salt, and set them on a chafing dish of coals[;] make not the yolks too hard, and in the doing cover them and make a sauce for them of an onion cut into round slices, and fried in sweet oyl or butter, then put to them verjuyce, grated nutmeg, a little salt, and so serve them.' Eggs were long regarded as aphrodisiacs.

122–3. *hot blood . . . crow*] bawdy. 'Took down' refers to detumescence and 'crow' to ejaculation.

132. *liberty*] the limits within which the warrant of a Justice of the Peace was valid (before 1850).

134. *merely*] extremely, altogether.

But when you come to love, there the soil alters;
Y' are in another country, where your laws
Are no more set by than the cacklings of geese
In Rome's great Capitol.

Fab. Marry him she shall then,
Let her agree upon love afterwards. *Exit.*

Liv. You speak now, brother, like an honest mortal
That walks upon th' earth with a staff; you were
Up i' th' clouds before. You'd command love—
And so do most old folks that go without it.
[*To Hippolito*] My best and dearest brother, I could dwell here;
There is not such another seat on earth
Where all good parts better express themselves.

Hip. You'll make me blush anon.

Liv. 'Tis but like saying grace before a feast then,
And that's most comely; thou art all a feast,
And she that has thee a most happy guest.
Prithee cheer up thy niece with special counsel. [*Exit* LIVIA.]

Hip. [*Aside*] I would 'twere fit to speak to her what I would; but
'Twas not a thing ordained, Heaven has forbid it;
And 'tis most meet that I should rather perish
Than the decree divine receive least blemish.

151. thy] *Dilke;* that *O.*

---

137. *set by*] valued, regarded.

137–8. *cacklings . . . Capitol*] In early Roman history sacred geese were kept on the Capitoline Hill. Middleton must be thinking only of their presence; it would be unapt to refer here to the familiar tale recording how their excited cackling woke the Roman defenders during a night-attack on the Capitol by invading Gauls in 390 or 387 B.C.

144. *dwell here*] i.e. 'dwell on' Hippolito's handsome appearance. Perhaps also suggesting 'seat' (compare 'country seat') in line 145.

147–8. *blush . . . grace*] punning on the two senses of 'grace'. Compare *Gent.* V. iv. 165: 'I think the boy hath grace in him; he blushes.'

151. *thy*] the reading of all modern editions. The compositor may have been influenced by 'that' in the previous line.

Feed inward you my sorrows; make no noise,
Consume me silent, let me be stark dead
Ere the world know I'm sick. You see my honesty;
If you befriend me, so.

Isab. [*Aside*] Marry a fool!
Can there be greater misery to a woman
That means to keep her days true to her husband,
And know no other man! So virtue wills it.
Why, how can I obey and honour him
But I must needs commit idolatry?
A fool is but the image of a man,
And that but ill made neither. Oh the heart-breakings
Of miserable maids, where love's enforced!
The best condition is but bad enough:
When women have their choices, commonly
They do but buy their thraldoms, and bring great portions
To men to keep 'em in subjection—
As if a fearful prisoner should bribe
The keeper to be good to him, yet lies in still,
And glad of a good usage, a good look sometimes.
By 'r Lady, no misery surmounts a woman's:
Men buy their slaves, but women buy their masters.

174–5. sometimes./By'r Lady,] *Dyce;* Sometimes by'r Lady; *O.* 175. woman's:] *Dilke;* womans. *O.*

158–9. *You . . . so.*] It is not clear to whom this is addressed. It cannot be Isabella; it is unlikely to be the audience; the immediately preceding 'you', his 'sorrows', would not give a particularly apt sense. He perhaps invokes Heaven as the power that imposes his 'honesty' of silence.

165. *image*] the outward semblance, statue or 'idol'. Hence 'idolatry' line 164.

170. *portions*] marriage-portions.

172–4.] The practice of bribing gaolers was widespread at this date, and their meanness was proverbial. Compare Hugh Dowriche, *The Iaylors Conversion* 1596 (sig. B.2.b.): 'The Iaylors make their Office odious, by vnmercifull abusing of the poore prisoners, robbing them by their great fees, selling them but a little libertie for a great deale of money . . .'

173. *lies in still*] remains in prison.

Yet honesty and love makes all this happy,
And, next to angels', the most blest estate.
That Providence that has made ev'ry poison
Good for some use, and sets four warring elements
At peace in man, can make a harmony
In things that are most strange to human reason.
Oh but this marriage! [*To him*] What, are you sad too, uncle?
'Faith, then there's a whole household down together!
Where shall I go to seek my comfort now
When my best friend's distressed? What is 't afflicts you, sir?

Hip. 'Faith, nothing but one grief that will not leave me,
And now 'tis welcome. Ev'ry man has something
To bring him to his end, and this will serve,
Joined with your father's cruelty to you—
That helps it forward.

Isab. Oh be cheered, sweet uncle!
How long has 't been upon you? I ne'er spied it;
What a dull sight have I. How long I pray, sir?

Hip. Since I first saw you, niece, and left Bologna.

Isab. And could you deal so unkindly with my heart
To keep it up so long hid from my pity?
Alas, how shall I trust your love hereafter?
Have we passed through so many arguments

179–80. *ev'ry poison . . . use*] Compare Middleton, *The Changeling*, II. ii. 46–7: 'Why, men of art make much of poison,/Keep one to expel another.' Bawcutt's note (*Revels* ed. p. 35) suggests that Middleton may have derived the doctrine that everything in nature has some use or purpose from Montaigne's *Essais*, Book III, ch. I 'De L'Utile et de L'Honneste' (*Oeuvres*, Paris, 1927, v. 3–4). But the doctrine is traditional.

180. *warring elements*] The elements (earth, air, fire and water) were thought of as being the component parts or aspects of matter, each having different and opposed qualities (earth cold and dry, air hot and moist, etc.). The most famous discussion of the 'warring elements' comes in Marlowe, *I Tamburlaine* II. vii. 18 ff.

194. *Bologna*] *T.H.* (see Introduction, pp. xliv, ff.) gives Bologna as Hippolito's birthplace.

198. *arguments*] themes, topics.

And missed of that still, the most needful one?
Walked out whole nights together in discourses;
And the main point forgot? We are to blame both;
This is an obstinate wilful forgetfulness,
And faulty on both parts. Let's lose no time now:
Begin, good uncle, you that feel 't, what is it?

Hip. You of all creatures, niece, must never hear on 't;
'Tis not a thing ordained for you to know.

Isab. Not I, sir! All my joys that word cuts off.
You made profession once you loved me best;
'Twas but profession!

Hip. Yes, I do 't too truly,
And fear I shall be chid for 't. Know the worst then:
I love thee dearlier than an uncle can.

Isab. Why so you ever said, and I believed it.

Hip. [*Aside*] So simple is the goodness of her thoughts,
They understand not yet th' unhallowed language
Of a near sinner. I must yet be forced
(Though blushes be my venture) to come nearer.
[*To her*] As a man loves his wife so love I thee.

Isab. What's that? Methought I heard ill news come toward me,
Which commonly we understand too soon,
Then over-quick at hearing. I'll prevent it,
Though my joys fare the harder, well fare it:

200 Walked] *O;* Wak'd *Dilke.* 220. hearing.] *Dilke subst.;* hearing, *O.*
221. well fare] *This ed.;* welcome *O.*

200. *Walked*] Dilke's 'Wak'd', in any case unnecessary, is proved wrong by I. ii. 65.

202. *obstinate wilful forgetfulness*] Forgetfulness as a *willed* blindness to the needs of others, self-absorption, is one of the charges brought against his own behaviour by the dying Hippolito (V. ii. 146 ff.).

216. *venture*] what is risked; a metaphor from commerce.

come nearer] be more explicit.

220. *prevent it*] anticipate its coming, deal with it before it comes (L. *prae* + *venire*).

221. *well fare*] = farewell. The octavo's 'welcome' gives precisely the opposite sense to that required. The compositor, as was common prac-

It shall ne'er come so near mine ear again.
Farewell all friendly solaces and discourses,
I'll learn to live without ye, for your dangers
Are greater than your comforts. What's become
Of truth in love, if such we cannot trust—
When blood that should be love is mixed with lust?
Exit.

Hip. The worst can be but death, and let it come;
He that lives joyless, ev'ry day's his doom. *Exit.*

[I. iii]

Enter LEANTIO *alone.*

Lean. Methinks I'm e'en as dull now at departure
As men observe great gallants the next day
After a revels; you shall see 'em look
Much of my fashion, if you mark 'em well.
'Tis e'en a second hell to part from pleasure
When man has got a smack on 't. As many holidays
Coming together makes your poor heads idle
A great while after, and are said to stick
Fast in their fingers' ends, e'en so does game

0.1. I. iii] Scaen. 3. *O.* 3. revels] *O;* revel *Dilke.*

---

tice, may have memorized lines 221 and 222, with two occurrences of 'fare' in the first and 'come' in the second. It would then have been easy to set 'welcome' in place of 'welfare' or 'well fare'. *O.E.D.* cites a similar use: 'Yet welfare another learned Jesuit that had been at Rome.' (T. James, *Corrupt. Script.* 1612, III. 35).

227.] Compare I. ii. 69–73n. 'Blood' may mean both 'affinity' and 'sexual desire', though Isabella intends only the first.

I. iii. 3. *revels*] any kind of merrymaking; 'revel' is used of 'a joyous love-making' (Partridge). Not in *O.E.D.* in this use.

6. *smack*] taste (G. *schmecken*).

8–9. *are said . . . fingers' ends*] Middleton seems to suggest the phrase was proverbial, but it does not occur in Tilley or the other large proverb collections. The meaning is plain: the revellers are hampered by the effects of the previous night's activities. The association of 'fingers' ends' with skilled crafts, especially of a delicate kind, was common; compare

In a new-married couple: for the time
It spoils all thrift, and indeed lies abed
To invent all the new ways for great expenses.

[*Enter*] BIANCA *and* MOTHER *above.*

See and she be not got on purpose now
Into the window to look after me.
I have no power to go now, and I should be hanged.
Farewell all business, I desire no more
Than I see yonder; let the goods at quay
Look to themselves; why should I toil my youth out?
It is but begging two or three year sooner,
And stay with her continually—is 't a match?
Oh fie, what a religion have I leaped into!
Get out again for shame; then man loves best
When his care's most: that shows his zeal to love.
Fondness is but the idiot to affection,
That plays at hot-cockles with rich merchants' wives—

10. couple:] *Dilke subst.;* couple *O.* 17. quay] *Dilke;* Key *O.* 22. then] *This ed.;* the *O.* 23. most:] *Dilke subst.;* most, *O.*

Tilley G88: 'The German hath his spirit at his fingers' ends, because he is a good Artificer.'

12. *expenses*] with a double sense, financial and sexual.

15. *and*] if.

16–17. *business . . . yonder*] Compare I. i. 108n.

20. *match*] agreement, bargain.

22. *then*] The octavo 'the' is very awkward; my emended reading makes 'when' much more natural, and gives 'that' (l. 23) a new forcefulness. On at least seven occasions the octavo certainly docks a word of its final letter, as it does, I assume, here.

23. *that*] his 'care', industry.

24. *Fondness . . . affection*] 'fondness (an over-strong, unreasoning, attachment) is the mere zany or fool that dogs the steps of, and caricatures, affection (a tempered, reasonable love).' Compare *Troil.*, II. i. 59, where Thersites, mocking Ajax as a mere caricature of the god of war, describes him as 'Mars his idiot.'

25. *hot-cockles*] Strutt p. 308 says that this pastime, deriving its name 'from the French *hautes-coquiles*, is a play in which one kneels, and covering his eyes lays his head in another's lap and guesses who struck him.' Only 'fond' lovers, says Leantio, can afford such foolish pastimes. Par-

Good to make sport withal when the chest's full,
And the long warehouse cracks. 'Tis time of day
For us to be more wise, 'tis early with us;
And if they lose the morning of their affairs
They commonly lose the best part of the day.
Those that are wealthy, and have got enough,
'Tis after sunset with 'em; they may rest,
Grow fat with ease, banquet and toy and play,
When such as I enter the heat o' th' day;
And I'll do 't cheerfully.

Bian. I perceive, sir,
Y' are not gone yet; I have good hope you'll stay now.

Lean. Farewell, I must not.

Bian. Come, come, pray return;
Tomorrow, adding but a little care more,
Will dispatch all as well; believe me 'twill, sir.

Lean. I could well wish myself where you would have me.
But love that's wanton must be ruled awhile
By that that's careful, or all goes to ruin:
As fitting is a government in love
As in a kingdom; where 'tis all mere lust
'Tis like an insurrection in the people,
That raised in self-will wars against all reason.
But love that is respective for increase

30. day.] *This ed.;* day, *O.* 31. enough,] *Dilke;* enough: *O.* 37. return;] *Dyce;* return *O.* 38. Tomorrow,] *Dyce;* tomorrow; *O.*

tridge (under 'cockles') explains that the phrase refers to 'intimate sexual handling by the old and impotent.'

27. *cracks*] bursts open, because so full of goods.

29. *they*] generic: 'one'; 'people.'

37–9. *Come . . . sir*] a good example of the octavo's line-by-line (or at least narrowly 'local') punctuation. Permitting 'tomorrow' to be read with 'pray return' makes perfectly good sense, except in relation to the larger context. (See Introduction, p. xxx.)

47. *is respective for increase*] is concerned to make a profit. Perhaps with a glance at 'increase' = procreation. 'For' is unexpected, possibly suggested by the root meaning 'to look (back) for, to have regard for' (L. *respicere*).

Is like a good king that keeps all in peace.
Once more farewell.

Bian. But this one night, I prithee.

Lean. Alas I'm in for twenty if I stay,
And then for forty more: I have such luck to flesh
I never bought a horse but he bore double.
If I stay any longer I shall turn
An everlasting spendthrift. As you love
To be maintained well do not call me again,
For then I shall not care which end goes forward—
Again farewell to thee.

Bian. Since it must, farewell too. *Exit* [LEANTIO.]

Moth. 'Faith, daughter, y' are to blame, you take the course
To make him an ill husband, troth you do.
And that disease is catching I can tell you,
Ay, and soon taken by a young man's blood,
And that with little urging. Nay fie, see now,
What cause have you to weep? Would I had no more
That have lived three score years—there were a cause
And 'twere well thought on. Trust me, y' are to blame,

51. forty more] *O;* forty *Dilke.* 57.1] *S.D. precedes Bianca's speech in O.*

---

48. *good king . . . peace*] perhaps intended as a compliment to James, renowned for his success in keeping peace. Middleton's *The Peacemaker* (1618) was written with James's full approval and backing (see Rhodes Dunlap, *Studies in the English Renaissance Drama*, ed. Bennett, Cargill and Hall, New York, 1959, pp. 82–94).

52. *bore double*] carried two riders. Leantio may be suggesting that Bianca will be doubly fertile; compare Thomas May, *The Heir* V. i.: (Shallow hoping for the birth of a child): 'I hope to have good luck to horse-flesh now, she is a parson's wife.' (*Ancient British Drama* 1810, vol. I, p. 215). Christopher Ricks thinks that Middleton intends a dramatic irony: Bianca on becoming the Duke's mistress does in fact 'bear double', having served two 'riders' (*R.E.S.*, n.s. XII, 1961, p. 249).

56. *which end goes forward*] *what* happens, *what* I do. The special connotation of the phrase at this date is given by Torriano, *A Common Place of Italian Proverbs*, 1666 (p. 133 note 29): 'Prodigals . . . care not which end goes formost.'

60. *that disease*] lethargy.

His absence cannot last five days at utmost.
Why should those tears be fetched forth? Cannot love
Be e'en as well expressed in a good look,
But it must see her face still in a fountain?
It shows like a country maid dressing her head
By a dish of water. Come, 'tis an old custom
To weep for love.

Enter two or three Boys, *and a* Citizen *or two, with an* Apprentice.

Boys. Now they come, now they come.
2 Boy. The Duke!
3 Boy. The State!
Cit. How near, boy?
1 Boy. I' th' next street, sir, hard at hand.
Cit. You sirrah, get a standing for your mistress
The best in all the city.
Apprent. I have 't for her, sir,
'Twas a thing I provided for her overnight,
'Tis ready at her pleasure.
Cit. Fetch her to 't then,
Away, sir.
Bian. What's the meaning of this hurry,
Can you tell, Mother?
Moth. What a memory
Have I! I see by that years come upon me.

73. *2 Boy.*] 2. *O.* 73. *3 Boy.*] 3. *O.* 73. State] *O;* states *Dilke.*

---

68. *good look*] a weak phrase; it is possible that Middleton wrote '*glad* look.'

69. *her*] the beloved woman.

still] always.

70–1. *dressing . . . water*] arranging her hair by the reflection in a bowl of water.

73. *The State*] collective singular (see *O.E.D.* under 'State' 26): 'the rulers, nobles or great men of a realm.' The singular is again used at ll. 83 and 102, but the plural at ll. 97 and 101.2.

75. *standing*] a place to stand, a vantage point.

76–8. *I have 't . . . pleasure*] The Apprentice plays on standing = sexual erection.

Why, 'tis a yearly custom and solemnity,
Religiously observed by th' Duke and State
To St. Mark's Temple, the fifteenth of April.
See if my dull brains had not quite forgot it.
'Twas happily questioned of thee, I had gone down else,
Sat like a drone below, and never thought on 't.
I would not to be ten years younger again
That you had lost the sight; now you shall see
Our Duke, a goodly gentleman of his years.

Bian. Is he old then?

Moth. About some fifty-five.

Bian. That's no great age in man, he's then at best
For wisdom, and for judgement.

Moth. The Lord Cardinal
His noble brother, there's a comely gentleman,
And greater in devotion than in blood.

Bian. He's worthy to be marked.

Moth. You shall behold
All our chief States of Florence; you came fortunately
Against this solemn day.

83. State] *O;* States *Dilke.*

82–4.] For a possible original of this procession see Moryson pp. 442–3: 'The fourth walke is to the *Church of St. Marke* [in Venice] vpon the *25th. of Aprill*, the Feast day of that Saynt . . . the sayde Feast is *yearely solemnized*, as the greatest of all the rest, and in greatest triumph, the Duke that day Feasting the Senate with great magnificence.' [my italics]. Middleton might conceivably have altered 25 to 15 April because Moryson explains at length that Italian dates may be converted to English by subtracting ten days. (St Mark's day is 25 April in *either* style, however.) The historical Bianca lived opposite the Church of S. Marco in Florence.

84. *To*] 'a procession' understood; implied in 'solemnity'.

86. *gone down*] from the balcony; they enter 'above' at line 12.1.

91. *fifty-five*] This and the observation that follows have been taken as a reference to James, 55 on 19 June, 1621 (see Introduction, p. xxxiv). Parker notes a similar remark in Middleton's *No Wit, No Help*, II. i. 412, dated by Bald 'c. 1615', roughly five years earlier (*Wks*, IV. 337): 'What's fifty years? 'tis man's best time and season.'

95. *blood*] birth.

98. *Against*] in time for.

Bian. I hope so always. *Music*
Moth. I hear 'em near us now; do you stand easily?
Bian. Exceeding well, good Mother.
Moth. Take this stool.
Bian. I need it not I thank you.
Moth. Use your will then.

Enter in great solemnity six Knights *bareheaded, then two* Cardinals, *and then the Lord* CARDINAL, *then the* DUKE; *after him the* States *of Florence by two and two, with variety of music and song. Exit.*

Moth. How like you, daughter?
Bian. 'Tis a noble State.
Methinks my soul could dwell upon the reverence
Of such a solemn and most worthy custom.
Did not the Duke look up? Methought he saw us.
Moth. That's ev'ry one's conceit that sees a duke;
If he look steadfastly, he looks straight at them;
When he perhaps, good careful gentleman,
Never minds any, but the look he casts
Is at his own intentions, and his object
Only the public good.
Bian. Mostly likely so.
Moth. Come, come, we'll end this argument below. *Exeunt.*

102. you, daughter] *O;* you [it], Daughter *Dilke.*

---

103. *reverence*] dignity, solemnity.
106. *conceit*] what is conceived; notion.
108. *careful*] having cares, responsibilities.
112. *argument*] subject of discussion. Compare I. ii. 198 and note.

Portrait of Francesco de' Medici by Bronzino

Act II

[Act II. Scene I.]

Enter HIPPOLITO, *and Lady* LIVIA *the Widow.*

Liv. A strange affection, brother! When I think on 't,
I wonder how thou camest by 't.
Hip. E'en as easily
As man comes by destruction, which oft-times
He wears in his own bosom.
Liv. Is the world
So populous in women, and creation
So prodigal in beauty and so various,
Yet does love turn thy point to thine own blood?
'Tis somewhat too unkindly. Must thy eye
Dwell evilly on the fairness of thy kindred,
And seek not where it should? It is confined
Now in a narrower prison than was made for 't—
It is allowed a stranger; and where bounty

1. brother! When I think on 't,] *Dilke subst.;* (Brother) When I think on 't! *O.* 5. creation] *Dilke;* Creation, *O.*

II. i. 2–4. *E'en . . . bosom*] The self-destructive nature of sin is a frequent topic with Middleton. Compare e.g. *The Mayor of Queenborough* V. ii. 76–7 (*Wks*, II. 109): 'See, sin needs/No other destruction than [what] it breeds/In its own bosom.'

7. *point*] alluding to the compass-needle. Cf. *The Changeling* III. iii. 216–17 (Revels ed. p. 55): 'The needle's point will to the fixed north;/ Such drawing arctics women's beauties are.'

blood] kin, relations.

8. *unkindly*] against kind, unnatural. With a punning glance at kind = family.

12. *stranger*] specifically anyone not a blood relation.

12–14. *where . . . spare*] 'where a great man's liberality is the reason for

Is made the great man's honour, 'tis ill husbandry
To spare, and servants shall have small thanks for 't.
So he heaven's bounty seems to scorn and mock
That spares free means, and spends of his own stock.

Hip. Never was man's misery so soon summed up,
Counting how truly.

Liv. Nay, I love you so
That I shall venture much to keep a change from you
So fearful as this grief will bring upon you.
'Faith it even kills me, when I see you faint
Under a reprehension, and I'll leave it,
Though I know nothing can be better for you.
Prithee, sweet brother, let not passion waste
The goodness of thy time, and of thy fortune.
Thou keep'st the treasure of that life I love
As dearly as mine own; and if you think

17. summed] *Dyce;* sow'd *O.*

---

his enjoying esteem, it is false economy to be frugal.' Moryson (p. 455) gives a striking instance of this view, which Middleton may have remembered. The careers of the Dukes of Venice, he says, were examined after their deaths by specially appointed officers: 'thus of late Duke Loredan, otherwise of singular goodness and wisdom, being founde to haue liued more sparingly then that his dignity required, was by the great Councell Fyned 1500. Ducates, which his hayres payd.'

16. *free means*] resources freely given: the whole of womankind.

stock] store; family.

17. *summed*] Dyce's emendation is almost certain. Misreading of copy would be particularly easy here: Middleton would probably have written 'sumde', and o/u and w/m misreadings are distinctly possible in his hand. Crane's spelling (see Introduction, pp. xxvi–xxvii) would have been 'som'd', requiring only an m/w misreading to give the octavo 'sow'd'.

19. *change*] much stronger in seventeenth-century than in present use: 'calamity'. Compare Celia sympathizing with Rosalind on her banishment, *AYL.* I. iii. 104–6: 'And do not seek to take your change upon you,/To bear your griefs yourself and leave me out;/For, by this heaven, now at our sorrows pale . . .'

22. *reprehension*] censure, reprimand.

24. *passion*] sorrow, fretful regret.

26. *Thou keep'st*] you preserve (in yourself).

My former words too bitter, which were ministered
By truth and zeal, 'tis but a hazarding
Of grace and virtue, and I can bring forth
As pleasant fruits as sensuality wishes
In all her teeming longings. This I can do.

Hip. Oh nothing that can make my wishes perfect!

Liv. I would that love of yours were pawned to 't, brother,
And as soon lost that way as I could win.
Sir, I could give as shrewd a lift to chastity
As any she that wears a tongue in Florence:
Sh' had need be a good horsewoman, and sit fast,
Whom my strong argument could not fling at last.
Prithee take courage, man: though I should counsel
Another to despair, yet I am pitiful
To thy afflictions, and will venture hard—
I will not name for what, 'tis not handsome.
Find you the proof, and praise me.

Hip. Then I fear me,
I shall not praise you in haste.

Liv. This is the comfort,
You are not the first, brother, has attempted
Things more forbidden than this seems to be.

28–9. *My . . . zeal*] The 'bitter words' were a medicine prescribed by truth and uprightness ('zeal'): contrast the 'cordials' of l. 48 and note. Livia sees herself as a skilled physician in these matters (see ll. 50–1).

32. *teeming*] fecund, ever-multiplying.

33. *perfect*] a usage between two *O.E.D.* senses: 'thoroughly performed, carried out' and 'in a state of complete satisfaction; satisfied, contented.'

34–5.] 'I wish I could make you forget your love for Isabella as easily as I could, if I wished, cause her to return it.'

36. *give . . . lift*] probably an ironic inversion of 'give a lift to' = 'lend a helping hand to.' Middleton is fond of this variety of sarcasm (see e.g. I. ii. 10 and note). Possibly 'give a lift *at*' = 'attack' is intended; the explicit metaphor from mounted combat in ll. 38–9 would then be a natural instead of a rather unexpected movement of thought. A further possibility is that 'lift' should be 'list', in the strong seventeenth-century sense of 'appetite', 'craving'; a punning verbal association of 'list' with 'lists' (the implied word in ll. 38–9) would be characteristic of Middleton.

39. *fling*] unseat, topple.

44.] 'when you have seen ('tried', 'proved') what I can do, praise me.'

I'll minister all cordials now to you
Because I'd cheer you up, sir.
Hip. I am past hope.
Liv. Love, thou shalt see me do a strange cure then,
As e'er was wrought on a disease so mortal,
And near akin to shame. When shall you see her?
Hip. Never in comfort more.
Liv. Y' are so impatient too.
Hip. Will you believe? 'Death, sh' has forsworn my company,
And sealed it with a blush.
Liv. So, I perceive
All lies upon my hands then; well, the more glory
When the work's finished.

Enter Servant.

How now, sir, the news!
Serv. Madam, your niece the virtuous Isabella,
Is 'lighted now to see you.
Liv. [*To Hippolito*] That's great fortune.
Sir, your stars bless; [*To Servant*] you simple, lead her in.
Exit Servant.

49. I'd] *This ed.;* I'll *O.* 54. believe?] *Dilke;* believe *O.* 57.1.] *S.D. follows end of line 57 in O.* 60. bless; you simple] *O;* bless you: Simple! *Dilke;* bless you simply.—*Bullen.*

---

48. *cordials*] lit. 'medicines stimulating to the heart' (L. *cor*), and then anything that comforts. The metaphor is carried on in 'cure' (l. 50), and 'disease so mortal' (l. 51).

49. *I'd*] Octavo 'I'll' makes little sense. Middleton always wrote 'Ide', and the 'd' very often approximates an 'l'.

54. *believe? 'Death*] Dilke's emendation is accepted, but the correct reading may be 'truth' not 'death' (*O*). In Middleton's hand r/e and u/a confusions are easily made, and an initial t/d misreading possible. 'truth' would give the line fluency, retain the compositor's punctuation, and avoid the weak expletive ''Death', a form very uncommon in Middleton.

55. *sealed*] confirmed.

59. *is 'lighted*] has arrived. See I. ii. 56 and note.

60. *your stars bless*] 'you' understood.

you simple] you blockhead.

Hip. What's this to me?
Liv. Your absence, gentle brother;
I must bestir my wits for you.
Hip. Ay, to great purpose.
Exit HIPPOLITO.
Liv. Beshrew you, would I loved you not so well.
I'll go to bed, and leave this deed undone.
I am the fondest where I once affect,
The carefull'st of their healths, and of their ease forsooth,
That I look still but slenderly to mine own.
I take a course to pity him so much now
That I have none left for modesty and myself.
This 'tis to grow so liberal—y' have few sisters
That love their brothers' ease 'bove their own honesties,
But if you question my affections,
That will be found my fault.

Enter ISABELLA *the niece.*

Niece, your love's welcome.
Alas, what draws that paleness to thy cheeks?
This enforced marriage towards?
Isab. It helps, good aunt,
Amongst some other griefs; but those I'll keep
Locked up in modest silence, for they're sorrows
Would shame the tongue more than they grieve the thought.

64. I'll] *O;* I'd *White.* 71. ease] *O;* case *Dilke.* 73.1.] *S.D. follows end of Livia's speech, line 75, in O.*

---

61. *What's . . . absence*] 'what does this ask of me?' 'It asks your absence.'

65. *fondest . . . affect*] Cf. I. iii. 24n.

70. *liberal*] bounteous, over-generous. With a glance at the frequent seventeenth-century sense of 'unrestrained by prudence or decorum, licentious' (*O.E.D.*). Compare *Oth.* III. iv. 38–40: '*Oth.* This argues fruitfulness and liberal heart:/Hot, hot, and moist: this hand of yours requires/A sequester from liberty, fasting and prayer.'

71. *ease*] Dilke and White read 'case', influenced probably by the octavo's badly worn initial 'e'.

Liv. Indeed the Ward is simple.
Isab. Simple! that were well:
Why one might make good shift with such a husband.
But he's a fool entailed, he halts downright in 't.
Liv. And knowing this, I hope 'tis at your choice
To take or refuse, niece.
Isab. You see it is not.
I loathe him more than beauty can hate death
Or age, her spiteful neighbour.
Liv. Let 't appear then.
Isab. How can I, being born with that obedience
That must submit unto a father's will?
If he command, I must of force consent.
Liv. Alas, poor soul, be not offended prithee,
If I set by the name of niece awhile,
And bring in pity in a stranger fashion—
It lies here in this breast, would cross this match.
Isab. How, cross it, aunt?
Liv. Ay, and give thee more liberty
Than thou hast reason yet to apprehend.
Isab. Sweet aunt, in goodness keep not hid from me
What may befriend my life.
Liv. Yes, yes, I must;

---

81. *a fool entailed*] To 'entail' is to make (someone) heir to a possession or condition, or to cause (him) to become (something) permanently. P. S. Clarkson and C. T. Warren (*The law of property in Shakespeare and the Elizabethan Drama*, Baltimore, 1942, p. 56) explain that the word is used of 'a trait, physical or mental, descending from an ancestor to his issue.' The Ward is a congenital idiot.

halts downright in 't] 'He comes to a full stop at "fool"; that's as far as his wit will carry him.' Cf. II. ii. 78–9.

84–5.] Age is *beauty's* 'spiteful neighbour.' Compare *The Changeling* II. ii. 66–7. (Revels ed., p. 36): 'Why, put case I loath'd him/As much as youth and beauty hates a sepulchre'.

90. *set by*] put aside, leave out of consideration.

93. *liberty*] Cf. II. i. 70 and note.

When I return to reputation,
And think upon the solemn vow I made
To your dead mother, my most loving sister—
As long as I have her memory 'twixt mine eyelids,
Look for no pity now.

Isab. Kind, sweet, dear aunt—

Liv. No, 'twas a secret I have took special care of,
Delivered by your mother on her death-bed;
That's nine years now, and I'll not part from 't yet,
Though ne'er was fitter time, nor greater cause for 't.

Isab. As you desire the praises of a virgin—

Liv. Good sorrow! I would do thee any kindness
Not wronging secrecy or reputation.

Isab. Neither of which, as I have hope of fruitfulness,
Shall receive wrong from me.

Liv. Nay, 'twould be your own wrong,
As much as any's, should it come to that once.

Isab. I need no better means to work persuasion then.

Liv. Let it suffice, you may refuse this fool,
Or you may take him, as you see occasion
For your advantage; the best wits will do 't.
Y' have liberty enough in your own will,
You cannot be enforced: there grows the flower
If you could pick it out, makes whole life sweet to you.
That which you call your father's command's nothing;
Then your obedience must needs be as little.
If you can make shift here to taste your happiness,
Or pick out aught that likes you, much good do you;

101. aunt—] *This ed.;* Aunt. *O.* 106. virgin—] *This ed.;* Virgin: *O.* 109. fruitfulness] *Dilke;* fruit-/ness *O.* 122. good do] *O;* good may't do *White.*

97. *reputation*] *five* syllables.
100. '*twixt mine eyelids*] in my mind, 'mind's eye'.
107. *Good sorrow*] Isabella is sorrow personified.
111. *once*] ever.
118. *sweet*] pleasant; sweet-scented.
122. *do you*] may it do you.

You see your cheer, I'll make you no set dinner.
Isab. And trust me, I may starve for all the good
I can find yet in this. Sweet aunt, deal plainlier.
Liv. Say I should trust you now upon an oath,
And give you in a secret that would start you,
How am I sure of you, in faith and silence?
Isab. Equal assurance may I find in mercy,
As you for that in me.
Liv. It shall suffice.
Then know, how ever custom has made good,
For reputation's sake, the names of niece
And aunt 'twixt you and I, w' are nothing less.
Isab. How's that?
Liv. I told you I should start your blood.
You are no more allied to any of us,
Save what the courtesy of opinion casts
Upon your mother's memory and your name,
Than the merest stranger is, or one begot
At Naples when the husband lies at Rome:
There's so much odds betwixt us. Since your knowledge
Wished more instruction, and I have your oath
In pledge for silence, it makes me talk the freelier:
Did never the report of that famed Spaniard,
Marquis of Coria, since your time was ripe
For understanding, fill your ear with wonder?

---

123. *cheer*] provisions, food.

127. *that*] that which.

start] startle.

129. *mercy*] divine mercy, specifically on the Day of Judgment.

138–9. *one begot . . . Rome*] In *T.H.* (see Introduction, p. xlv) Isabella is made to believe that Fabrico (her real father) was on business in Rome at the time she was begotten in Naples by the 'Marquis of Coria' (see below l. 144).

140. *There's . . . us*] 'There is that much distance (in relationship) between us.'

144. *Marquis of Coria*] The name comes from Middleton's source. The Marquisate of Coria was in history the possession of the Dukes of Alva (or Alba), and named from the town of Coria (where the Dukes owned a palace) in the Carceres province of Spain. The most celebrated

Isab. Yes, what of him? I have heard his deeds of honour
Often related when we lived in Naples.
Liv. You heard the praises of your father then.
Isab. My father!
Liv. That was he. But all the business
So carefully and so discreetly carried
That fame received no spot by 't, not a blemish.
Your mother was so wary to her end
None knew it but her conscience and her friend,
Till penitent confession made it mine,
And now my pity yours. It had been long else—
And I hope care and love alike in you,
Made good by oath, will see it take no wrong now.
How weak his commands now, whom you call father?
How vain all his enforcements, your obedience?
And what a largeness in your will and liberty,
To take, or to reject, or to do both?
For fools will serve to father wise men's children.
All this y' have time to think on. Oh my wench,
Nothing o'erthrows our sex but indiscretion;
We might do well else of a brittle people

Marquis was Fernando Alvarez de Toledo (1507–82), tyrant of the Netherlands under Philip II of Spain, and victor of many battles there and in Italy and Portugal. The source-reference may be either to this man or to his father, Fadrique Alvares de Toledo (d. 1531), the second Duke.

149. *business*] as often, with a sexual connotation.

149–53. *all the . . . friend*] an implied example for Isabella.

153. *friend*] referring to a sexual relationship. Compare *Meas.* I. iv. 29: 'He hath got his friend with child.'

154. *penitent confession*] a phrase more appropriate to the Nun of Middleton's source than to Livia (see Introduction, p. xlv).

157. *now*] The awkward and redundant 'now', chiming with 'now' in the following line, might perhaps be deleted on the assumption that the compositor failed to remember copy accurately.

163–4. *Oh my . . . indiscretion*] precisely the sentiment of the common tag *Si non caste, tamen caute.* Compare Middleton, *A Game at Chess* II. i. 173–7 (*Wks,* VII. 38): '*Qui caute, caste;* that's my motto ever.'

165. *of a brittle people*] 'for a frail, mortal, race.' For a similar defining function for 'of a' compare *Wint.* III. ii. 187: 'That did but show thee, of a fool, inconstant.'

As any under the great canopy.
I pray forget not but to call me aunt still;
Take heed of that, it may be marked in time else.
But keep your thoughts to yourself, from all the world,
Kindred, or dearest friend, nay, I entreat you
From him that all this while you have called uncle;
And though you love him dearly, as I know
His deserts claim as much e'en from a stranger,
Yet let not him know this, I prithee do not—
As ever thou hast hope of second pity,
If thou shouldst stand in need on 't, do not do 't.

Isab. Believe my oath, I will not.

Liv. Why, well said.
[*Aside*] Who shows more craft t' undo a maidenhead,
I'll resign my part to her.

Enter HIPPOLITO.

[*To him*] She's thine own, go.

Exit [LIVIA].

Hip. [*Aside*] Alas, fair flattery cannot cure my sorrows!

Isab. [*Aside*] Have I passed so much time in ignorance,
And never had the means to know myself
Till this blest hour? Thanks to her virtuous pity
That brought it now to light. Would I had known it
But one day sooner, he had then received
In favours, what, poor gentleman, he took
In bitter words—a slight and harsh reward
For one of his deserts.

179.1] '*Enter* HIPPOLITO.' *follows end of Livia's speech in O.*

---

166. *the great canopy*] the sky. Compare W. Parry, *Travels of Sir Anthony Shirley*, 1601: 'those resplendent and crystalline heavens over-canopying the earth.' (Quoted J. D. Wilson, 'New Cambridge' *Hamlet*, 2nd ed., Cambridge 1954, p. 175).

168. *marked*] noticed.

175. *hope of second pity*] hope of my befriending you again.

181–3. *Have I . . . hour*] heavily ironic; only now has she, literally, lost knowledge of who she *is*.

Hip. [*Aside*] There seems to me now
More anger and distraction in her looks.
I'm gone, I'll not endure a second storm;
The memory of the first is not past yet.
Isab. [*Aside*] Are you returned, you comforts of my life,
In this man's presence? I will keep you fast now,
And sooner part eternally from the world
Than my good joys in you. [*To him*] Prithee forgive me,
I did but chide in jest; the best loves use it
Sometimes, it sets an edge upon affection.
When we invite our best friends to a feast
'Tis not all sweetmeats that we set before them,
There's somewhat sharp and salt, both to whet appetite,
And make 'em taste their wine well. So methinks
After a friendly, sharp and savoury chiding
A kiss tastes wondrous well, and full o' th' grape. [*Kisses him*]
How think'st thou, does 't not?
Hip. 'Tis so excellent,
I know not how to praise it, what to say to 't.
Isab. This marriage shall go forward.
Hip. With the Ward?
Are you in earnest?
Isab. 'Twould be ill for us else.
Hip. [*Aside*] For us? How means she that?
Isab. [*Aside*] Troth I begin
To be so well methinks within this hour,
For all this match able to kill one's heart,
Nothing can pull me down now. Should my father

192. life,] *Dyce;* life? *O.* 193. presence?] *Dyce;* presence, *O.* 204. does 't] *Dilke;* do'st *O.* 210. heart,] *Dilke;* heart. *O.* 211. now.] *Dilke;* now; *O.*

196–203.] Isabella uses one of the play's standard idioms for sexuality, the vocabulary of food and eating. (See Introduction, pp. lxi–lxii.)
197. *sets . . . affection*] makes desire sharper.
213. *either*] just as willingly.
215. *want*] lack.
So] provided that.

Provide a worse fool yet, which I should think
Were a hard thing to compass, I'd have him either:
The worse the better, none can come amiss now,
If he want wit enough. So discretion love me,
Desert and judgment, I have content sufficient.
[*To him*] She that comes once to be a housekeeper
Must not look every day to fare well, sir,
Like a young waiting-gentlewoman in service:
For she feeds commonly as her lady does,
No good bit passes her, but she gets a taste on 't.
But when she comes to keep house for herself,
She's glad of some choice cates then once a week,
Or twice at most, and glad if she can get 'em:
So must affection learn to fare with thankfulness.
Pray make your love no stranger, sir, that's all.
[*Aside*] Though you be one yourself, and know not on 't,
And I have sworn you must not. *Exit.*

Hip. This is beyond me!
Never came joys so unexpectedly
To meet desires in man. How came she thus?
What has she done to her, can any tell?
'Tis beyond sorcery this, drugs, or love-powders.
Some art that has no name sure, strange to me

215–16. *discretion . . . Desert . . . judgment*] referring to Hippolito.

217. *housekeeper*] a woman in charge of her own household, a housewife.

217–25.] an elaborate application of the food/sexual experience metaphor. The distinction between the 'young waiting-gentlewoman' (the unmarried girl) who partakes freely of the rich fare of her mistress' household, and the 'housekeeper' (a position Isabella will take up on marriage) who has to make do with occasional delicacies, is that between Isabella as she now is, able to meet with Hippolito when she will, and Isabella as the Ward's wife, making infrequent opportunities to enjoy her lover's company.

223. *cates*] delicacies. These were usually bought, in contrast to home-made food, and were often elaborate; see, for example, the recipes in Sir H. Plat, *Delights for Ladies*, 1609.

231. *she*] Livia.

233.] An art without a name was thought of as more mysterious and terrible than a named one. Compare *Mac.* IV. i. 48–9: '*Macb.* How now,

Of all the wonders I e'er met withal
Throughout my ten years' travels; but I'm thankful for 't.
This marriage now must of necessity forward,
It is the only veil wit can devise
To keep our acts hid from sin-piercing eyes. *Exit.*

[II. ii]

Enter GUARDIANO *and* LIVIA.

Liv. How, sir, a gentlewoman so young, so fair
As you set forth, spied from the widow's window!
Guard. She!
Liv. Our Sunday-dinner woman?
Guard. And Thursday-supper woman, the same still.
I know not how she came by her, but I'll swear
She's the prime gallant for a face in Florence;
And no doubt other parts follow their leader.
The Duke himself first spied her at the window,
Then in a rapture, as if admiration
Were poor when it were single, beckoned me,
And pointed to the wonder warily
As one that feared she would draw in her splendour
Too soon, if too much gazed at. I ne'er knew him
So infinitely taken with a woman,

0.1. II. ii] Scaen. 2. *O.*

---

you secret, black, and midnight hags!/What is't you do? *All.* A deed without a name.'

II. ii. 2. *spied from*] seen at. 'From' is suggested by the implied 'looking'.
3. *She!*] the widow, not the gentlewoman.
3–4. *Sunday-dinner . . . Thursday-supper*] Presumably the Mother ate these meals at Livia's house, as a poor neighbour might; or perhaps helped serve or prepare them.
6. *gallant*] used of both sexes; a handsome person.
7. *follow their leader*] are as attractive as her face.
9. *admiration*] wonder (L. *admirari*).
10. *single*] unshared.

Nor can I blame his appetite, or tax
His raptures of slight folly: she's a creature
Able to draw a State from serious business,
And make it their best piece to do her service.
What course shall we devise? 'Has spoke twice now.

Liv. Twice?

Guard. 'Tis beyond your apprehension
How strangely that one look has catched his heart;
'Twould prove but too much worth in wealth and favour
To those should work his peace.

Liv. And if I do 't not,
Or at least come as near it, if your art
Will take a little pains and second me,
As any wench in Florence of my standing,
I'll quite give o'er, and shut up shop in cunning.

Guard. 'Tis for the Duke, and if I fail your purpose
All means to come by riches or advancement
Miss me, and skip me over.

Liv. Let the old woman then
Be sent for with all speed, then I'll begin.

Guard. A good conclusion follow, and a sweet one,
After this stale beginning with old ware.
Within there!

Enter Servant.

Serv. Sir, do you call?

Guard. Come near, list hither.
[*Talks aside with Servant*]

20. apprehension] *Dyce;* apprehension. *O.* 26. standing,] *Dilke;* standing. *O.*

---

16. *slight folly*] the foolishness of being occupied with a trivial object.
18. *best piece*] most important concern, proudest achievement.
23. *work his peace*] meet his wishes, satisfy him.
28. *your purpose*] in assisting you to your aim.
33. *stale . . . old ware*] referring to the Mother. 'Stale' is often used of someone past the prime of life; 'ware' is applied jocularly and unflatteringly to women.

Liv. I long myself to see this absolute creature,
That wins the heart of love and praise so much.
Guard. Go, sir, make haste.
Liv. Say I entreat her company;
Do you hear, sir?
Serv. Yes, madam. *Exit.*
Liv. That brings her quickly.
Guard. I would 'twere done; the Duke waits the good hour
And I wait the good fortune that may spring from 't.
I have had a lucky hand these fifteen year
At such court passage with three dice in a dish.

Enter FABRITIO.

Signor Fabritio!
Fab. Oh sir, I bring an alteration in my mouth now.
Guard. An alteration! [*Aside*] No wise speech I hope;
He means not to talk wisely, does he trow?
[*To him*] Good! What's the change I pray, sir?
Fab. A new change.
Guard. [*Aside*] Another yet! Faith there's enough already.

42. three] *Dilke;* theee *O.* 42.1.] *S.D. follows line 43* in *O.*

---

35. *absolute*] absolute in quality, perfect.

42. *court passage*] 'Passage is a game at dice, to be played at but by two, and it is performed with three dice. The caster throws continually till he hath thrown doublets under ten, and then he is out and loseth; or doublets above ten, and then he passeth and wins'. *Compleat Gamester* 1680 p. 119 (Dilke). Guardiano also alludes to a secondary meaning of 'passage': 'an interchange of . . . amorous relations' or 'an amorous fence or encounter' (*O.E.D.*). The 'three dice' might be the Mother, Bianca and the Duke, though no identification is necessary.

44–6. *alteration . . . trow?*] Fabritio means a change in Isabella's attitude to the Ward; Guardiano deliberately misunderstands him to mean a change in his own manner of address—perhaps taking 'to alter' in the obsolete sense of 'to affect mentally' (*O.E.D.* sense 3), and thinking therefore of a change (from idiocy to wisdom) in Fabritio's mentality.

46. *does he trow?*] do you think?

47–8. *A new change . . . enough already*] Guardiano mocks the redundancy of a *new* change. Just possibly there may also be a reference to the New 'Change' (i.e. Exchange) opened in the Strand on 11 April 1609. As

Fab. My daughter loves him now.
Guard. What does she, sir?
Fab. Affects him beyond thought, who but the Ward forsooth!
No talk but of the Ward—she would have him
To choose 'bove all the men she ever saw.
My will goes not so fast as her consent now;
Her duty gets before my command still.
Guard. Why then, sir, if you'll have me speak my thoughts,
I smell 'twill be a match.
Fab. Ay, and a sweet young couple,
If I have any judgment.
Guard. [*Aside*] 'Faith that's little.
[*To him*] Let her be sent tomorrow before noon,
And handsomely tricked up; for 'bout that time
I mean to bring her in, and tender her to him.
Fab. I warrant you for handsome. I will see
Her things laid ready, every one in order,
And have some part of her tricked up tonight.
Guard. Why, well said.
Fab. 'Twas a use her mother had,
When she was invited to an early wedding:
She'd dress her head o'er night, sponge up herself,
And give her neck three lathers—
Guard. [*Aside*] Ne'er a halter?

67. lathers—] *This ed.;* lathers. *O.*

H. B. Wheatley (*London Past and Present*, 1891, II. 581) explains: 'It was long before the New Exchange attained to any great degree of favour or trade. London was not then large enough for more than one structure of the kind [the Royal Exchange being already in existence]'. Guardiano in that case feigns surprise at Fabritio's mention of 'another yet': 'there's enough already' with two.

54. *gets before*] goes ahead of.

56. *smell*] predict, infer. In Fabritio's response 'sweet' (l. 56) picks up the literal sense of 'smell'.

59. *tricked up*] dressed in finery. 'Tricks' (l. 69) = trinkets, baubles.

64. *use*] custom.

67. *halter*] noose; a simple anagram of 'lather'.

Fab. On with her chain of pearl, her ruby bracelets,
Lay ready all her tricks, and jiggam-bobs—
Guard. So must your daughter.
Fab. I'll about it straight, sir.
Exit FABRITIO.
Liv. How he sweats in the foolish zeal of fatherhood
After six ounces an hour, and seems
To toil as much as if his cares were wise ones!
Guard. Y' have let his folly blood in the right vein, lady.
Liv. And here comes his sweet son-in-law that shall be.
They're both allied in wit before the marriage;
What will they be hereafter, when they are nearer?
Yet they can go no further than the fool:
There's the world's end in both of 'em.

Enter WARD *and* SORDIDO, *one with a shuttlecock, the other a battledore.*

Guard. Now young heir!
Ward. What's the next business after shuttlecock now?
Guard. Tomorrow you shall see the gentlewoman
Must be your wife.

69. jiggam-bobs—] *This ed.;* Jiggam-bobs. *O.* 79.1, 80. *shuttlecock*] *Shittlecock O.*

---

69. *jiggam-bobs*] 'tricks'; see l. 59n. above.
72. *After*] at the rate of; usually of money.
six ounces an hour] This may have been a conventional amount; see Middleton, *The Witch* I. ii. 99–100 (*Wks*, V. 371): 'Sweat thy six ounces out about the vessel,/And thou shalt play at midnight.'
74.] referring to the old surgical operation of 'letting blood', i.e. draining quantities of blood from the body in certain disorders. Guardiano means that Livia has defined Fabritio's foolishness precisely.
79. *world's end*] as far as they can go; they can't be more foolish than they are.
79.1–2. shuttlecock . . . battledore] equipment used in a distant precursor (still played) of the modern game of badminton. The 'shuttlecock' was 'a small piece of cork, or similar light material, fitted with a crown or circle of feathers' (*O.E.D.*), and the 'battledore' a small racquet used to strike it. The game's object was to keep the shuttlecock in the air as long as possible, either with one's own racquet or by hitting it to and fro between two players.

Ward. [*Aside*] There's e'en another thing too
Must be kept up with a pair of battledores.
[*To him*] My wife! What can she do?
Guard. Nay, that's a question you should ask yourself, Ward,
When y'are alone together. [*Livia and Guardiano talk apart.*]
Ward. That's as I list.
A wife's to be asked anywhere I hope;
I'll ask her in a congregation, if I have a mind to 't, and
so save a licence. My guardianer has no more wit than
an herb-woman,
That sells away all her sweet herbs and nose-gays,
And keeps a stinking breath for her own pottage.
Sord. Let me be at the choosing of your beloved,
If you desire a woman of good parts.
Ward. Thou shalt, sweet Sordido.
Sord. I have a plaguy guess:
Let me alone to see what she is; if I but look upon her—
'way, I know all the faults to a hair that you may refuse
her for.
Ward. Dost thou! I prithee let me hear 'em, Sordido.
Sord. Well, mark 'em then; I have 'em all in rhyme.

87. asked] *Dilke;* ask *O.*

82–3.] presumably with a sexual innuendo, perhaps referring to the testes.

86–92. *That's . . . pottage*] The odd typographical arrangement here, prose and verse together, attempts to follow the rhythms of the passage. To set the whole of this speech as verse (as some editors do) produces a number of extraordinary verse-lines.

88. *ask . . . congregation*] referring to 'asking the banns' of marriage in Church. If the banns were not 'asked', a licence had to be obtained from the Archbishop of Canterbury, or other appointed cleric. Hence the Ward's 'and so save a licence' (ll. 88–9).

92. *pottage*] here probably = soup (generally a thick soup with vegetables). The Ward is thinking of the habit of blowing on soup to cool it.

95. *plaguy guess*] shrewd judgment. 'Plaguy' (lit. 'of the plague') was used colloquially merely as an intensive. See *O.E.D.* sense 2b.

97. *'way*] away; leave it to me.

The wife your guardiner ought to tender
Should be pretty, straight and slender;
Her hair not short, her foot not long,
Her hand not huge, nor too too loud her tongue;
No pearl in eye, nor ruby in her nose,
No burn or cut, but what the catalogue shows.
She must have teeth, and that no black ones,
And kiss most sweet when she does smack once;
Her skin must be both white and plumped,
Her body straight, not hopper-rumped,
Or wriggle sideways like a crab;
She must be neither slut nor drab,
Nor go too splay-foot with her shoes,
To make her smock lick up the dews.
And two things more, which I forgot to tell ye
She neither must have bump in back, nor belly—
These are the faults that will not make her pass.

Ward. And if I spy not these, I am a rank ass.

109. plumped] *Dyce;* plump *O.*

101–117.] Sordido debases an old tradition. Many of the features he mentions appear in mediaeval catalogues of female beauty, such as those in the work of Matthew of Vendome and Geoffrey of Vinsauf. (See further D. S. Brewer, 'The Ideal of Feminine Beauty in Mediaeval Literature', *M.L.R.*, L (1955), 257–69.).

105. *pearl in eye*] Clifford Leech (New Arden *Gent.*, V. ii. 11–12n.) refers to 'the Elizabethan doctor Vicary using the term "pearl on the eye" in the sense of "cataract" '; this appears to have been the usual meaning.

ruby] a red pimple or swelling.

106. *burn*] associated with venereal disease.

108. *smack*] in kissing.

109. *plumped*] well filled out. The octavo 'plump' makes sense, but a rhyme is required, and the octavo frequently drops final letters.

110. *hopper-rumped*] with protruberant buttocks. The 'hopper' was the wide funnel-like container into which corn was poured prior to grinding. Its to-and-fro motion as well as its shape may have suggested the association with large buttocks.

113. *splay-foot*] with clumsy, flat feet, especially of feet turned outwards in walking.

116.] must be neither hump-backed nor pregnant.

Sord. Nay more: by right, sir, you should see her naked,
For that's the ancient order.
Ward. See her naked?
That were good sport, i' faith. I'll have the books turned over,
And if I find her naked on record,
She shall not have a rag on. But stay, stay,
How if she should desire to see me so too? I were in a
sweet case then, such a foul skin.
Sord. But y' have a clean shirt, and that makes amends, sir.
Ward. I will not see her naked for that trick though.
Exit [WARD.]
Sord. Then take her with all faults, with her clothes on!
And they may hide a number with a bum-roll.
'Faith, choosing of a wench in a huge farthingale is like
the buying of ware under a great penthouse:
What with the deceit of one,

119–25.] More's *Utopia* mentions a custom of this kind: 'In chuesinge wyfes and husbandes they obserue earnestly and straytelye a custome, whiche semed to us very fonde and folyshe. For a sad and an honest matrone sheweth the woman, be she mayde or widdowe, naked to the wower. And lykwyse a sage and discrete man exhibyteth the wower naked to the woman.' (*Utopia* tr. Ralph Robinson, 1556, ed. E. Arber, 1869, VI. 123). The *Utopia* was reprinted in 1624. This passage appears to have been singularly popular for it is alluded to elsewhere in seventeenth-century writings, e.g. by Heylyn.

125. *case*] quibbling: (1) situation (2) garment, suit.

such . . . skin] having such a blemished (and perhaps diseased) skin.

127. *for that trick*] the 'trick' of asking him to strip in turn.

129. *bum-roll*] 'a stuffed cushion worn by women about the hips, over which the pleated skirt of their kirtle was allowed to fall' (*O.E.D.*) Properly called a 'French farthingale' (see l. 130 and Linthicum, p. 181, n.2).

130. *farthingale*] a framework of hoops, usually of whalebone, worked into some kind of cloth, and used for extending the skirts of women's dresses.

131. *penthouse*] a sloping roof attached to the wall of the main building over a door or window; a shop fitted with one would be dark inside, impairing customers' judgement of goods. Cf. Dekker, *Westward Ho!* I. i. 151–6: (*Wks*, II. 323): '[they] weare their hats ore their eye-browes, like pollitick penthouses, which commonly make the shop of a Mercer, or a Linnen Draper, as dark as a roome in Bedlam.'

And the false light of th' other, mark my speeches,
He may have a diseased wench in 's bed,
And rotten stuff in 's breeches. *Exit.*

Guard. It may take handsomely.

Liv. I see small hindrance:

Enter [Servant *with*] MOTHER [*following*].

[*To Servant*] How now, so soon returned?

Guard. She's come.

Liv. That's well.

[*Exit* Servant.]

[*To Mother*] Widow, come, come, I have a great quarrel to you;
'Faith, I must chide you, that you must be sent for!
You make yourself so strange, never come at us,
And yet so near a neighbour, and so unkind.
Troth y' are to blame, you cannot be more welcome
To any house in Florence, that I'll tell you.

Moth. My thanks must needs acknowledge so much, madam.

Liv. How can you be so strange then? I sit here
Sometime whole days together without company,
When business draws this gentleman from home;
And should be happy in society,
Which I so well affect as that of yours.
I know y' are alone too; why should not we
Like two kind neighbours then supply the wants
Of one another, having tongue-discourse,

136.1.] *S.D. follows* 'returned' *line 137 in O.*

---

133. *false light*] the meagre and deceptive light in a shop with a 'pent-house'.

135. *rotten stuff*] literally 'rotten cloth', but with an allusion to venereal disease.

136. *take*] succeed.

140. *so strange*] so much a stranger, so unsociable.

152. *tongue-discourse*] perhaps not only 'conversation, gossip' but '"the gift of the gab"', 'facility in speech'.

Experience in the world, and such kind helps
To laugh down time, and meet age merrily?
Moth. Age! Madam, you speak mirth! 'Tis at my door,
But a long journey from your ladyship yet.
Liv. My faith, I'm nine and thirty, ev'ry stroke, wench;
And 'tis a general observation
'Mongst knights' wives, or widows, we account ourselves
Then old when young men's eyes leave looking at 's.
'Tis a true rule amongst us, and ne'er failed yet
In any but in one that I remember—
Indeed she had a friend at nine and forty;
Marry, she paid well for him, and in th' end
He kept a quean or two with her own money,
That robbed her of her plate, and cut her throat.
Moth. She had her punishment in this world, madam,
And a fair warning to all other women
That they live chaste at fifty.

154. merrily] *Dilke;* meerly *O.* 159. knights' wives, or widows] *This ed.;* Knights, Wives, or Widows *O;* knights—wives or widows *Dyce.* 159. account] accompt *O.*

---

154. *merrily*] Octavo 'meerly' may represent a misreading of copy. Middleton would probably have written 'merrilie'; in a context of many short strokes an i/e confusion is very simple, as is an e/r confusion: the compositor may have read 'meerelie'. Crane spells 'merily'; to read this as 'merely' would be very simple.

157.] Middleton was himself thirty-nine between April 1619 and April 1620. He may be casting a rueful glance at his own ageing here. 'Stroke' = hour.

159. *knights' wives, or widows*] The octavo prints a comma after 'knights', making the three nouns seem in apposition, and this has caused a good deal of editorial confusion. But Middleton did not use apostrophes in possessive words, to the puzzlement, here, of the compositor. Livia is ranking herself among aristocratic widows (she says she's a widow at I. ii. 50) appropriately to her position in the source of the main plot, if not so clearly in the play.

163. *friend*] lover.

165. *quean*] whore.

168.] perhaps alluding to the popular play *A Warning for Fair Women* (1599). A more specific reference to that play seems intended in *The Witch* IV. i. 12–16 (*Wks*, V. 419).

Liv. Ay, or never, wench.
Come, now I have thy company I'll not part with 't
Till after supper.
Moth. Yes, I must crave pardon, madam.
Liv. I swear you shall stay supper. We have no strangers, woman,
None but my sojourners and I, this gentleman
And the young heir his ward; you know our company.
Moth. Some other time I will make bold with you, madam.
Guard. Nay, pray stay, widow.
Liv. 'Faith, she shall not go;
Do you think I'll be forsworn?
Moth. 'Tis a great while
Till supper-time; I'll take my leave then now, madam,
And come again i' th' evening, since your ladyship
Will have it so.
Liv. I' th' evening! By my troth, wench,
I'll keep you while I have you; you have great business sure
To sit alone at home, I wonder strangely
What pleasure you take in 't! Were 't to me now,
I should be ever at one neighbour's house
Or other all day long. Having no charge,
Or none to chide you, if you go, or stay,
Who may live merrier, ay, or more at heart's ease?
Come, we'll to chess, or draughts; there are an hundred tricks
To drive out time till supper, never fear 't wench.

174. our] *O;* your *Lamb.* 180. evening!] *Dilke subst.;* evening *O.* 185. charge,] *Dilke;* charge. *O.*

---

173. *sojourners*] guests staying at a close acquaintance's house.
177. *forsworn*] see l. 172.
182. *strangely*] greatly, exceedingly.
183. *Were 't to me*] were it my case.
188. *chess*] not a game in which the seventeenth-century Englishman excelled, and thought of primarily as an Italian or Spanish pastime. J. R.

Moth. I'll but make one step home, and return straight,
madam.

Liv. Come, I'll not trust you; you use more excuses
To your kind friends than ever I knew any.
What business can you have, if you be sure
Y' have locked the doors? And that being all you have
I know y' are careful on 't. One afternoon
So much to spend here! Say I should entreat you now
To lie a night or two, or a week with me,
Or leave your own house for a month together—
It were a kindness that long neighbourhood
And friendship might well hope to prevail in.
Would you deny such a request? I' faith,
Speak truth, and freely.

Moth. I were then uncivil, madam.

Liv. Go to then, set your men; [*Points to a 'Table and Chess'*]
we'll have whole nights
Of mirth together, ere we be much older, wench.

Moth. [*Aside*] As good now tell her then, for she will know 't;
I have always found her a most friendly lady.

Liv. Why, widow, where's your mind?

Moth. Troth e'en at home, madam.
To tell you truth, I left a gentlewoman
E'en sitting all alone, which is uncomfortable,
Especially to young bloods.

Liv. Another excuse!

Moth. No, as I hope for health, madam, that's a truth;
Please you to send and see.

203.1.] '*Table and Chess*' *set in righthand margin opposite line 177 in O.*

Moore (*P.M.L.A.*, L, 1935, pp. 761–8) shows that Middleton was knowledgeable enough however to shape *A Game at Chess* round one of the best games of the greatest player of the century, an Italian subject of the Spanish King named Greco (resident in England from 1622–4). The references of the present scene show at the least a knowledge of technical terms.

203. *men*] chessmen.

Liv. What gentlewoman? Pish.
Moth. Wife to my son indeed, but not known, madam,
To any but yourself.
Liv. Now I beshrew you,
Could you be so unkind to her and me
To come and not bring her? 'Faith, 'tis not friendly.
Moth. I feared to be too bold.
Liv. Too bold? Oh what's become
Of the true hearty love was wont to be
'Mongst neighbours in old time?
Moth. And she's a stranger, madam.
Liv. The more should be her welcome. When is courtesy
In better practice, than when 'tis employed
In entertaining strangers? I could chide i' faith—
Leave her behind, poor gentlewoman, alone too!
Make some amends, and send for her betimes, go.
Moth. Please you command one of your servants, madam.
Liv. Within there.

Enter Servant.

Serv. Madam.
Liv. Attend the gentlewoman.
Moth. [*Aside*] It must be carried wondrous privately
From my son's knowledge, he'll break out in storms else.
[*To Servant*] Hark you, sir.
[*They talk apart; exit* Servant.]
Liv. Now comes in the heat of your part.
Guard. True, I know it, lady, and if I be out
May the Duke banish me from all employments,
Wanton, or serious.
Liv. So, have you sent, widow?

222. i' faith] *O;* ye in faith *Lamb.*

229–30. *part . . . be out*] Guardiano interprets 'part' as meaning a theatrical 'part'. To 'be out' is to forget one's lines, and hence to be nonplussed. 'The heat of' = the most demanding aspect of.

Moth. Yes, madam, he's almost at home by this.
Liv. And 'faith let me entreat you that henceforward
All such unkind faults may be swept from friendship,
Which does but dim the lustre. And think thus much,
It is a wrong to me, that have ability
To bid friends welcome, when you keep 'em from me;
You cannot set greater dishonour near me
For bounty is the credit and the glory
Of those that have enough. I see y' are sorry,
And the good 'mends is made by 't.
Moth. Here she's, madam.

Enter BIANCA *and* Servant.

Bian. [*Aside*] I wonder how she comes to send for me now?
[*Exit* Servant.]
Liv. Gentlewoman, y' are most welcome, trust me y' are,
As courtesy can make one, or respect
Due to the presence of you.
Bian. I give you thanks, lady.
Liv. I heard you were alone, and 't had appeared
An ill condition in me, though I knew you not,
Nor ever saw you—yet humanity
Thinks ev'ry case her own—to have kept your company
Here from you, and left you all solitary.
I rather ventured upon boldness then
As the least fault, and wished your presence here—
A thing most happily motioned of that gentleman,
Whom I request you, for his care and pity
To honour and reward with your acquaintance:
A gentleman that ladies' rights stands for,
That's his profession.

237–41.] Cf. II. i. 12–14 and note.
242. *'mends*] amends.
249. *humanity*] humaneness, concern for others.
254. *motioned of*] suggested by.
258. *profession*] perhaps double-edged: (1) occupation (2) assertion, pose. For the latter cf. I. ii. 208–9.

Bian. 'Tis a noble one,
And honours my acquaintance.
Guard. All my intentions
Are servants to such mistresses.
Bian. 'Tis your modesty
It seems, that makes your deserts speak so low, sir.
Liv. Come, widow. [*To Bianca*] Look you, lady, here's our business. [*Pointing to the* '*Table and Chess*']
Are we not well employed, think you? An old quarrel
Between us, that will never be at an end.
Bian. No, and methinks there's men enough to part you, lady.
Liv. Ho! but they set us on, let us come off
As well as we can, poor souls, men care no farther.
I pray sit down forsooth, if you have the patience
To look upon two weak and tedious gamesters.
Guard. 'Faith, madam, set these by till evening,
You'll have enough on 't then; the gentlewoman
Being a stranger, would take more delight
To see your rooms and pictures.
Liv. Marry, good sir,
And well remembered, I beseech you show 'em her—
That will beguile time well. Pray heartily do, sir,
I'll do as much for you; here take these keys,
Show her the Monument too—and that's a thing
Everyone sees not, you can witness that, widow.
Moth. And that's worth sight indeed, madam.
Bian. Kind lady,
I fear I came to be a trouble to you.
Liv. Oh nothing less forsooth.
Bian. And to this courteous gentleman,

---

259. *intentions*] endeavours (L. *intendere* = 'aim at', 'endeavour').
265. *men*] the chessmen.
266. *set us on*] incite us (to quarrel). 'Come off' = emerge, come through. Both phrases hint at sexual play.
277. *the Monument*] usually a carved figure in wood or stone; though anything that served as a memento of a past occasion could be called a 'monument'.

That wears a kindness in his breast so noble
And bounteous to the welcome of a stranger.
Guard. If you but give acceptance to my service
You do the greatest grace and honour to me
That courtesy can merit.
Bian. I were to blame else,
And out of fashion much. I pray you lead, sir.
Liv. After a game or two, w' are for you, gentlefolks.
Guard. We wish no better seconds in society
Than your discourses, madam, and your partner's there.
Moth. I thank your praise. I listened to you, sir,
Though when you spoke there came a paltry rook
Full in my way, and chokes up all my game.
Exit GUARDIANO *and* BIANCA.
Liv. Alas, poor widow, I shall be too hard for thee.
Moth. Y' are cunning at the game, I'll be sworn, madam.
Liv. It will be found so, ere I give you over.
She that can place her man well—
Moth. As you do, madam.
Liv. As I shall, wench, can never lose her game.
Nay, nay, the black king's mine.

293. chokes] *O;* chok'd *Dilke.* 297. well—] *This ed.;* well, *O.*

---

285. *grace and honour*] Guardiano thinks of the rewards he may expect from the Duke.

288. *w' are . . . you*] we shall join you.

292. *rook*] the chessman now usually called the 'castle'. It was previously also called the 'Duke', a fact Middleton expects his audience to know (see l. 300). Cf. *A Game at Chess*, Induction ll. 55–7 (Middleton, *Wks*, VII. 12): '*Ignatius.* Dukes? they're called Rooks by some./*Error.* Corruptedly; *Le roc* the word, *custode de la roche*,/The keeper of the forts.' *O.E.D.* derives the word ultimately from the Persian 'rukh', originally the fabulous bird the 'roc'.

295.] with a glance at 'the game' = amorous intrigue. The Mother is of course unconscious of this second sense; Livia however takes it up in her reply, and it occurs several times in the following dialogue.

296. *give you over*] am finished with you.

297. *place her man*] the Duke.

299. *the black king*] suggesting evil. Contrasted with the 'white king' described (l. 306) as 'your saintish king.'

Moth. Cry you mercy, madam.
Liv. And this my queen.
Moth. I see 't now.
Liv. Here's a duke
Will strike a sure stroke for the game anon—
Your pawn cannot come back to relieve itself.
Moth. I know that, madam.
Liv. You play well the whilst.
How she belies her skill! I hold two ducats
I give you check and mate to your white king,
Simplicity itself, your saintish king there.
Moth. Well, ere now lady
I have seen the fall of subtlety. Jest on.
Liv. Ay, but simplicity receives two for one.
Moth. What remedy but patience!

Enter above GUARDIANO *and* BIANCA.

Bian. Trust me, sir,
Mine eye ne'er met with fairer ornaments.
Guard. Nay, livelier, I'm persuaded, neither Florence
Nor Venice can produce.
Bian. Sir, my opinion
Takes your part highly.
Guard. There's a better piece
Yet than all these.

[*Enter*] DUKE *above* [*behind* GUARDIANO *and* BIANCA.]

309. simplicity] *O corr.* (Simplicitie); Simplicities *O uncorr.* 315.1.] '*Duke above*' *set in right-hand margin in O.*

302.] Bianca, like the pawn in chess, can only move forward, without the option of retreat.
304. *hold*] wager.
309.] presumably 'two blows for one': simple honesty is always worsted.
312. *livelier*] perhaps hinting at the living 'monument'.
313. *Venice*] Bianca's birthplace. See I. i. 49.
314. *Takes your part*] supports you.
315.1.] Dyce suggests that Guardiano 'draws a curtain and discovers

Bian. Not possible, sir!
Guard. Believe it;
You'll say so when you see 't. Turn but your eye now
Y' are upon 't presently. *Exit.*
Bian. [*Seeing the Duke*] Oh sir.
Duke. He's gone, beauty!
Pish, look not after him. He's but a vapour
That when the sun appears is seen no more.
Bian. Oh treachery to honour!
Duke. Prithee tremble not.
I feel thy breast shake like a turtle panting
Under a loving hand that makes much on 't.
Why art so fearful? As I'm friend to brightness,
There's nothing but respect and honour near thee.
You know me, you have seen me; here's a heart
Can witness I have seen thee.
Bian. The more's my danger.
Duke. The more's thy happiness. Pish, strive not, sweet;
This strength were excellent employed in love now,
But here 'tis spent amiss. Strive not to seek
Thy liberty, and keep me still in prison.
[*Draws her arms round him*]
I' faith you shall not out, till I'm released now;

329. here 'tis] *Dilke;* here's 'tis *O.*

---

the Duke' (at l. 317, 'presently'), but a simple entry behind an unsuspecting Bianca, seen by the audience but not by her, requires no change in the placing of the octavo entry, and offers a much better dramatic effect.

317. *presently*] at once.

319. *the sun*] the very common Renaissance figure for the prince or ruler.

321. *like . . . panting*] Compare De Flores carrying off Beatrice (*Changeling* III. iv. 170; Revels ed. p. 66): ''Las, how the turtle pants.' Turtle = turtledove.

323. *brightness*] beauty. (See *O.E.D.* 'bright' sense 3).

330. *still in prison*] always in your arms. Compare Dekker, *If this be not a good play*, I. ii. 252–4 (*Wks*, III. 136): *King*. . . . You haue stolne vpon vs (Ladie)./*Erminghild*. You haue good law against me, (playing the thiefe)/Your Grace may keepe mee prisoner. *King*. In these Armes.'

We'll be both freed together, or stay still by 't;
So is captivity pleasant.
Bian. Oh my lord.
Duke. I am not here in vain; have but the leisure
To think on that, and thou'lt be soon resolved.
The lifting of thy voice is but like one
That does exalt his enemy, who proving high
Lays all the plots to confound him that raised him.
Take warning I beseech thee; thou seem'st to me
A creature so composed of gentleness,
And delicate meekness—such as bless the faces
Of figures that are drawn for goddesses
And makes art proud to look upon her work—
I should be sorry the least force should lay
An unkind touch upon thee.
Bian. Oh my extremity!
My lord, what seek you?
Duke. Love.
Bian. 'Tis gone already,
I have a husband.
Duke. That's a single comfort;
Take a friend to him.
Bian. That's a double mischief,
Or else there's no religion.
Duke. Do not tremble
At fears of thine own making.
Bian. Nor, great lord,
Make me not bold with death and deeds of ruin

---

332. *still*] ever; unmoving.

336–8.] a cumbrous simile: Bianca's screams would merely bring about her own downfall—like the unfortunate man who secures high position for an acquaintance, only to find the other's new influence used against himself.

347. *single comfort*] a poor comfort, because one only (*O.E.D.* 'one', sense 12b); with a play on single = unmarried.

348. *to*] in addition to.

350–8. *Nor . . . virtue*] 'bold with' = callous towards; 'fear' = frighten. The meaning of this rather awkward passage depends upon an association

Because they fear not you; me they must fright.
Then am I best, in health—should thunder speak
And none regard it, it had lost the name
And were as good be still. I'm not like those
That take their soundest sleeps in greatest tempests;
Then wake I most, the weather fearfullest,
And call for strength to virtue.

Duke. Sure I think
Thou know'st the way to please me. I affect
A passionate pleading 'bove an easy yielding,
But never pitied any—they deserve none—
That will not pity me. I can command,
Think upon that. Yet if thou truly knewest
The infinite pleasure my affection takes
In gentle, fair entreatings, when love's businesses
Are carried courteously 'twixt heart and heart,
You'd make more haste to please me.

Bian. Why should you seek, sir,
To take away that you can never give?

Duke. But I give better in exchange: wealth, honour.
She that is fortunate in a duke's favour
Lights on a tree that bears all women's wishes;
If your own mother saw you pluck fruit there
She would commend your wit, and praise the time
Of your nativity. Take hold of glory.

374. nativity.] *Dilke subst.;* Nativity *O.*

---

between bad weather ('thunder' 'greatest tempests') and moral judgements (a metaphor quite frequent in the play). Bianca says *she* is sensitive to moral order (acknowledges bad weather when it comes) while the Duke ignores it. 'Then am I best, in health' may mean 'I'm at my best when in health' using 'health' as synonymous with fair weather; but a phrase parallel to, and contrasted with, 'the weather fearfullest' may have dropped out. (There is however no obvious textual dislocation.)

369–87.] Compare Gratiana's and the disguised Vindice's incitements to Castiza in *Revenger's Tragedy* II. i. 145–244 (Revels ed. pp. 38–42).

371–2.] An allusion to the Fall is almost certain; the Duke is no doubt unconscious that he casts himself for the role of serpent.

Do not I know y' have cast away your life
Upon necessities, means merely doubtful
To keep you in indifferent health and fashion—
A thing I heard too lately, and soon pitied?
And can you be so much your beauty's enemy
To kiss away a month or two in wedlock,
And weep whole years in wants for ever after?
Come play the wise wench, and provide for ever;
Let storms come when they list, they find thee sheltered.
Should any doubt arise, let nothing trouble thee;
Put trust in our love for the managing
Of all to thy heart's peace. We'll walk together,
And show a thankful joy for both our fortunes.

Exit above.

Liv. Did not I say my duke would fetch you over, widow?
Moth. I think you spoke in earnest when you said it, madam.
Liv. And my black king makes all the haste he can too.
Moth. Well, madam, we may meet with him in time yet.
Liv. I have given thee blind mate twice.
Moth. You may see, madam,
My eyes begin to fail.
Liv. I'll swear they do, wench.

Enter GUARDIANO.

382. wise] *Dilke;* wife *O.*

---

376. *merely*] extremely, wholly.

383.] Cf. I. i. 51–3 and line 356 above.

388. *fetch you over*] get the better of you.

391. *meet with*] encounter, oppose; perhaps, be even with (see *O.E.D.* 'meet' senses 11c and 11i).

392. *I . . . twice*] the Mother has been hoodwinked. Saul's *Famous Game of Chesse-Play*, 1614, explains: 'A Blinde Mate is, when thy Adversary giueth thee a check, such as thou canst not avoid . . . which is indeed an absolute Mate: but in so much as he not seeing it to be a Mate, cries onely Checke to thee, it is therefore called *A blinde Mate*, as who should say, a Mate giuen by a Blinde man (at least in skill.)' (Ed. Jo. Barbier, 1640 sig. Gl*v*.). The 'blindness' here is however the Mother's, not Livia's.

Guard. [*Aside*] I can but smile as often as I think on 't:
How prettily the poor fool was beguiled,
How unexpectedly; it's a witty age.
Never were finer snares for women's honesties
Than are devised in these days; no spider's web
Made of a daintier thread, than are now practised
To catch love's flesh-fly by the silver wing.
Yet to prepare her stomach by degrees
To Cupid's feast, because I saw 'twas queasy,
I showed her naked pictures by the way:
A bit to stay the appetite. Well, advancement,
I venture hard to find thee; if thou comest

---

395. *the poor fool*] a term of pity not contempt.

396. *witty*] living by its wits.

397–9.] a favourite image with Middleton. Compare e.g. *A Mad World* I. i. 153–5, (*Wks*, III. 259): 'Every part of the world shoots up daily into more subtlety; the very spider weaves her cauls with more art and cunning to entrap the fly.'

400. *flesh-fly*] blow-fly; one that deposits its eggs in animal carcasses. 'Flesh' has strong sexual connotations; for the association between lust and a fly-blown carcass see *Ham.* II. ii. 181–7. Cf. *The Roaring Girl* I. ii. 125–6 (Dekker *Wks*, III. 20): *Gosh.* What then could vex his father so. *Alex.* Oh a woman./*Seb.* A flesh fly, that can vex any man.'

silver wing] rather cryptic; perhaps 'silver' to suggest the attractive glitter of lust. Not an entomologist's description.

401. *stomach*] appropriate to the play's food-imagery; also used for 'inclination' (compare 'against one's stomach').

402. *queasy*] (1) liable to nausea (2) scrupulous, nice. Compare II. ii. 471–3, note and quotation.

403.] apparently standard practice. Compare *The Woman Hater* II. i. (Beaumont and Fletcher, *Wks*, X. 85), a woman's amorous advances being repulsed: 'Why should you come to me? I have no Galleries, nor banqueting houses, nor bawdy pictures to shew your Ladyship.'

404. *A bit . . . appetite*] The usual phrase is 'to stay the stomach', meaning to appease its cravings, to quiet it (and thus avoid queasiness). Middleton might however be referring to a secondary meaning of 'to stay' = to strengthen, and mean 'to encourage the appetite (for sexual pleasure), to whet it by titillation.' (See *O.E.D.* 'stay' v.[1] sense 29 and v.[2] sense 1.).

404–9.] It is difficult not to suspect some bungling here. As the text stands 'that first cross' (l. 407) makes no sense. (Parker suggests various interpretations, but none convinces.) The phrase is meaningful only after Bianca's outburst at ll. 426–44, which makes it tempting to guess that the whole passage is displaced, perhaps because of a slip of paper carrying the

With a greater title set upon thy crest,
I'll take that first cross patiently, and wait
Until some other comes greater than that—
I'll endure all.

Liv. The game's e'en at the best now; you may see, widow,
How all things draw to an end.

Moth. E'en so do I, madam.

Liv. I pray take some of your neighbours along with you.

Moth. They must be those are almost twice your years then,
If they be chose fit matches for my time, madam.

Liv. Has not my duke bestirred himself?

Moth. Yes 'faith, madam,
'Has done me all the mischief in this game.

Liv. 'Has showed himself in 's kind.

Moth. In 's kind, call you it?
I may swear that.

Liv. Yes 'faith, and keep your oath.

Guard. [*Aside*] Hark, list, there's somebody coming down; 'tis she.

Enter BIANCA.

Bian. [*Aside*] Now bless me from a blasting; I saw that now

---

relevant lines being inserted at an incorrect point in the manuscript. Another possibility is that ll. 404–9 were intended to *replace* (or be replaced by) ll. 444–7. With no parallel emergencies elsewhere in the text it would however be irresponsible to emend.

406.] the promise, or award, of greater favours. A metaphor from heraldry: the 'crest' is 'the figure or device . . . placed on a wreath, coronet or chapeau, and borne above the shield and helmet in a coat of arms' (*O.E.D.*); the 'title' is the inscription on the crest.

411–12. *E'en . . . with you*] 'I draw to an end also (approach my death).' 'Remember that some of your neighbours (e.g. I myself) do so too.' Livia no doubt means 'draw to an end' (l. 411) as a *double entendre*.

414. *time*] age.

417. *in's kind*] lit. 'as his nature prompted.' Probably with a sexual reference; compare *Mer. V.* I. iii. 83–6: ' . . . when the work of generation was/Between these woolly breeders in the act,/ . . . in the doing of the deed of kind . . .'

420–2. *blasting . . . mildews*] Mildew is a destructive growth of minute

Fearful for any woman's eye to look on.
Infectious mists and mildews hang at 's eyes,
The weather of a doomsday dwells upon him.
Yet since mine honour's leprous, why should I
Preserve that fair that caused the leprosy?
Come poison all at once. [*Aside to Guardiano*] Thou in whose baseness
The bane of virtue broods, I'm bound in soul
Eternally to curse thy smooth-browed treachery,
That wore the fair veil of a friendly welcome,
And I a stranger; think upon 't, 'tis worth it.
Murders piled up upon a guilty spirit
At his last breath will not lie heavier
Than this betraying act upon thy conscience.
Beware of off'ring the first-fruits to sin:
His weight is deadly, who commits with strumpets
After they have been abased, and made for use;
If they offend to th' death, as wise men know,

424. why] *Dilke;* who *O.*

---

fungi on plants; then used metaphorically of disease in human beings. The fungi are contagious; mildew therefore became associated with 'blasting', the active transference of infection, in plants and in humans. Compare *Ham.* III. iv. 64–5: 'Here is your husband; like a mildew'd ear,/ Blasting his wholesome brother.'

422. *Infectious mists*] Mists and fogs were thought to spread disease. Compare *Lr.* II. iv. 168–70: 'Infect her beauty,/You fen suck'd fogs, drawn by the powerful sun,/To fall and blast her pride!' One of the allegorical figures in Middleton's *The Triumphs of Truth* (1613) appears to have been costumed with 'mists hanging at his eyes.' (*Wks*, VII. 241).

424–5.] In leprosy the skin is coated with silvery scales; mildew (l. 422) forms a similar coating on the plants it destroys. Leprosy is a familiar metaphor for moral foulness.

428. *smooth-browed*] The forehead was considered the place where the various emotions were registered. 'Smooth-browed' therefore means 'unruffled', 'calm.'

429. *fair veil*] 'Vail' (the octavo spelling), meaning a doffing of one's hat in respectful greeting, may also have been in Middleton's mind, suggested by 'friendly welcome'.

435–8.] freely constructed. 'They' in l. 437 refers to those who 'commit

How much more they then that first make 'em so?
I give thee that to feed on. I'm made bold now;
I thank thy treachery, sin and I'm acquainted,
No couple greater. And I'm like that great one
Who making politic use of a base villain,
He likes the treason well, but hates the traitor.
So I hate thee, slave.

Guard. [*Aside*] Well, so the Duke love me,
I fare not much amiss then: two great feasts
Do seldom come together in one day,
We must not look for 'em.

Bian. What at it still, Mother?

Moth. You see we sit by 't. Are you so soon returned?

Liv. [*Aside*] So lively and so cheerful, a good sign that.

Moth. You have not seen all since sure?

Bian. That have I, Mother,
The Monument and all. I'm so beholding
To this kind, honest, courteous gentleman,
You'd little think it, Mother, showed me all,
Had me from place to place, so fashionably—
The kindness of some people, how 't exceeds!
'Faith, I have seen that I little thought to see,
I' th' morning when I rose.

---

with strumpets', ''em' (l. 438) to the 'strumpets' themselves. Bianca's point is the much greater culpability of those who 'make' strumpets, as compared with those who merely 'use' them; she is not (as one reading of the syntax would suggest) condemning the strumpets themselves. 'Weight' = responsibility; 'to th' death' = mortally, with mortal sin.

443.] The italics indicate the proverbial or at least familiar character of the line. Cf. Dekker, *The Honest Whore*, IV. iv. 49–50 (*Wks*, II. 87): 'This principle is olde but true as fate,/Kings may loue treason, but the traitor hate.' (Quoted by Parker.).

445. *fare*] The secondary sense 'to eat' provides the transition to 'feasts'. The 'two feasts' would be the Duke's gratitude (already gained) and Bianca's (refused).

454. *Had*] *who* had; cf. Abbott, section 244, pp. 164–6.

456–7. *'Faith . . . rose*] As Parker notes, a similar dramatic irony is found in *The Changeling* III. ii. 1–2 (Revels ed. p. 45): '*De Flores*. [about to murder Alonzo] All this is nothing; you shall see anon/A place you little dream on.'

Moth. Nay, so I told you
Before you saw 't, it would prove worth your sight.
I give you great thanks for my daughter, sir,
And all your kindness towards her.
Guard. Oh good widow!
Much good may 't do her—[*Aside*] forty weeks hence, i' faith.

Enter Servant.

Liv. Now, sir.
Serv. May 't please you, madam, to walk in?
Supper's upon the table.
Liv. Yes, we come; [*Exit* Servant.]
Will 't please you, gentlewoman?
Bian. Thanks, virtuous lady.
[*Aside to Livia*] Y' are a damned bawd. [*Aloud*] I'll follow you forsooth;
Pray take my mother in. [*Aside to Livia*] An old ass go with you.
[*Aloud*] This gentleman and I vow not to part.
Liv. Then get you both before.
Bian. [*Aside*] There lies his art.
Exeunt [BIANCA *and* GUARDIANO.]

Liv. Widow, I'll follow you. [*Exit* MOTHER.]
Is 't so: damned bawd?
Are you so bitter? 'Tis but want of use—
Her tender modesty is sea-sick a little,
Being not accustomed to the breaking billow
Of woman's wavering faith, blown with temptations.

461. may 't] *Dyce;* may *O.* 464 Will 't] *Dilke;* Wilt *O.*

468.] Bianca's riposte is probably indecent, but she may mean that Guardiano 'precedes' the Duke as his pander.

471–3.] The implied 'voyage' is a common metaphor for a sexual encounter. Cf. Middleton, *Michaelmas Term* I. ii. 10–12 (*Wks*, I. 233): 'But why sad now? Yet indeed 'tis the fashion of any courtesan to be sea-sick i' th' first voyage.' (Quoted by Parker).

'Tis but a qualm of honour, 'twill away,
A little bitter for the time, but lasts not.
Sin tastes at the first draught like wormwood water,
But drunk again, 'tis nectar ever after. *Exit.*

---

474. *qualm of honour*] nausea induced by regard for honour.

476. *wormwood water*] a drink prepared (like absinthe or vermouth) from wormwood, a herb proverbial for its bitterness.

Act III

[Act III. Scene I.]

Enter MOTHER.

Moth. I would my son would either keep at home,
Or I were in my grave;
She was but one day abroad, but ever since
She's grown so cutted, there's no speaking to her.
Whether the sight of great cheer at my lady's
And such mean fare at home work discontent in her
I know not, but I'm sure she's strangely altered.
I'd ne'er keep daughter-in-law i' th' house with me again, if I had an hundred. When read I of any that agreed long together, but she and her mother fell out in the first quarter—nay, sometime a grudging of a scolding the first week, by 'r Lady?
So takes the new disease methinks in my house.
I'm weary of my part, there's nothing likes her,

8. I'd] *This ed.;* I'll *O.* 11. of] *O;* or *conj. Dyce, Bullen.*

III. i. 4. *cutted*] abrupt, curt, querulous (*O.E.D.* sense 3b).

8. *I'd*] Grammar and logic require this reading in place of the octavo's 'I'll'. See II. i. 49n.

11. *a grudging*] a slight symptom of an approaching illness; a small portion of anything.

13. *takes*] takes root, catches hold.

the new disease] An uncertainly diagnosed fever that made its appearance in England during the latter half of the sixteenth century. Jonson (*Every Man in his Humour* 1616 Folio version II. i. 46) gives a violent headache corruption of the memory and the judgement, and finally a distempering of all the mind's functions as the stages in the progress of the disease. (See *Wks*, III. 329–30 and the Yale edition of *E.M.I.H.* p. 193).

I know not how to please her here a-late;
And here she comes.

Enter BIANCA.

Bian. This is the strangest house
For all defects as ever gentlewoman
Made shift withal to pass away her love in.
Why is there not a cushion-cloth of drawn work,
Or some fair cut-work pinned up in my bedchamber,
A silver-and-gilt casting-bottle hung by 't?
Nay, since I am content to be so kind to you
To spare you for a silver basin and ewer,
Which one of my fashion looks for of duty—
She's never offered under, where she sleeps—
Moth. [*Aside*] She talks of things here my whole state's not worth.
Bian. Never a green silk quilt is there i' th' house, Mother,
To cast upon my bed?
Moth. No, by troth is there,
Nor orange tawny neither.

25. sleeps—] *This ed.;* sleeps: *O.*

---

19. *cushion-cloth*] 'apparently a cushion case or covering' (Nares).
drawn work] 'ornamental work done in textile fabrics by drawing out some of the threads of warp and woof, so as to form patterns, with or without the addition of needlework or other accessories' (*O.E.D.*).

20. *cut-work*] openwork lace popular in the seventeenth century, the pattern being *cut* rather than woven into the material. Often associated with Italy. With Bianca's demands that her chamber should be elaborately adorned compare Moryson's *Itinerary*: 'the houses of gentlewemen brought to bed, and espetially the Chambers wherein they lye, are richly sett forth with costly hangings . . .' (Moryson, p. 453).

21. *casting-bottle*] a bottle for sprinkling perfumes.

23. *To . . . for*] not to demand from you.

24. *of duty*] as something due to her.

25. *offered under*] offered less. Parker thinks Middleton leads the audience to expect that Bianca will mention a chamberpot.

26. *state*] estate.

29. *orange tawny*] Linthicum (pp. 45–6) notes this as 'a gay colour, usually associated with courtiers.' She makes and then half-withdraws the

Bian. Here's a house
For a young gentlewoman to be got with child in.
Moth. Yes, simple though you make it, there has been three
Got in a year in 't, since you move me to 't;
And all as sweet-faced children, and as lovely,
As you'll be mother of. I will not spare you.
What, cannot children be begot think you,
Without gilt casting-bottles? Yes, and as sweet ones:
The miller's daughter brings forth as white boys,
As she that bathes herself with milk and bean-flour.
'Tis an old saying, one may keep good cheer
In a mean house; so may true love affect
After the rate of princes, in a cottage.
Bian. Troth, you speak wondrous well for your old house here;
'Twill shortly fall down at your feet to thank you,
Or stoop when you go to bed, like a good child
To ask you blessing. Must I live in want,
Because my fortune matched me with your son?
Wives do not give away themselves to husbands,
To the end to be quite cast away; they look
To be the better used, and tendered rather,
Highlier respected, and maintained the richer—
They're well rewarded else for the free gift
Of their whole life to a husband. I ask less now

---

suggestion that it symbolized pride, citing the present passage among others.

31. *Yes*] The true reading may be 'Yet'; the compositor was prone to context-influence and the next word begins with an 's'. A misreading of Middleton's final 't' as an 's' would be just possible.

31–2.] Either the house was shared, or she exaggerates.

37. *white boys*] a term of endearment or praise; with a rather clumsy reference to the whiteness of flour ('miller's daughter').

38.] unbelievable extravagance in an age in which few baths of any kind were taken (though Mary Queen of Scots is said to have claimed an extra allowance of wine for hers).

40. *affect*] love, express itself.

41. *After . . . princes*] on a princely scale, as much as any prince.

44. *stoop*] bow.

48. *To the end*] with the intention.

Than what I had at home when I was a maid,
And at my father's house; kept short of that
Which a wife knows she must have, nay, and will,
Will, Mother, if she be not a fool born;
And report went of me, that I could wrangle
For what I wanted when I was two hours old,
And by that copy, this land still I hold.
You hear me, Mother. *Exit.*

Moth. Ay, too plain methinks;
And were I somewhat deafer when you spake,
'Twere ne'er a whit the worse for my quietness.
'Tis the most sudden'st, strangest alteration,
And the most subtlest that e'er wit at threescore
Was puzzled to find out. I know no cause for 't; but
She's no more like the gentlewoman at first
Than I am like her that never lay with man yet;
And she's a very young thing where'er she be.
When she first lighted here, I told her then
How mean she should find all things; she was pleased forsooth,
None better. I laid open all defects to her,
She was contented still. But the devil's in her,
Nothing contents her now. Tonight my son
Promised to be at home; would he were come once,
For I'm weary of my charge, and life too.
She'd be served all in silver by her good will,
By night and day; she hates the name of pewter

77. pewter] *Oliphant;* Pew-/terer *O.*

59.] referring to the legal status of copy-holder, a householder or property-owner possessing a transcript from the court-roll of the manor in which his property lay. The transcript (his 'copy') secured him from eviction: Bianca means that she has long established a right to 'wrangle', and will not forgo it.

71. *defects*] cf. I. i. 123 and note.

74. *once*] now.

76. *by . . . will*] if she had her will.

77. *pewter*] The metal out of which *inferior* kitchen ware was made.

More than sick men the noise, or diseased bones
That quake at fall o' th' hammer, seeming to have
A fellow-feeling with 't at every blow.
What course shall I think on? She frets me so. [*Exit.*]

[III. ii]

Enter LEANTIO.

Lean. Ho̩w near am I now to a happiness
That earth exceeds not! Not another like it;
The treasures of the deep are not so precious
As are the concealed comforts of a man,
Locked up in woman's love. I scent the air
Of blessings when I come but near the house.
What a delicious breath marriage sends forth—

0.1. III. ii] *Oliphant; not in O.*

Oliphant's emendation (for octavo 'Pewterer') gives better rhythm and better sense. The doubling of final 'er' would be a simple mechanical error on the part of scribe, compositor or indeed author. A misreading is also just possible; if Middleton wrote 'Pewtere' there would be a confusing number of short strokes in the last three letters, and the 'e' and 'r' forms are very alike in Middleton's hand.

78. *the noise*] perhaps referring to 'the noises': 'sounds supposed to have been heard before the death of any person' (*English Dialect Dictionary*). I have not found the singular used elsewhere (possibly a compositor-error here; the compositors were prone to omit a final 's'). But 'noise' may have the normal meaning.

80. *fellow . . . with 't*] feel the same jolts as the hammer when it strikes.

III. ii. 0.1] Oliphant first introduced a new scene here. If we are right in giving the Mother an exit after her speech, the new scene-arrangement is technically correct, for the stage is clear before Leantio enters. It should be noted, however, that we also have to supply a re-entry for the Mother as well as Bianca (who certainly leaves the stage at III. i. 60.1) later in the current scene (line 27.1). It is possible therefore that the Mother simply retires to the back of the stage as Leantio enters.

5–6. *I scent . . . house*] modelled perhaps on Duncan's equally ill-placed confidence, *Mac.* I. vi. 1–3: 'This castle hath a pleasant seat; the air/Nimbly and sweetly recommends itself/Unto our gentle senses.'

The violet-bed's not sweeter. Honest wedlock
Is like a banqueting-house built in a garden,
On which the spring's chaste flowers take delight
To cast their modest odours; when base lust
With all her powders, paintings, and best pride,
Is but a fair house built by a ditch side.
When I behold a glorious dangerous strumpet,
Sparkling in beauty and destruction too,
Both at a twinkling, I do liken straight
Her beautified body to a goodly temple
That's built on vaults where carcasses lie rotting;
And so by little and little I shrink back again,
And quench desire with a cool meditation;
And I'm as well methinks. Now for a welcome
Able to draw men's envies upon man:
A kiss now that will hang upon my lip
As sweet as morning dew upon a rose,
And full as long. After a five days' fast

---

9. *banqueting-house*] a favourite feature of Jacobean gardens, built usually of wood and of a semi-permanent nature. They were frequently used as places of assignation. Compare Stubbes, *Anatomy of Abuses*, 1585: 'In the suburbes of the citie . . . they [women] have their banqueting houses, with galleries, turrets, and what not, therein sumptuously erected, wherein they may, and doubtless do, many of them, play the filthy persons.' Middleton's audience would probably note the unintended irony of Leantio's comparison.

12. *pride*] display, finery.

13.] Middleton may have in mind the City Ditch or Town Ditch built originally as a means of defence, but by the early seventeenth century fallen into a dilapidated and foul condition. John Stowe (*Survey of London* 1633 ed. p. 26) notes that 'Gardens [are] planted, & houses builded thereon, even to the Wall and in many places upon both Ditch and Wall, houses are builded.'

14–15.] The strumpet's combining beauty and menace was a commonplace subject of remark.

17–18. *goodly . . . rotting*] Compare Matthew xxiii, 27: 'Woe unto you, scribes and Pharisees, hypocrites! for ye are like unto whited sepulchres, which indeed appear beautiful outward, but are within full of dead men's bones, and of all uncleanness.'

24–5. *As sweet . . . long*] a frequent metaphor in Middleton, most successful in *A Game at Chess* I. i. 77–80, (*Wks*, VII. 17): 'Upon those

She'll be so greedy now, and cling about me,
I take care how I shall be rid of her;

[*Enter* BIANCA *and* MOTHER.]

And here 't begins.
Bian. Oh sir, y' are welcome home.
Moth. Oh is he come? I am glad on 't.
Lean. Is that all?
[*Aside*] Why this as dreadful now as sudden death
To some rich man, that flatters all his sins
With promise of repentance when he's old,
And dies in the midway before he comes to 't.
Sure y' are not well, Bianca! How dost, prithee?
Bian. I have been better than I am at this time.
Lean. Alas, I thought so.
Bian. Nay, I have been worse too,
Than now you see me, sir.
Lean. I'm glad thou mend'st yet,
I feel my heart mend too. How came it to thee?

30. this as] *This ed., suggested by F. D. Hoeniger;* this? as *O;* this is *Dilke, Dyce;* this is as *White.*

---

lips, the sweet fresh buds of youth,/The holy dew of prayer lies, like pearl/Dropt from the opening eyelids of the morn/Upon the bashful rose.' Here 'full as long' must be ironic; dew soon evaporates.

30–3.] Compare the complacent rich man in Luke xii, 14–21.

30. *this*] this is. The octavo reading looks like a misunderstanding of copy. Middleton sometimes completely elided 'is' after 'this' for metrical reasons. Thus the holograph *Game at Chess* (Bald, V. ii. 85) has 'This a strange game, did not I lye with you?' The scribes of other manuscripts, presumably thinking this too eccentric, read: 'Here's a strange game . . .' Newcomb's compositor may have tried the query as a way out. Crane could be equally puzzling; in his transcript of *The Witch* (Malone Society Reprints l. 162) he has: 'this' the worst fright that could come . . .' A compositor might well interpret an apostrophe as an exclamation mark or query. Comparable readings are found in several First Folio texts, e.g. *Shr.*, I. ii. 45 (sig. S4v): 'Why this a heauie chance'; and *Meas.* V. i. 131 (sig. G4v): 'This' a good Fryer belike'. 'This' for 'this is' survived from Middle English; see e.g. Chaucer, *Knight's Tale* l. 2761.

Has anything disliked thee in my absence?
Bian. No, certain, I have had the best content
That Florence can afford.
Lean. Thou makest the best on 't;
Speak, Mother, what's the cause? You must needs know.
Moth. Troth I know none, son, let her speak herself.
[*Aside*] Unless it be the same gave Lucifer
A tumbling cast: that's pride.
Bian. Methinks this house stands nothing to my mind;
I'd have some pleasant lodging i' th' high street, sir,
Or if 'twere near the court, sir, that were much better:
'Tis a sweet recreation for a gentlewoman
To stand in a bay-window, and see gallants.
Lean. Now I have another temper, a mere stranger
To that of yours, it seems; I should delight
To see none but yourself.
Bian. I praise not that:
Too fond is as unseemly as too churlish.
I would not have a husband of that proneness
To kiss me before company, for a world.
Beside 'tis tedious to see one thing still, sir,
Be it the best that ever heart affected;
Nay, were 't yourself, whose love had power you know

---

39. *disliked*] displeased.

45. *tumbling cast*] fall, overthrow (*O.E.D.*).

49–50.] the opposite of strict respectability in Renaissance Italy. Compare Moryson, p. 151: 'the poore [Italian] wife sitts alone at home, locked vpp and kept by old women [compare I. i. 173–6], not having liberty to looke out of the windowe, especially if it be towards the streete.' Several Jacobean plays set in Italy make much of the restrictions imposed upon women's liberty, and of the window as a means of circumventing them. (See e.g. *Volpone* I. v. 118 ff. and *The Broken Heart* II. i. 1 ff.).

51. *another temper*] a different disposition.

54.] With this and ll. 84–9 compare I. iii. 22 ff.: Leantio's maxims are being quoted back at him.

55–6.] apparently a cause for complaint at the time. Swetnam (sig. H3) writes: 'those that play and dally with them [their wives] before company, they doe thereby set other mens teeth on edge, and make their Wives the less shamefast.'

55. *proneness*] inclination, disposition.

To bring me from my friends, I would not stand thus,
And gaze upon you always. Troth, I could not, sir;
As good be blind, and have no use of sight
As look on one thing still. What's the eye's treasure,
But change of objects? You are learned, sir,
And know I speak not ill; 'tis full as virtuous
For woman's eye to look on several men
As for her heart, sir, to be fixed on one.

Lean. Now thou comest home to me; a kiss for that word.

Bian. No matter for a kiss, sir; let it pass,
'Tis but a toy, we'll not so much as mind it;
Let's talk of other business, and forget it.
What news now of the pirates, any stirring?
Prithee discourse a little.

Moth. [*Aside*] I am glad he's here yet
To see her tricks himself; I had lied monstrously,
If I had told 'em first.

65. 'tis] *Dilke;* 'till *O.*

63–4. *What's . . . learned*] Bianca may be crediting Leantio with a (no doubt secondhand) knowledge of Euripides' line (*Orestes* l. 234) 'Variety is sweet in all things', or of Plutarch's similar 'Monotony in everything is tiresome and repellent, but variety is agreeable' (*Moralia* ch. 9 sec. 7c on 'the education of children'.) The saying occurs also in Aristotle (*Rhetoric* I. ii. 20) and in Erasmus (*Adagia* i. vii. 63), this last no doubt the most accessible source for the Renaissance reader.

65. *'tis*] The octavo 'till' is one of the clearest cases of context-influence in the play: the double l in 'ill' and 'full' remained in the compositor's mind.

70. *mind it*] think of it.

72.] Pirates were much in the news at this date: on 12 October 1620 a fleet under Sir Robert Mansell left Plymouth in an attempt to scatter them. It returned, after partial success, in June and July 1621 (see *Naval Tracts of Sir William Monson*, Navy Records Society, 1913, III, 98–118.) Middleton may have had a special interest in this expedition: his curiosity about Gondomar, the Spanish ambassador, is fully shown by *A Game at Chess*, and early historians believed that Gondomar (as Bald notes, p. 148) was behind the venture. (Bald mistakenly dates the fleet's departure 'August 1620').

any stirring] 'anything happening?'; or 'are any active?'

73. *yet*] at this point (see *O.E.D.* sense 5b).

Lean. Speak, what's the humour, sweet,
You make your lip so strange? This was not wont.
Bian. Is there no kindness betwixt man and wife,
Unless they make a pigeon-house of friendship,
And be still billing? 'Tis the idlest fondness
That ever was invented, and 'tis pity
It's grown a fashion for poor gentlewomen;
There's many a disease kissed in a year by 't,
And a French curtsy made to 't. Alas, sir,
Think of the world, how we shall live; grow serious;
We have been married a whole fortnight now.
Lean. How, a whole fortnight! Why is that so long?
Bian. 'Tis time to leave off dalliance; 'tis a doctrine
Of your own teaching, if you be remembered,
And I was bound to obey it.
Moth. [*Aside*] Here's one fits him;
This was well catched i' faith son, like a fellow
That rids another country of a plague,
And brings it home with him to his own house.
Knock within.
Who knocks?
Lean. Who's there now? Withdraw you, Bianca,
Thou art a gem no stranger's eye must see,
How e'er thou art pleased now to look dull on me.
Exit [BIANCA.]

84. live;] *Dyce;* live, *O.* 95. thou art] *This ed.;* thou *O;* thou ['rt] *Dyce.*

---

76. *strange*] not friendly and encouraging. (*O.E.D.* sense 11b).

79. *idlest fondness*] Cf. I. iii. 24 and note.

83. *French curtsy*] The French were associated with elaborate manners; cf. *R3* I. iii. 47–9: '*Gloucester*: . . . Because I cannot flatter and speak fair,/Smile in men's faces, smooth, deceive and cog,/Duck with French nods and apish courtesy . . .'. Middleton no doubt also refers to the 'French pox', venereal disease (see 'disease' l. 82 and compare 'stoop gallantly' I. ii. 111–12 and note).

92.] as Leantio brought Bianca.

95. *thou art pleased*] I accept Dyce's emendation (except in spelling out 'art'); the compositor may have inadvertently omitted 'art', having

Enter Messenger.

Y' are welcome, sir; to whom your business, pray?
Mess. To one I see not here now.
Lean. Who should that be, sir?
Mess. A young gentlewoman I was sent to.
Lean. A young gentlewoman?
Mess. Ay, sir, about sixteen;
Why look you wildly, sir?
Lean. At your strange error.
Y' have mistook the house, sir. There's none such here,
I assure you.
Mess. I assure you too,
The man that sent me cannot be mistook.
Lean. Why, who is 't sent you, sir?
Mess. The Duke.
Lean. The Duke?
Mess. Yes, he entreats her company at a banquet
At Lady Livia's house.
Lean. Troth shall I tell you, sir,
It is the most erroneous business
That e'er your honest pains was abused with.
I pray forgive me, if I smile a little;
I cannot choose i' faith, sir, at an error
So comical as this—I mean no harm though.
His Grace has been most wondrous ill informed,
Pray so return it, sir. What should her name be?
Mess. That I shall tell you straight too: Bianca Capella.

114 *and* 116. Capella] *O;* Capello *Dyce.*

---

already set it in the previous line. An apparently neater solution, 'please' for 'pleas'd', is possible: in Middleton's hand the 'umbrella' of the 's' can arch over a final 'e' and suggest a 'd'. 'Art pleased' however picks up more neatly the present tense of line 94.

103. *cannot be mistook*] cannot err.

114, 116. *Capella*] a form found in the Italian manuscripts (see Introduction pp. xliii–xliv), and quite possibly Middleton's own. There is no need to emend.

Lean. How, sir, Bianca? What do you call th' other?
Mess. Capella. Sir, it seems you know no such then?
Lean. Who should this be? I never heard o' th' name.
Mess. Then 'tis a sure mistake.
Lean. What if you enquired
In the next street, sir? I saw gallants there
In the new houses that are built of late.
Ten to one, there you find her.
Mess. Nay, no matter,
I will return the mistake, and seek no further.
Lean. Use your own will and pleasure, sir, y' are welcome.
Exit Messenger.
What shall I think of first? Come forth, Bianca—

Enter BIANCA.

Thou art betrayed I fear me.
Bian. Betrayed! How, sir?
Lean. The Duke knows thee.
Bian. Knows me! How know you that, sir?
Lean. 'Has got thy name.
Bian. [*Aside*] Ay, and my good name too,
That's worse o' th' twain.
Lean. How comes this work about?
Bian. How should the Duke know me? Can you guess, Mother?
Moth. Not I with all my wits, sure we kept house close.
Lean. Kept close! Not all the locks in Italy
Can keep you women so; you have been gadding,

124.1.] *S.D. follows* 'fear me.' *line 125 in O.* 127. 'Has] *This ed.;* Has *O*

---

122. *return the mistake*] return and make known the mistake.

126. *Knows me*] Bianca fears Leantio may mean 'knows carnally' (see 'my good name'—reputation—l. 127).

128. *this work*] these events; but possibly 'this affliction', 'this trouble' (*O.E.D.* sense 6a).

130. *kept house close*] remained indoors in concealment.

132. *gadding*] roving, wandering idly; condemned by early seventeenth-century moralists as inappropriate to faithful wives. Compare e.g. Thomas Gataker (*Marriage Duties*, 1620): 'Againe, here commeth to bee con-

And ventured out at twilight to th' court-green yonder,
And met the gallant bowlers coming home—
Without your masks too, both of you, I'll be hanged else.
Thou hast been seen Bianca by some stranger,
Never excuse it.
Bian. I'll not seek the way, sir.
Do you think y' have married me to mew me up
Not to be seen; what would you make of me?
Lean. A good wife, nothing else.
Bian. Why, so are some
That are seen ev'ry day, else the devil take 'em.
Lean. No more then, I believe all virtuous in thee
Without an argument; 'twas but thy hard chance
To be seen somewhere, there lies all the mischief.
But I have devised a riddance.
Moth. Now I can tell you, son,
The time and place.
Lean. When, where?
Moth. What wits have I?
When you last took your leave, if you remember,
You left us both at window.
Lean. Right, I know that.

---

demned the practise of such wives as are gadders abroad . . . the wise man maketh such *gadding abroad* a note of a light and lewd housewife.'

133–4.] Bowls were popular with the Jacobean nobility. 'Court-bowl', a version of the game mentioned by Marvell (*The Rehearsal Transpros'd*, *First Part* p. 60—*O.E.D.*), perhaps gives the name 'Court-green.' More simply, it may refer to a bowling-green attached to the court. The game was in poor repute with moralists: compare T. Taylor *Commentary upon the Epistle of Paul to Titus* 1612, ii. 14: 'Cards, dice, bowls, bouls, vnprofitable Companie.' (*O.E.D.*)

135. *Without your masks*] Modest Italian women wore masks or veils out of doors. Compare Moryson p. 410: 'their [Italian] wiues and virgins are . . . watched by their wemen attending them abroade, [and] have their faces covered with a vaile not to be seen . . .' Upper-class English women of this period also wore masks, especially at balls and other entertainments (see Linthicum pp. 271–2).

138. *mew . . . up*] in hawking, to shut the hawk in a cage or 'mew' while moulting.

Moth. And not the third part of an hour after,
The Duke passed by in a great solemnity,
To St. Mark's temple, and to my apprehension
He looked up twice to th' window.
Lean. Oh there quickened
The mischief of this hour!
Bian. [*Aside*] If you call 't mischief—
It is a thing I fear I am conceived with.
Lean. Looked he up twice, and could you take no warning!
Moth. Why, once may do as much harm, son, as a thousand:
Do not you know one spark has fired an house
As well as a whole furnace?
Lean. My heart flames for 't.
Yet let's be wise, and keep all smothered closely;
I have bethought a means; is the door fast?
Moth. I locked it myself after him.
Lean. You know, Mother,
At the end of the dark parlour there's a place
So artificially contrived for a conveyance,
No search could ever find it. When my father
Kept in for manslaughter, it was his sanctuary.
There will I lock my life's best treasure up,
Bianca.

166–7. up,/Bianca.] *This ed.;* up./*Brancha?* O.

---

151. *apprehension*] understanding, knowledge.

152–4. *quickened . . . conceived*] quibbling on 'quicken' = (1) come into being, begin (2) become pregnant (lit. to reach the stage in pregnancy when the embryo shows signs of life.).

159. *smothered closely*] carrying on the 'fire' metaphor.

163. *conveyance*] a passage or corridor; a secret passage. Compare R. Carpenter, *Experience* 1642, iv. p. vii: 'Scarce a House . . . which they have not fitted with private doores and conveyances.' (*O.E.D.*)

165. *Kept in*] remained indoors; 'for manslaughter' = when he had committed manslaughter.

167. *Bianca.*] Parker thinks this an exclamation evoked by some gesture of impatience on Bianca's part (the octavo has a full-stop after 'up' l. 166.) I prefer to take the word in apposition to 'life's best treasure.'

Bian. Would you keep me closer yet?
Have you the conscience? Y' are best e'en choke me up, sir!
You make me fearful of your health and wits,
You cleave to such wild courses; what's the matter?
Lean. Why, are you so insensible of your danger
To ask that now? The Duke himself has sent for you
To Lady Livia's, to a banquet forsooth.
Bian. Now I beshrew you heartily, has he so!
And you the man would never yet vouchsafe
To tell me on't till now. You show your loyalty
And honesty at once; and so farewell, sir.
Lean. Bianca, whither now?
Bian. Why to the Duke, sir:
You say he sent for me.
Lean. But thou dost not mean
To go, I hope.
Bian. No? I shall prove unmannerly,
Rude, and uncivil, mad, and imitate you.
Come, Mother, come, follow his humour no longer,
We shall be all executed for treason shortly.
Moth. Not I, i' faith. I'll first obey the Duke,
And taste of a good banquet; I'm of thy mind.
I'll step but up, and fetch two handkerchiefs
To pocket up some sweetmeats, and o'ertake thee. *Exit.*
Bian. [*Aside*] Why here's an old wench would trot into a bawd now,

---

173. *banquet*] in seventeenth-century usage either a substantial meal or a much slighter one of sweetmeats only. The latter seems intended here: there are frequent references to sweetmeats (and none to other foods) in the following lines, and in the next scene. This would have obvious advantages in stage-performance. Parker quotes Gervase Markham, *The English Housewife:* 'I will now proceed to the ordering or setting forth of a Banquet, wherein you will observe, that Marchpanes have the first place, the middle place and last place.'

186. *handkerchiefs*] often used for carrying small items. Compare the christening scene in *A Chaste Maid in Cheapside* (III. ii.) where the 'gossips' store away delicacies in their handkerchiefs.

188. *trot into*] readily turn into.

For some dry sucket, or a colt in marchpane. *Exit.*
Lean. Oh thou the ripe time of man's misery, wedlock,
When all his thoughts like over-laden trees
Crack with the fruits they bear, in cares, in jealousies.
Oh that's a fruit that ripens hastily,
After 'tis knit to marriage; it begins
As soon as the sun shines upon the bride
A little to show colour. Blessed Powers,
Whence comes this alteration? The distractions,
The fears and doubts it brings are numberless,
And yet the cause I know not. What a peace
Has he that never marries! If he knew
The benefit he enjoyed, or had the fortune
To come and speak with me, he should know then
The infinite wealth he had, and discern rightly
The greatness of his treasure by my loss.
Nay, what a quietness has he 'bove mine
That wears his youth out in a strumpet's arms,
And never spends more care upon a woman
Than at the time of lust; but walks away,
And if he find her dead at his return,
His pity is soon done—he breaks a sigh
In many parts, and gives her but a piece on 't!
But all the fears, shames, jealousies, costs and troubles,

---

189. *dry sucket*] Sir Hugh Plat (*Delights for Ladies*, 1609) has several recipes for this. Any kind of fruit, lettuce stalks or even 'greene wallnuts' served as core; these were boiled, and left to stand in a Rosewater syrup 'between hot and cold.' The solidifying of the syrup round the core produced the 'dry sucket.'

colt in marchpane] a figure of a (young) horse in marzipan. 'Marchpane' is the native English form, 'marzipan' a German introduction. Plat (*op. cit.*) includes in his recipe for 'marchpane' two pounds of almonds, two pounds of sugar, and two or three spoonfuls of Rosewater 'that will keep your almonds from oiling.' He adds: 'you may also print off this Marchpane paste in your molds for banquetting dishes.'

194. *knit*] The word was also used of the begetting of children: compare Donne *The Extasie* (ll. 61–4): 'As our blood labours to beget/Spirits, as like soules as it can,/Because such fingers need to knit/That subtile knot, which makes us man.'

And still renewed cares of a marriage bed
Live in the issue, when the wife is dead.

Enter Messenger.

Mess. A good perfection to your thoughts.
Lean. The news, sir?
Mess. Though you were pleased of late to pin an error on me,
You must not shift another in your stead too:
The Duke has sent me for you.
Lean. How, for me, sir?
[*Aside*] I see then 'tis my theft; w' are both betrayed.
Well, I'm not the first has stol'n away a maid,
My countrymen have used it. [*To him*] I'll along with
you, sir. *Exeunt.*

[III. iii]

A banquet prepared.

Enter GUARDIANO *and* WARD.

Guard. Take you especial note of such a gentlewoman,
She's here on purpose; I have invited her,
Her father, and her uncle, to this banquet.
Mark her behaviour well, it does concern you,
And what her good parts are, as far as time
And place can modestly require a knowledge of,
Shall be laid open to your understanding.

0.1. III. iii] *Oliphant;* Scaen 2. *O.*

---

215. *perfection*] conclusion, outcome.

217.] 'to shift' is to substitute, with overtones of shift = a cunning trick. 'Another' probably means another *person*: Leantio sent the Messenger to look for someone else in Bianca's place ('stead'). If 'another' = another *trick* (something that causes an 'error', l. 216), 'shift' means 'to practise (a trick)' and 'stead' means 'advantage', 'defence.'

221. *used*] practised.

III. iii. 3. *this banquet*] as mentioned in the previous scene.

You know I'm both your guardian and your uncle,
My care of you is double, ward and nephew,
And I'll express it here.

Ward. 'Faith, I should know her
Now by her mark among a thousand women:
A little pretty deft and tidy thing you say.

Guard. Right.

Ward. With a lusty sprouting sprig in her hair.

Guard. Thou goest the right way still; take one mark more:
Thou shalt ne'er find her hand out of her uncle's,
Or else his out of hers, if she be near him.
The love of kindred never yet stuck closer
Than theirs to one another; he that weds her
Marries her uncle's heart too.

Ward. Say you so, sir,
Then I'll be asked i' th' church to both of them.

Cornets [*sound.*]

Guard. Fall back, here comes the Duke.

Ward. [*Aside*] He brings a gentlewoman,
I should fall forward rather.

Enter DUKE, BIANCA, FABRITIO, HIPPOLITO, LIVIA, MOTHER, ISABELLA, *and* Attendants.

Duke. Come, Bianca,
Of purpose sent into the world to show
Perfection once in woman; I'll believe
Henceforward they have ev'ry one a soul too

20.1.] *S.D. in right-hand margin opposite* 'heart too' *line 19 in O.*

---

10. *express*] show.
11. *her mark*] the distinctive features of her appearance and behaviour.
12. *deft*] dainty, 'petite.' Ray's definition (*A Collection of English Words*, 1691) is 'little and pretty, or neat.' (Quoted *O.E.D.*).
13. *lusty*] large (*O.E.D.* sense 9).
sprig] an ornament made from the 'sprig' (or 'spray') of a plant.
20. *asked*] compare II. ii. 88 and note.
22. *fall forward*] bawdy; fall on her.
24–7. *I'll . . . 'em*] Whether women possessed souls was a lively debating-point at this date. The author of *Swetnam the Woman Hater Arraigned by*

'Gainst all the uncourteous opinions
That man's uncivil rudeness ever held of 'em.
Glory of Florence, light into mine arms!

Enter LEANTIO.

Bian. Yon comes a grudging man will chide you, sir;
The storm is now in 's heart, and would get nearer,
And fall here if it durst—it pours down yonder.
Duke. If that be he, the weather shall soon clear.
List, and I'll tell thee how. [*Whispers in her ear*]
Lean. [*Aside*] A-kissing too?
I see 'tis plain lust now, adultery boldened.
What will it prove anon, when 'tis stuffed full
Of wine and sweetmeats, being so impudent fasting?
Duke. [*To Leantio*] We have heard of your good parts, sir, which we honour
With our embrace and love—[*To Attendants*] Is not the captainship
Of Rouans citadel, since the late deceased,
Supplied by any yet?

40. Supplied] *Dilke;* Suppli' *O.*

Women (1620) attacks Swetnam because 'He cares not to defame their [women's] very soules,/But that he's of the Turke's opinion:/They have none.' (III. i.) A note to Jonson's *Masque of Beauty* (*Wks*, IX, 464) says that the 'profane paradox' *Mulieres Homines non esse* appeared at Leipzig in 1595 (?1495). Its logic is given in Donne's *To the Countess of Huntingdon* (*Works* ed. Grierson, I. 201): 'Man to Gods image; *Eve*, to mans was made,/Nor finde wee that God breath'd a soule in her.'

28. *light*] see I. ii. 56n.

33. *A-kissing*] Leantio mistakes for kissing the Duke's whispering in Bianca's ear.

39. *Rouans citadel*] For a possible source of this puzzling proper name see Moryson, *Itinerary*, I. 318: 'The Citie [Florence] is of a round forme, and upon the walles thereof lie eight Fortes, whereof the greatest and strongest lies towards the South . . . and in that part there is a place vulgarly called le Ruinate, that is, the ruinous.' Five lines (represented by dots) are omitted, so the connection is not as close as this extract suggests. As none of the Forts is named, however, 'le Ruinate' is the single proper name in this context, and may have lodged in Middleton's mind; he may

Gentlemen. By none, my lord.
Duke. [*To Leantio*] Take it, the place is yours then, and as faithfulness
And desert grows, our favour shall grow with 't:
[*Leantio kneels.*]
Rise now the Captain of our fort at Rouans.
Lean. The service of whole life give your Grace thanks.
Duke. Come sit, Bianca.
Lean. [*Aside*] This is some good yet,
And more than e'er I looked for; a fine bit
To stay a cuckold's stomach. All preferment
That springs from sin and lust, it shoots up quickly,
As gardeners' crops do in the rotten'st grounds;
So is all means raised from base prostitution,
E'en like a sallet growing upon a dunghill.
I'm like a thing that never was yet heard of,
Half merry and half mad: much like a fellow
That eats his meat with a good appetite,
And wears a plague-sore that would fright a country;
Or rather like the barren, hardened ass
That feeds on thistles till he bleeds again—
And such is the condition of my misery.
Liv. Is that your son, widow?
Moth. Yes, did your ladyship
Never know that till now?
Liv. No, trust me did I.
[*Aside*] Nor ever truly felt the power of love

---

even have seen an irony in calling Leantio's fort 'le Ruinate', the ruinous. Sugden says 'Rovezzano seems to be meant', but gives no evidence.

46–7. *fine . . . stomach*] a tasty morsel to appease a cuckold's hunger (to make more palatable being a cuckold). Cf. II. ii. 404 and note.

50. *means*] advantage, gain.

51. *a sallet*] any green vegetable or herb used in preparing a 'salad'.

56. *barren*] stupid (*O.E.D.* sense 8).

56–7.] Another metaphor for Leantio's paradoxical state, with a half-reference to the proverb 'the Ass though laden with gold still eats thistles'. (Tilley A 360).

57. *again*] as a result (see *O.E.D.* sense 2).

And pity to a man, till now I knew him—
I have enough to buy me my desires,
And yet to spare; that's one good comfort. [*To Leantio*]
Hark you,
Pray let me speak with you, sir, before you go.
Lean. With me, lady? You shall, I am at your service.
[*Aside*] What will she say now, trow, more goodness yet?
Ward. I see her now I'm sure: the ape's so little,
I shall scarce feel her; I have seen almost
As tall as she sold in the fair for ten pence.
See how she simpers it, as if marmalade
Would not melt in her mouth. She might have the kindness i' faith

62. knew] *O;* know *Dilke, White.* 70. ten pence] *O;* twopence *White.*

---

67. *goodness*] kindness; gifts.

68. *ape*] a term of endearment; but in the Ward's mouth derisory, as if Isabella were merely counterfeiting ('aping') a woman.

70. *ten pence*] White's 'twopence' may be correct. Although 'ten pence' can be explained (see below), 'two pence' was and still is the more common term of derision; the seventeenth-century reader 'Arthur Rylard' who scribbled remembered fragments of the play on the end papers of a British Museum copy (162.d.28) recalled 'two pence' and not 'ten pence' in this line. Misreading of copy is just possible: Middleton's miniscule 'w' is often extremely careless, occasionally looking like an 'e'; if the 'o' were interpreted as an 'n' the octavo 'ten' would emerge. Precisely this mistake ('10' for 'two') is press-corrected in *The White Devil* sig. G4 (V. i. 207, Revels ed. p. 135).

Ten pence (compare modern 'tuppence') was used as a term of belittlement (often of a Turk). Compare Marlowe, *The Jew of Malta*, IV. iv. 43–4 (ed. Bennett): '*Ithamore*. Gentleman! he flouts me; what gentry can be in a poor Turk of tenpence!' and Middleton, *A Fair Quarrel*, III. i. 73 (*Wks*, IV. 208): 'Give me a valiant Turk, though not worth tenpence.' The Ward may have in mind 'Bartholomew babies', mentioned in the prologue to Jonson's *Bartholomew Fair*, l. 5, and twice in the text, Induction l. 165 and II. ii. 30 (Revels ed. pp. 3, 13, 45). These were small-sized dolls (a word not itself in use till *c.* 1700) sold at the Fair for a few coppers. (See Jonson, *Wks*, X. 171).

71. *marmalade*] according to Markham (see note at III. ii. 173) one of the dishes at a 'banquet' might well be '*Marmalades*', or sweet confections made by boiling down fruit (plums, quinces etc.).

To send me a gilded bull from her own trencher,
A ram, a goat, or somewhat to be nibbling—
These women when they come to sweet things once,
They forget all their friends, they grow so greedy;
Nay, oftentimes their husbands.

Duke. Here's a health now, gallants,
To the best beauty at this day in Florence.

Bian. Whoe'er she be, she shall not go unpledged, sir.

Duke. Nay, you're excused for this.

Bian. Who, I, my lord?

Duke. Yes, by the law of Bacchus—plead your benefit;
You are not bound to pledge your own health, lady.

Bian. That's a good way, my lord, to keep me dry.

Duke. Nay, then I will not offend Venus so much,

---

73. *gilded bull*] one of the shapes into which the 'marchpane' had been cast. (Cf. III. ii. 189 and note.) The three shapes, bull, ram and goat all have suitably lecherous associations. Marzipan and other sweetmeats were often 'gilded' i.e. decorated with a golden colouring matter. H. C. Hart says that 'no gold was used in this gilding. . . . Yolk of egg, quicksilver and salt armoniak are the ingredients.' (Quoted in *Love's Labour's Lost*, New Arden ed., V. ii. 637n.) Presumably this potentially lethal mixture was used in very small quantities.

79–86. *Whoe'er . . . Bianca*] Middleton may have in mind a publication of 1616 entitled: 'Disputatio Inauguralis Theoretico-Practica. Ius potandi, cum omnibus solemnitatibus & controversiis occurrentibus secundum Ius civile discussis, breviter adumbrans.' Written throughout in Latin, the book (or large pamphlet) is a burlesque of the academic inaugural disputation. Translated in 1617, it affects in part to define the correct behaviour of freshmen and seniors at drinking-parties. One question of etiquette discussed (sig. B6) is: '*Whether one may with modesty suffer his owne health to be drunke in his presence!*' The writer (Richard Brathwaite according to *S.T.C.*) answers that one may: 'Yet it is by a more especiall charter granted to all *Lovers* and *Servants* of *Venus* to instill such wished healths as these, as sacrifices to the health of their pretty Ducklings, even in their presence: for these kind of healthes use to stirre in them ferverous desires, and to pierce their hearts and veines.' The Duke would be here taking advantage of that 'more especiall charter.'

81. *plead your benefit*] usually referring to Benefit of Clergy or Benefit of Peerage. 'To plead benefit' is to claim exemption from some duty or penalty by virtue of belonging to a privileged class. Bianca is herself the 'first beauty' and therefore exempt from drinking the toast.

83–4.] In Renaissance astrology Venus was represented by 'warm and moist'.

Let Bacchus seek his 'mends in another court.
Here's to thyself, Bianca.

Bian. Nothing comes
More welcome to that name than your Grace.

Lean. [*Aside*] So, so;
Here stands the poor thief now that stole the treasure,
And he's not thought on. Ours is near kin now
To a twin-misery born into the world:
First the hard-conscienced worldling, he hoards wealth up,
Then comes the next, and he feasts all upon 't—
One's damned for getting, th' other for spending on 't.
Oh equal justice, thou hast met my sin
With a full weight; I'm rightly now oppressed;
All her friends' heavy hearts lie in my breast.

Duke. Methinks there is no spirit amongst us, gallants,
But what divinely sparkles from the eyes
Of bright Bianca; we sat all in darkness,
But for that splendour. Who was 't told us lately
Of a match-making right, a marriage tender?

Guard. 'Twas I, my lord.

Duke. 'Twas you indeed; where is she?

Guard. This is the gentlewoman.

---

89. *Ours*] i.e. I and those like me.

94. *equal*] impartial.

96.] I'm now myself suffering as much grief as all her friends did when I 'stole' her from them.

99. *sat*] should have sat.

100–1. *Who . . . tender*] a reflection, with the following events, of Italian custom. See Moryson, p. 453: 'The Bridegrome and bride were wont to visit the Duke, to make him wittness of the maryage.'

101. *match-making right*] perhaps = rite, as K. Deighton (*The Old Dramatists: Conjectural Readings*, 1896) suggests. But 'right' may mean 'privilege or permission' to celebrate the marriage, and could be defended. The spelling 'right' for 'rite' occurs in the 1600 Q. of *MND* (IV. i. 129–30): 'No doubt they rose vp early, to observe/The right of May.' The opposite confusion ('rites' where we would expect 'rights') is found in *Dr. Faustus* (Greg's parallel text edition, B text l. 958, III. i.). The two words were not perhaps always kept distinct in seventeenth-century usage.

marriage tender] betrothal. In law a 'tender' is a 'formal offer duly made by one party to another.' (*O.E.D.*)

Fab. My lord, my daughter.
Duke. Why, here's some stirring yet.
Fab. She's a dear child to me.
Duke. That must needs be; you say she is your daughter.
Fab. Nay, my good lord, dear to my purse I mean—
Beside my person, I ne'er reckoned that.
She has the full qualities of a gentlewoman:
I have brought her up to music, dancing, what not
That may commend her sex, and stir her husband.
Duke. And which is he now?
Guard. This young heir, my lord.
Duke. What is he brought up to?
Hip. [*Aside*] To cat-and-trap.
Guard. My lord, he's a great ward, wealthy, but simple;
His parts consist in acres.
Duke. Oh, wise-acres.
Guard. Y' have spoke him in a word, sir.
Bian. 'Las poor gentlewoman,
She's ill bestead, unless sh' has dealt the wiselier
And laid in more provision for her youth:
Fools will not keep in summer.
Lean. [*Aside*] No, nor such wives

110. husband.] *Dilke;* husband? *O.* 114. parts consist] *O;* part consists *Ellis.*

---

104. *stirring*] excitement.
106.] the affection/economics ambivalence at a ludicrous level.
107.] 'and also to me as a man; I didn't count that in.'
110. *stir*] excite sexually.
112. *cat-and-trap*] see I. ii. 87.1n.
114. *parts*] accomplishments, 'qualities' (cf. l. 108).
wise-acres] derived from the Middle Dutch *wijsseger* 'a soothsayer' (*O.E.D.*). With the Duke's witticism compare *Ham.* V. ii. 89–90: ''tis a chough; but, as I say, spacious in the possession of dirt.'
118. *Fools . . . summer*] quibbling on 'fool' = a kind of delicacy or trifle (compare I. ii. 116 and note), the 'clouted creame' of which certainly would not 'keep' (i.e. would turn sour) in hot weather. 'Keep' might also mean 'keep house'. Prof. M. C. Bradbrook points out (privately) that fools and simpletons strayed over the countryside in summer.
118–19. *No . . . winter*] presumably just a bitter echo of Bianca's

From whores in winter.
Duke. [*Talking with Fabritio*] Yea, the voice too, sir!
Fab. Ay, and a sweet breast too, my lord, I hope,
Or I have cast away my money wisely.
She took her pricksong earlier, my lord,
Than any of her kindred ever did:
A rare child, though I say 't—but I'd not have
The baggage hear so much, 'twould make her swell
straight;
And maids of all things must not be puffed up.
Duke. Let's turn us to a better banquet then,
For music bids the soul of man to a feast,
And that's indeed a noble entertainment,
Worthy Bianca's self. [*To Bianca*] You shall perceive,
beauty,
Our Florentine damsels are not brought up idly.

128. of man] *Dyce;* of a man *O.*

---

remark, but it is just possible that 'whores' is a quibble on its homophone 'hoar' = (1) frost (2) the mould (cf. 'blue mould') that forms on stale 'provisions.' For the latter compare Thomas, *Italian Dictionary* (1548–67): '*Muffa,* the hoare that is seene in stale breade.' (*O.E.D.*; no plural usage).

120. *a sweet breast*] a pleasant singing voice. Compare Fletcher, *The Pilgrim* III. vi (Beaumont and Fletcher, *Wks*, V. 192): 'let's hear him sing, h'as a fine breast.'

121. *wisely*] ironic: foolishly.

122. *pricksong*] 'harmony written or pricked down, in opposition to plain-song, where the descant rested with the will of the singer'. (Bullen, quoting Chappell's *Popular Music* i. 51). The indecent pun in *prick*song is very common.

125. *baggage*] used playfully of a young woman. Shakespeare always (with one doubtful exception in *Per.*) uses the word abusively.

125–6. *swell . . . puffed up*] (1) with pride (2) with child. Compare *The Witch* II. i. 97–9: (Middleton, *Wks*, V. 384): '*Isa.* Were I conceiv'd with child,/Beshrew my heart, I should be so proud on't!/*Fran.* That's natural; pride is a kind of swelling'.

127–8.] The ultimate origin of this fairly common view may be Plato, *The Republic*, III. 401: 'Is it then, Glaucon, on these accounts that we attach such supreme importance to a musical education, because rhythm and harmony sink most deeply into the recesses of the soul, and take most powerful hold of it?' (tr. Davies and Vaughan, 1925, p. 97).

Bian. They are wiser of themselves, it seems, my lord,
And can take gifts when goodness offers 'em. *Music*
Lean. [*Aside*] True, and damnation has taught you that wisdom;
You can take gifts too. Oh that music mocks me!
Liv. [*Aside*] I am as dumb to any language now
But love's, as one that never learned to speak.
I am not yet so old but he may think of me;
My own fault, I have been idle a long time,
But I'll begin the week, and paint tomorrow,
So follow my true labour day by day—
I never thrived so well as when I used it.

SONG.

What harder chance can fall to woman
Who was born to cleave to some man,
Than to bestow her time, youth, beauty,
Life's observance, honour, duty,
On a thing for no use good,
But to make physic work, or blood

140–1. *paint . . . true labour*] a sharp irony. 'Painting' (using cosmetics) is often condemned in Jacobean drama, an attitude going back at least as far as Tertullian's *De Cultu Feminarum;* cf. *Ham.*, III. i. 148–52, *The Duchess of Malfi*, II. i. 21–40 (Revels ed., pp. 40–1) and *The Revenger's Tragedy*, I. i. 14–25 (Revels ed. p. 4.). Moryson (p. 412) writes of Florentine women: 'Both honest and dishonest women are Lisciate fin' alla fossa, that is paynted to the very grave'.

143–52.] The song may have been written or pasted into the copy: the octavo prints it to the left of a vertical rule, with the Ward's following speech (ll. 153–6) to the right. This may explain the octavo's garbled lineation: if the song was crammed into the left-hand margin in the copy it would be difficult to sort out correct line-lengths. I have given three short lines to close the song, which offers a fairly metrical arrangement, but Oliphant may be right in assuming that 'probably a line and a half' has dropped out.

146. observance] dutiful service (*O.E.D.* sense II. 3).

148. to make physic work] Cf. Chapman, *Bussy D'Ambois* I. i. 92–4, (Revels ed. p. 9): '[should I] please portly Ladies/With a good carriage, tell them idle tales,/To make their physic work.' Evidently the Jacobeans held that the purgative effect of 'physic' was increased by mild excite-

Force fresh in an old lady's cheek?
She that would be
Mother of fools,
Let her compound with me.

Ward. Here's a tune indeed! Pish, I had rather hear one ballad sung i' th' nose now, of the lamentable drowning of fat sheep and oxen, than all these simpering tunes played upon cats' guts, and sung by little kitlings.

Fab. How like you her breast now, my lord?
Bian. [*Aside*] Her breast?
He talks as if his daughter had given suck
Before she were married, as her betters have;
The next he praises sure will be her nipples.
Duke. [*Aside to Bianca*] Methinks now, such a voice to such a husband
Is like a jewel of unvalued worth,
Hung at a fool's ear.
Fab. May it please your Grace
To give her leave to show another quality.
Duke. Marry as many good ones as you will, sir,
The more the better welcome.
Lean. [*Aside*] But the less
The better practised: that soul's black indeed
That cannot commend virtue; but who keeps it?
The extortioner will say to a sick beggar,
Heaven comfort thee, though he give none himself:

---

ment, such as, says Isabella, the Ward is capable of stimulating: he could make an *old* lady blush (ll. 148–9). But he would be incapable, she implies, of provoking real desire.

152. compound with] join with.

157. *Her breast?*] Bianca's exclamation perhaps indicates that even in the 1620's 'breast' meaning 'voice' was obsolescent, regarded as odd or affected. *O.E.D.* quotes one later example only (in 1711) and then in the semi-technical sense of a boy's (unbroken) voice.

161. *to*] compared to, set beside.

163. *Hung . . . ear*] Earrings were commonly worn by men in Jacobean England.

168. *keeps*] practises.

This good is common.
Fab. Will it please you now, sir,
To entreat your ward to take her by the hand,
And lead her in a dance before the Duke?
Guard. That will I, sir, 'tis needful; hark you, nephew.
Fab. Nay, you shall see, young heir, what y' have for your money,
Without fraud or imposture.
Ward. Dance with her!
Not I, sweet guardiner, do not urge my heart to 't,
'Tis clean against my blood; dance with a stranger!
Let whoso will do 't, I'll not begin first with her.
Hip. [*Aside*] No, fear 't not, fool, sh' has took a better order.
Guard. Why, who shall take her then?
Ward. Some other gentleman.
Look, there's her uncle, a fine-timbered reveller;
Perhaps he knows the manner of her dancing too—
I'll have him do 't before me, I have sworn, guardiner,
Then may I learn the better.
Guard. Thou'lt be an ass still.
Ward. Ay, all that, uncle, shall not fool me out:
Pish, I stick closer to myself than so.

179. whoso] *Dyce;* who's *O;* who *White, Ellis.* 184. guardiner] *Dyce;* Gardiner *O.*

173.] apparently common practice at noble weddings in Renaissance Italy. Signora 'Loredana' (pseud., *Bianca Cappello*, Rome 1936, p. 8) says that after exchanging a kiss with her bridegroom in the Duke's presence a noble Venetian girl 'doveva ballare tre danze figurate in segno di letizia.' Guardiano's ''tis needful' (l. 174) may imply that Middleton knew of this custom.

178. *blood*] inclination, disposition.

179. *whoso*] The octavo 'who's' probably represents Middleton's careless placing of the apostrophe.

180.] She had 'danced' with Hippolito first.

181. *take*] hinting at 'take' meaning 'take sexually' (Partridge).

182. *fine-timbered*] neatly made; well-built.

186. *out*] out of my resolve.

187. *stick closer to myself*] 'am not so easily persuaded to alter by resolutions'; 'have more sense of self-interest.' Compare the Latin tag (a

Guard. I must entreat you, sir, to take your niece
And dance with her; my ward's a little wilful,
He would have you show him the way.
Hip. Me, sir?
He shall command it at all hours, pray tell him so.
Guard. I thank you for him, he has not wit himself, sir.
Hip. [*To Isabella*] Come, my life's peace. [*Aside*] I have a strange office on 't here:
'Tis some man's luck to keep the joys he likes
Concealed for his own bosom, but my fortune
To set 'em out now, for another's liking—
Like the mad misery of necessitous man
That parts from his good horse with many praises,
And goes on foot himself; need must be obeyed
In ev'ry action, it mars man and maid.

Music. A dance [*by Hippolito and Isabella*], *making honours to the Duke and curtsy to themselves, both before and after.*

Duke. Signor Fabritio, y' are a happy father,
Your cares and pains are fortunate you see,
Your cost bears noble fruits. Hippolito, thanks.
Fab. Here's some amends for all my charges yet:
She wins both prick and praise, where'er she comes.
Duke. How likest, Bianca?

200.1–3] '*A dance . . . after*' *printed in right-hand margin in O. opposite lines 201–3.*

---

misquotation from Terence's *Andria* IV. i. 12) in *The Jew of Malta*, I. i. 187 (ed. Bennett): 'Ego mihimet sum semper proximus.'

193. *office*] duty (L. *officium*).

194. *some man's*] 'some' followed by a singular noun and 'used with an indefinite or generalizing force' (*O.E.D.* sense B.I. 3) was possible, though rare, seventeenth-century usage. Shakespeare (see Abbott pp. 30–1) used 'some' in this way only with nouns of time: compare e.g. *Rom.* V. iii. 257–8: 'But when I came, some minute ere the time/Of her awaking.'

205. *prick and praise*] 'praise for the highest excellence.' The 'prick' is the centre of the target in archery, and 'to prick' = to select, by making a mark against, or 'pricking down', the outstanding names in a list. An indecent allusion is also meant.

Bian. All things well, my lord;
But this poor gentlewoman's fortune, that's the worst.
Duke. There is no doubt, Bianca, she'll find leisure
To make that good enough; he's rich and simple.
Bian. She has the better hope o' th' upper hand indeed,
Which women strive for most.
Guard. [*To Ward*] Do 't when I bid you, sir.
Ward. I'll venture but a hornpipe with her, guardiner,
Or some such married man's dance.
Guard. Well, venture something, sir.
Ward. I have rhyme for what I do.
Guard. [*Aside*] But little reason, I think.
Ward. Plain men dance the measures, the cinquepace the gay:
Cuckolds dance the hornpipe, and farmers dance the hay:
Your soldiers dance the round, and maidens that grow big:

213. Well] *Dilke;* We'll *O.*

210–11. *She . . . most*] almost proverbial. Cf. *Blurt Master-Constable* III. iii. 70–1 (Middleton, *Wks*, I. 62): 'a woman's only desire is to have the reins in her own white hand.'

212. *hornpipe*] a lively, vigorous dance usually performed by a single dancer. Alluding here to the cuckold's horns.

214.] The phrase 'neither rhyme nor reason' is quasi-proverbial. (Tilley R 98).

215. *the measures*] a slow and stately dance in five movements (see further Dolmetsch, pp. 49–54). Compare *Ado* II. i. 79–80: 'the wedding, mannerly-modest as a measure, full of state and ancientry.'

the cinquepace] 'the primitive galliard, without the later elaborations and gymnastic feats which weighted it and retarded its swift movement. The fundamental five steps consisted firstly of four 'zoppetti' or *limping hops* . . . while the fifth step . . . was the 'cadenza' or falling step, composed of a jump.' (Dolmetsch, p. 51).

216. *the hay*] a country dance with a winding, serpentine movement. Furness (Variorum annotation of *LLL*. V. i. 161 'let them dance the hay') quoting Arbeau *Orchesographie* (1588), describes the *Braule de la Haye* as similar to the grand chain in a quadrille. It is uncertain whether this is the English hay, however. A variant known as the Irish hay is mentioned by Dekker in *The Strange Horse-Race*. (See further Richard David's note *loc. cit.* in the New Arden *LLL*.).

217. *the round*] a dance in which the performers move in a circle. Danced by 'soldiers' because 'certain soldiers of inferior rank . . . whose office it was to go *round* and inspect the sentinels, watches and advanced guard, were called *gentlemen of the round*.' (Dyce).

Your drunkards the canaries, your whore and bawd the jig.
Here's your eight kind of dancers, he that finds the ninth, let him pay the minstrels.

Duke. Oh here he appears once in his own person;
I thought he would have married her by attorney,
And lain with her so too.

Bian. Nay, my kind lord,
There's very seldom any found so foolish
To give away his part there.

Lean. [*Aside*] Bitter scoff!
Yet I must do 't—with what a cruel pride
The glory of her sin strikes by my afflictions!

Music. [*The*] *Ward and Isabella dance; he ridiculously imitates Hippolito.*

Duke. This thing will make shift, sirs, to make a husband,
For ought I see in him; how think'st Bianca?

Bian. 'Faith an ill-favoured shift, my lord, methinks;
If he would take some voyage when he's married,
Dangerous, or long enough, and scarce be seen
Once in nine year together, a wife then

218. Your . . . your] *Dilke;* You . . . you *O.* 227.1–2.] *S.D. printed opposite lines 227–8 in O.*

---

218. *canaries*] (1) 'a lively Spanish dance, the idea of which is said to have been derived from the aborigines of the Canary Islands' (*O.E.D.*) (2) a light sweet wine imported from those Islands. The earliest reference to the dance is in *LLL.* III. i. 11–13: '. . . but to jig off a tune at the tongue's end, canary to it with your feet . . .'

218. *the jig*] This lively dance was often associated with lewdness (as was the song-and-dance act of the same name on the stage). Compare *Ham.* II. ii. 522–3: 'he's for a jig or a tale of bawdry, or he sleeps'.

222. *by attorney*] by proxy.

227. *glory*] boastfulness, showiness.

strikes by] 'thrusts aside', 'consigns to oblivion'; *O.E.D.* marks this usage *Sc*[*otch*], and gives one example only (from the *Dunfermline Register* of 1457), yet it is plainly the correct meaning here.

230. *shift*] (1) an insecure attempt or endeavour (2) chemise, or other under-garment. 'Ill-favoured' = offensive to any of the senses, here (with 'shift' (2)) that of smell.

Might make indifferent shift to be content with him.
Duke. A kiss [*kisses Bianca*]; that wit deserves to be made much on.
Come, our caroch.
Guard. Stands ready for your Grace.
Duke. My thanks to all your loves. Come, fair Bianca,
We have took special care of you, and provided
Your lodging near us now.
Bian. Your love is great, my lord.
Duke. Once more our thanks to all.
Omnes. All blest honours guard you.

Cornets flourish.

Exeunt all but LEANTIO *and* LIVIA.

Lean. [*Aside*] Oh hast thou left me then, Bianca, utterly!
Bianca, now I miss thee! Oh return,
And save the faith of woman. I ne'er felt
The loss of thee till now; 'tis an affliction
Of greater weight than youth was made to bear,
As if a punishment of after-life
Were fallen upon man here; so new it is
To flesh and blood, so strange, so insupportable
A torment, e'en mistook, as if a body
Whose death were drowning, must needs therefore suffer it
In scalding oil.
Liv. Sweet sir!
Lean. [*Aside*] As long as mine eye saw thee,
I half enjoyed thee.
Liv. Sir?
Lean. [*Aside*] Canst thou forget

---

236. *caroch*] a stately and luxurious coach.

238–9.] Malespini (see Introduction, p. xli) and all the relevant manuscripts report this change in Bianca's residence.

241–62.] Leantio's speeches are marked *Aside*, since he is addressing no other character; they are, however, overheard by Livia. Hence her 'This makes me madder to enjoy him now' (l. 263), referring to the apparent strength of his attachment to Bianca.

249. *mistook*] inappropriate.

The dear pains my love took? How it has watched
Whole nights together, in all weathers for thee,
Yet stood in heart more merry than the tempests
That sung about mine ears—like dangerous flatterers
That can set all their mischief to sweet tunes—
And then received thee from thy father's window
Into these arms at midnight; when we embraced
As if we had been statues only made for 't,
To show art's life, so silent were our comforts,
And kissed as if our lips had grown together!

Liv. [*Aside*] This makes me madder to enjoy him now.

Lean. [*Aside*] Canst thou forget all this? And better joys
That we met after this, which then new kisses
Took pride to praise?

Liv. [*Aside*] I shall grow madder yet. [*To him*] Sir.

Lean. [*Aside*] This cannot be but of some close bawd's working.
[*To her*] Cry mercy, lady. What would you say to me?
My sorrow makes me so unmannerly,
So comfort bless me, I had quite forgot you.

Liv. Nothing but e'en in pity to that passion
Would give your grief good counsel.

Lean. Marry, and welcome, lady,
It never could come better.

Liv. Then first, sir,
To make away all your good thoughts at once of her,
Know most assuredly she is a strumpet.

Lean. Ha? Most assuredly! Speak not a thing
So vile so certainly, leave it more doubtful.

Liv. Then I must leave all truth, and spare my knowledge;
A sin which I too lately found and wept for.

266. yet.] *Dyce;* yet, *O.* 271. to] *Dilke;* too, *O.*

---

253. *watched*] kept awake and alert. Compare *R2*, II. i. 77: 'For sleeping England long time have I watch'd'.

260.] figures sculpted in that position. 'For 't' = for embracing.

261. *show art's life*] perhaps 'to serve as a model for art'.

267. *close*] furtive.

Lean. Found you it?
Liv. Ay, with wet eyes.
Lean. Oh perjurious friendship!
Liv. You missed your fortunes when you met with her, sir:
Young gentlemen that only love for beauty,
They love not wisely; such a marriage rather
Proves the destruction of affection—
It brings on want, and want's the key of whoredom.
I think y' had small means with her.
Lean. Oh not any, lady.
Liv. Alas poor gentleman, what meant'st thou, sir,
Quite to undo thyself with thine own kind heart?
Thou art too good and pitiful to woman.
Marry, sir, thank thy stars for this blest fortune
That rids the summer of thy youth so well
From many beggars that had lain a-sunning
In thy beams only else, till thou hadst wasted
The whole days of thy life in heat and labour.
What would you say now to a creature found
As pitiful to you, and as it were
E'en sent on purpose from the whole sex general,
To requite all that kindness you have shown to 't?
Lean. What's that, madam?
Liv. Nay, a gentlewoman, and one able
To reward good things; ay, and bears a conscience to 't.
Couldst thou love such a one, that, blow all fortunes,
Would never see thee want?
Nay more, maintain thee to thine enemy's envy?

---

280. *Oh perjurious friendship*] perhaps double-edged: Leantio complains about Bianca's infidelity, but the comment applies equally to Livia's 'perjurious (false, deceitful) friendship' towards the Mother and, through her, towards Bianca.

285. *want's . . . whoredom*] in that it opens the way to that occupation, or makes it a necessity.

297. *sex general*] the generality of women, every woman.

301. *blow all fortunes*] let Fate do what it will. An unemphatic use 'blow') of the storm image: compare I. i. 51–2 and note.

And shalt not spend a care for 't, stir a thought,
Nor break a sleep; unless love's music waked thee,
No storm of fortune should. Look upon me,
And know that woman.

Lean. Oh my life's wealth, Bianca!

Liv. [*Aside*] Still with her name? Will nothing wear it out?
[*To him*] That deep sigh went but for a strumpet, sir.

Lean. It can go for no other that loves me.

Liv. [*Aside*] He's vexed in mind; I came too soon to him;
Where's my discretion now, my skill, my judgment?
I'm cunning in all arts but my own love.
'Tis as unseasonable to tempt him now
So soon, as for a widow to be courted
Following her husband's corse, or to make bargain
By the grave side, and take a young man there:
Her strange departure stands like a hearse yet
Before his eyes; which time will take down shortly. *Exit.*

Lean. Is she my wife till death, yet no more mine?
That's a hard measure; then what's marriage good for?
Methinks by right, I should not now be living,
And then 'twere all well. What a happiness
Had I been made of, had I never seen her;

304. shalt] *O;* shall *Ellis, Oliphant.* 305. sleep;] *This ed.;* sleep, *O.* 305. thee,] *Dilke;* thee; *O.* 306. should.] *Dilke subst.;* should *O.* 313. own] *Dyce;* own, *O.* 315. for] *Dilke; not in O.*

---

304. *shalt*] a rather unprepared use of the second person singular. With these lines compare II. ii. 379–86.

314–17.] Compare *R3*, I. ii. 228–34: 'Was ever woman in this humour woo'd ?/Was ever woman in this humour won ?/ . . . The bleeding witness of her hatred by.'

318. *strange*] not yet made familiar by the passage of time.

hearse] an ornamental structure of wood, carried in royal and noble funerals, and temporarily erected ('which time will take down shortly' l. 319) in the dead person's Parish Church. Compare John Chamberlain to Dudley Carleton, 14 May, 1619: 'Yt was full sixe a clocke at night before all the solemnitie was don at church, where the herse [Queen Anne's] is to continue till the next terme, the fairest and stateliest that I thincke was ever seene there.' (ed. N. E. McClure, Philadelphia, 1939, II. 237).

For nothing makes man's loss grievous to him
But knowledge of the worth of what he loses;
For what he never had he never misses.
She's gone for ever, utterly; there is
As much redemption of a soul from hell
As a fair woman's body from his palace.
Why should my love last longer than her truth?
What is there good in woman to be loved,
When only that which makes her so has left her?
I cannot love her now, but I must like
Her sin, and my own shame too, and be guilty
Of law's breach with her, and mine own abusing—
All which were monstrous. Then my safest course,
For health of mind and body, is to turn
My heart, and hate her, most extremely hate her;
I have no other way. Those virtuous powers
Which were chaste witnesses of both our troths
Can witness she breaks first. And I'm rewarded
With captainship o' th' fort; a place of credit
I must confess, but poor; my factorship
Shall not exchange means with 't. He that died last in 't,
He was no drunkard, yet he died a beggar

328. ever, utterly;] *Dilke;* ever; utterly *O.*

325–6.] This is Middleton's view of the torments of the damned, and so perhaps suggesting 'redemption . . . from hell' l. 329. Cf. *The Witch* II. i. 217–21 (*Wks*, V. 390): 'What makes the greatest torment 'mongst lost souls?/'Tis not so much the horror of their pains,/Though they be infinite, as the loss of joys;/It is that deprivation is the mother/Of all the groans in hell . . .' (Quoted by Parker).

328–30. *there . . . palace*] Tilley (R 60) gives 'There is no redemption from Hell' as a common saying. The L. form (*ab Inferno nulla est redemptio*) appears in Thomas Robinson's *The Anatomie of the English Nunnerie at Lisbon* (1622, p. 9), a book Middleton read before writing *A Game at Chess* (see Bald p. 13 and p. 156 quotation). Sir John Harington (*Metamorphosis of Ajax*, 1596) says roundly (ed. E. S. Donno, p. 138): 'As for that Scripture, *ex inferno nulla redemptio*, I have heard it oft alleadged by great clerkes, but I thinke it is in the Epistle of S. Paule to the Laodiceans, or in Nicodemus Gospel: for I never yet could find it in the Bible'.

344–5. *my factorship . . . with 't*] 'what I earn as a merchant more than

For all his thrift; besides the place not fits me—
It suits my resolution, not my breeding.

Enter LIVIA.

Liv. [*Aside*] I have tried all ways I can, and have not power
To keep from sight of him. [*To him*] How are you now, sir?
Lean. I feel a better ease, madam.
Liv. Thanks to blessedness.
You will do well I warrant you, fear it not, sir;
Join but your own good will to 't. He's not wise
That loves his pain or sickness, or grows fond
Of a disease, whose property is to vex him,
And spitefully drink his blood up. Out upon 't, sir,
Youth knows no greater loss. I pray let's walk, sir;
You never saw the beauty of my house yet,
Nor how abundantly fortune has blessed me
In worldly treasure; trust me I have enough, sir,
To make my friend a rich man in my life,
A great man at my death—yourself will say so.
If you want anything, and spare to speak,
Troth I'll condemn you for a wilful man, sir.
Lean. Why, sure this can be but the flattery of some dream.
Liv. Now by this kiss, my love, my soul and riches,
'Tis all true substance. [*Kisses him*]
Come, you shall see my wealth; take what you list;
The gallanter you go, the more you please me.

---

equals it in value.' 'Shall' perhaps because he has not yet taken up the Captainship.

347–8. *besides . . . breeding*] Leantio thinks of himself as a brave man ('resolution'), but reflects that he has not been bred a soldier.

356. *drink his blood up*] In Renaissance physiology ardent or unrequited love was thought to have this effect. Compare Burton, *Anatomy of Melancholy* Part 3, Section 2 Member 3 (Ed. Dell and Jordan-Smith, p. 721): 'Symptoms [of love] are either of Body or Mind; of body, Paleness, Leanness, dryness &c. . . . A reason of all this, Jason Pratensis gives, because of the distraction of the spirits, the Liver doth not perform his part, nor turns the aliment into blood as it ought.'

358.] deliberately recalling the circumstances of Bianca's seduction.

I will allow you, too, your page and footman,
Your race-horses, or any various pleasure
Exercised youth delights in; but to me
Only, sir, wear your heart of constant stuff—
Do but you love enough, I'll give enough.

Lean. Troth then, I'll love enough, and take enough.

Liv. Then we are both pleased enough. *Exeunt.*

[III. iv]

Enter GUARDIANO *and* ISABELLA *at one door, and the* WARD *and* SORDIDO *at another.*

Guard. Now nephew, here's the gentlewoman again.

Ward. Mass, here she's come again; mark her now, Sordido.

Guard. This is the maid my love and care has chose
Out for your wife, and so I tender her to you;
Yourself has been eye-witness of some qualities
That speak a courtly breeding, and are costly.
I bring you both to talk together now,
'Tis time you grew familiar in your tongues;
Tomorrow you join hands, and one ring ties you,
And one bed holds you, if you like the choice.
Her father and her friends are i' th' next room,
And stay to see the contract ere they part.
Therefore dispatch, good Ward, be sweet and short;
Like her, or like her not, there's but two ways—
And one your body, th' other your purse pays.

0.1. III. iv] *Oliphant;* Scaen 3. *O.*

---

373. *constant stuff*] as contrasted with 'changeable stuff', e.g. 'changeable taffeta' a glossy silk that altered its colour when viewed in different lights (cf. 'shot silk').

III. iv. 12. *contract*] marriage-contract, betrothal.

14–15.] If you like her it will pay (please, satisfy) your body; if you don't, it will satisfy your purse anyway.

Ward. I warrant you, guardiner, I'll not stand all day thrumming,
But quickly shoot my bolt at your next coming.
Guard. Well said: good fortune to your birding then.
[*Exit* GUARDIANO.]
Ward. I never missed mark yet.
Sord. Troth I think, master, if the truth were known,
You never shot at any but the kitchen-wench,
And that was a she-woodcock, a mere innocent,
That was oft lost and cried, at eight and twenty.
Ward. No more of that meat, Sordido, here's eggs o' th' spit now,

16. guardiner] *Dyce;* Gardiner *O.*

---

16. *thrumming*] idling. *O.E.D.* explains the word as referring to strumming of an instrument, and then talking monotonously. Parker however quotes Linthicum (p. 232): *s.v.* Thrummed hats: 'Thrums were the unwoven threads at the ends of cloth or silk. . . . Since the nap or thrum on a hat was raised by rubbing, any turning of a hat around in the hands was called thrumming. "Thrumming of hats", therefore, became proverbial for indecision or time wasting.' Linthicum's explanation is confirmed by *The Wild-Goose Chase* II. iii.: '*Belleur*. . . . How has *Pinne* performed [his wooing]? *Mirabel.* He has won already:/He stands not thrumming of caps thus.'

17. *shoot my bolt*] give my decision. Probably with an allusion (unconscious on the Ward's part) to the common proverb (Tilley F 515) 'a fool's bolt is soon shot.' And with a bawdy reference to copulation.

18. *birding*] fowling. Guardiano takes up 'bolt' = bird-bolt, the blunt-headed arrow used by fowlers. The bird-bolt was frequently associated with Cupid; 'birding' could apparently mean 'following after women', 'wenching.' Compare *Misogonus* (1577) II. iii. 105–8: '*Cacurgus.* Ile. tell ye vort, a went in right now a burdinge/ . . . I am sure I heis gone a very horehuntinge.' (R. Warwick Bond, *Early Plays from the Italian*, Oxford 1911, pp. 202–3).

22. *she-woodcock*] a bird easy to snare; hence an 'innocent' or 'simpleton.' Compare *Ham.* V. ii. 317: '*Laertes.* Why, as a woodcock to mine own springe, Osric'.

23. *cried*] publicly announced by the town crier as lost; small children were 'cried' if they strayed.

24. *eggs o' th' spit*] Usually 'to have eggs on the spit' means to have business that requires constant attention. Here, additionally, the delicacy of the operation is referred to ('turn gingerly' l. 25). Isabella will require more adept wooing than the kitchen-wench.

We must turn gingerly. Draw out the catalogue
Of all the faults of women.

Sord. How, all the faults! Have you so little reason to think so much paper will lie in my breeches? Why, ten carts will not carry it, if you set down but the bawds. All the faults? Pray let's be content with a few of 'em; and if they were less, you would find 'em enough I warrant you. Look you, sir. [*They scrutinize her intently.*]

Isab. [*Aside*] But that I have th' advantage of the fool,
As much as woman's heart can wish and joy at,
What an infernal torment 'twere to be
Thus bought and sold, and turned and pried into; when alas
The worst bit is too good for him! And the comfort is
'Has but a cater's place on 't, and provides
All for another's table; yet how curious
The ass is, like some nice professor on 't,
That buys up all the daintiest food i' th' markets,
And seldom licks his lips after a taste on 't!

Sord. Now to her, now y' have scanned all her parts over.

Ward. But at what end shall I begin now, Sordido?

44. what] *This ed.; not in O;* which *Dilke.*

27–9. *How . . . bawds*] Sordido draws here on an old formula. The late medieval 'Bannatyne Manuscript' (Hunterian Club, 1896, IV. 755) offers parallel sentiments: 'Gif all the erth war perchmene scribable,/Maid to the hand and all maner of wud/War hewit, and proportionat pennis able,/All watter ynk in dame or in flude,/And every man a perfyt scryb and guid,/The cursitnes and disset of wemen/Cowld not be schawin be the mene of pen.' F. P. Wilson (Intro. to *The batchelars banquet*, Oxford 1929, p. xvii) notes that the same hyperbole is found also in *Les Lamentations de Matheolus* (*c.* 1295–1300) and was 'ancient' even then. It turns up again, among Middleton's probable reading, in Swetnam, sig. F1.

38. *cater's*] the person in charge of buying 'cates', (provisions), for a large household. ('Caterer', though derivative, has a different sense.)

40. *nice*] exact, pedantic.

professor] one who claims ('professes') close knowledge of any subject, in this case food.

44. *at what end*] slightly more plausible than 'at which end' as a necessary emendation of octavo 'at end'; the compositor after setting 'at' might by a simple mental leap think he had also set 'what'.

Sord. Oh ever at a woman's lip, while you live, sir, do you ask that question?

Ward. Methinks, Sordido, sh' has but a crabbed face to begin with.

Sord. A crabbed face? That will save money.

Ward. How! Save money, Sordido?

Sord. Ay, sir: for having a crabbed face of her own, she'll eat the less verjuice with her mutton; 'twill save verjuice at year's end, sir.

Ward. Nay, and your jests begin to be saucy once, I'll make you eat your meat without mustard.

Sord. And that in some kind is a punishment.

Ward. Gentlewoman, they say 'tis your pleasure to be my wife, and you shall know shortly whether it be mine or no, to be your husband; and thereupon thus I first enter upon you. [*Kisses her*] Oh most delicious scent! [*Aside*] Methinks it tasted as if a man had stepped into a comfit-maker's shop to let a cart go by, all the while I kissed her. [*To her*] It is reported, gentlewoman, you'll run mad for me, if you have me not.

Isab. I should be in great danger of my wits, sir;

54. once] *O;* ones *White.* 65. sir;] *This ed.;* Sir, *O.*

47–53.] quibbling on 'crab' = crab-apple, 'verjuice' being a sauce or *purée* made by crushing this fruit.

54. *once*] now, at this point.

54–6.] An anecdote in *Pierce Pennilesse* (Nashe, ed. McKerrow, I. 171) helps to explain this exchange. A 'mad ruffion' in danger of shipwreck, vows never to eat 'Haberdine' (dried cod) again if he is saved. The storm drops 'and this carelesse wretch . . . readie to set foote a Land cryed out: not without Mustard, good Lord, not without Mustard: as though it had been the greatest torment in the world, to haue eaten Haberdine without Mustard'. 'Meat without mustard' may have become a jocular phrase for apparent, not real, penance. ('After meat comes mustard' was a common saying—Tilley M 809.) Middleton's *The Blacke Book* (if it *is* his) is a sequel or reply to *Pierce Pennilesse.*

61–2. *a comfit-maker's shop*] A 'comfit' was a sweetmeat made of fruit preserved with ginger: a shop selling them would have a fragrant smell.

[*Aside*] For being so forward, should this ass kick backward now.

Ward. Alas poor soul! And is that hair your own?

Isab. Mine own? Yes sure, sir, I owe nothing for 't.

Ward. 'Tis a good hearing, I shall have the less to pay when I have married you. [*To Sordido*] Look, does her eyes stand well?

Sord. They cannot stand better than in her head, I think; where would you have them? And for her nose, 'tis of a very good last.

Ward. I have known as good as that has not lasted a year though.

Sord. That's in the using of a thing; will not any strong bridge fall down in time, if we do nothing but beat at the bottom? A nose of buff would not last always, sir,

---

66.] Previous editors have marked only the second phrase '*aside*'. But presumably Isabella intends the Ward to think of her being 'in great danger of [her] wits' due to unrequited love, while remarking *aside* that her madness would really be attested by her being 'forward' (oncoming) towards such a brute. She then quibbles on the literal sense of 'forward' suggesting that pressing too close to 'this ass' might put her in danger of lashing hoofs.

67.] an indirect enquiry, perhaps, about Isabella's purity: venereal disease destroyed the hair. But the line may have had added point for Middleton's audience. Swetnam's notorious anti-feminist pamphlet of 1615 (sig. G3v) instructed each man to enquire whether the woman he addressed was 'wearing but her own proper hair'; the play written in reply, *Swetnam the Woman-Hater Arraigned by Women*, acted in 1620, took up in mockery (p. 47) this absurd enquiry. The subject was evidently much discussed. *Haec Vir*, a pamphlet of 1620, attacks women for ostentation and extravagance in wearing 'a shorne, powdered, borrowed Hayre'; Isabella (l. 68) claims she owns her hair outright. The boy player would of course be wearing a wig.

71. *stand well?*] are they well placed?

74. *last*] shape. From the cobbler's 'last', used to stretch a shoe to its correct shape. Compare Middleton, *Michaelmas Term* I. i. 47–9 (*Wks*, I. 221): 'Here's gallants of all sizes, of all lasts;/Here you may fit your foot, make choice of those/Whom your affection may rejoice in.'

77–9.] with reference to venereal disease, which sometimes caused the bone-structure of the nose ('bridge') to collapse.

79. *of buff*] of great strength, resilience. 'Buff' was a durable leather, normally of ox-hide (originally *buffalo* hide). The word was then used of a soldier's uniform (made of that material); hence 'camp' l. 80.

especially if it came into th' camp once.

Ward. But, Sordido, how shall we do to make her laugh, that I may see what teeth she has? For I'll not bate her a tooth, nor take a black one into th' bargain.

Sord. Why, do but you fall in talk with her, you cannot choose but one time or other, make her laugh, sir.

Ward. It shall go hard but I will. [*To her*] Pray what qualities have you beside singing and dancing? Can you play at shuttlecock forsooth?

Isab. Ay, and at stool-ball too, sir; I have great luck at it.

Ward. Why, can you catch a ball well?

Isab. I have catched two in my lap at one game.

Ward. What have you, woman? I must have you learn
To play at trap too, then y' are full and whole.

Isab. Anything that you please to bring me up to
I shall take pains to practise.

Ward. [*Aside to Sordido*] 'Twill not do, Sordido, we shall never get her mouth opened wide enough.

Sord. No, sir? That's strange! Then here's a trick for your learning. *He yawns;* [*Isabella yawns also.*]
Look now, look now; quick, quick there.

Ward. Pox of that scurvy mannerly trick with handkerchief;

88. shuttlecock] Shittlecock *O.*

82–3. *bate . . . a tooth*] accept one less than the full number.

83. *th'*] The corrected forme (see press-variants, Appendix III) lacks the apostrophe, presumably because it fell out when the chase was unlocked; the word stands at the end of a line in the octavo.

88. *shuttlecock*] Cf. II. ii. 79.1–2, note.

89. *stool-ball*] a game, normally indoor, played mainly by women. Strutt (p. 77) describes a simple form in which one player defends a stool from the ball thrown by her opponent—a sort of primitive cricket. She is 'out' if the ball hits the stool or is caught direct from her hand (cf. 'can you catch a ball well?' l. 90). Herrick (*Hesperides*, 1648), in verses entitled *Stool-ball*, speaks of the 'trundling of the ball'; he is perhaps alluding to the variant form of the game mentioned by Ellis: 'The object of the game was to drive the ball from stool to stool.'

91.] with a bawdy innuendo.

93. *trap*] the game of cat-and-trap. Cf. I. ii. 87. 1n.

100. *mannerly . . . handkerchief*] Isabella politely covers her yawn with her handkerchief.

It hindered me a little, but I am satisfied.
When a fair woman gapes, and stops her mouth so,
It shows like a cloth-stopple in a cream-pot;
I have fair hope of her teeth now, Sordido.

Sord. Why, then y' have all well, sir; for aught I see
She's right and straight enough, now as she stands.
They'll commonly lie crookèd, that's no matter:
Wise gamesters never find fault with that, let 'em lie still so.

Ward. I'd fain mark how she goes, and then I have all. For of all creatures I cannot abide a splay-footed woman, she's an unlucky thing to meet in a morning; her heels keep together so, as if she were beginning an Irish dance still, and the wriggling of her bum playing the tune to 't. But I have bethought a cleanly shift to find

113. the] *Dilke;* he *O.*

---

103. *cloth-stopple*] a plug or stopper of cloth.

107–8.] With Sordido's insinuation compare Webster, *Duchess of Malfi* III. ii. 11–14 (Revels ed. p. 74): '*Cari.* My Lord, I lie with her often; and I know/She'll much disquiet you:—*Ant.* See, you are complain'd of./*Cari.* For she's the sprawling'st bedfellow./*Ant.* I shall like her the better for that.'

108. *gamesters*] players of the game of sex.

still] always.

109. *goes*] walks, bears herself in walking.

110–11. *I cannot . . . in a morning*] Parker quotes Ford, *The Broken Heart* V. i. (*Wks,* I. 306): 'The doubles of a hare,—or, in a morning,/ Salutes from a splay-footed witch, . . ./Are not so boding mischief as thy crossing,/My private meditations.' 'Splay-feet' (with toes pointing outwards in walking) were 'unlucky' because regarded as one of the features distinctive of a witch. (Compare Sidney, *Arcadia,* I. iii.: 'onely her face and her splayfoote have made her accused for a witch.' (ed. Feuillerat, Cambridge 1912, I. 21)).

111–13. *heels . . . dance*] the position still adopted by dancers about to commence one of the traditional Irish dances (the heel of the right foot is normally tucked against the instep of the left). P. and G. O'Raftery (*Dances of Ireland,* 1953, p. 8) quoting Fynes Moryson (*Manners and Customs of the Irish*) say that 'Irish music and dancing were much in vogue in England during the last years of Elizabeth's reign.'

113. *still*] always.

114. *cleanly shift*] an honest trick.

it: dab down as you see me, and peep of one side,
when her back's toward you; I'll show you the way.

Sord. And you shall find me apt enough to peeping,
I have been one of them has seen mad sights
Under your scaffolds.

Ward. [*To Isabella*] Will it please you walk forsooth,
A turn or two by yourself? You are so pleasing to me,
I take delight to view you on both sides.

Isab. I shall be glad to fetch a walk to your love, sir;
'Twill get affection a good stomach, sir.
[*Aside*] Which I had need have, to fall to such coarse victuals.

Ward. Now go thy ways for a clean-treading wench,
As ever man in modesty peeped under.

Sord. I see the sweetest sight to please my master:
Never went Frenchman righter upon ropes
Than she on Florentine rushes.

Ward. [*To Isabella*] 'Tis enough forsooth.

Isab. And how do you like me now, sir?

Ward. 'Faith so well,
I never mean to part with thee, sweetheart,
Under some sixteen children, and all boys.

Isab. You'll be at simple pains, if you prove kind,

---

115. *dab down*] duck down; not in this sense in *O.E.D.*

119. *your*] in a general sense: scaffolds as you know them.

scaffolds] probably the temporary wooden platforms erected to give spectators a better view of a procession or spectacle. Being 'under' one of these would put the eyes on a level with the hemline of a lady's skirts, just as the Ward's instruction to 'dab down' would do. Early stages for plays were also called 'scaffolds' and these may be meant.

125. *clean-treading*] walking straight and true.

128. *Frenchman . . . ropes*] on the tightrope. 'Walking' or 'dancing' on the ropes was a popular Jacobean entertainment; Frenchmen seem to have been especially proficient at it. Compare Jonson, *Epicoene* II. ii. 60–2 (*Wks*, V. 180): 'If, after you are married, your wife doe run away with a vaulter, or the Frenchman that walkes upon ropes . . .' Herford and Simpson (Jonson, *Wks*, X. 15) note that on 12 May 1600 Queen Elizabeth 'appoints to see a *Frenchman* doe Feates upon a Rope, in the Conduit Court.'

133. *simple*] great.

And breed 'em all in your teeth.

Ward. Nay by my faith,
What serves your belly for? 'Twould make my cheeks
Look like blown bagpipes.

Enter GUARDIANO.

Guard. How now, ward and nephew,
Gentlewoman and niece! Speak, is it so or not?

Ward. 'Tis so, we are both agreed, sir.

Guard. In to your kindred then;
There's friends, and wine, and music waits to welcome you.

Ward. Then I'll be drunk for joy.

Sord. And I for company,
I cannot break my nose in a better action. *Exeunt.*

---

134. *breed . . . teeth*] 'In allusion to a superstitious idea, that an affectionate husband had the toothache while his wife was breeding.' (Dilke).

141.] I cannot suffer in a better cause. 'To have one's nose put out of joint' (compare Tilley N 219) is to be injured, offended. There may also be a bawdy play on 'nose'.

Act IV

[Act IV. Scene I.]

Enter BIANCA *attended by two* Ladies.

Bian. How goes your watches, ladies? What's o' clock now?
1 *Lady.* By mine full nine.
2 *Lady.* By mine a quarter past.
1 *Lady.* I set mine by St Mark's.
2 *Lady.* St Anthony's they say
Goes truer.
1 *Lady.* That's but your opinion, madam,
Because you love a gentleman o' th' name.
2 *Lady.* He's a true gentleman then.
1 *Lady.* So may he be
That comes to me tonight, for aught you know.
Bian. I'll end this strife straight. I set mine by the sun,

IV. i. 1–5.] *The Honest Whore, Part Two* has a passage (III. i. 108–27; Dekker, *Wks*, II. 168–9) very similar to the present in defining sexual relations by reference to good and bad time-keeping (compare l. 8, note). The well-known lines in *LLL.* (III. i. 192–5), 'A woman, that is like a German clock . . .', seem to have begun a spate of comparisons in the drama between clocks and women's amorous behaviour. Richard David (New Arden ed. pp. 59–60) refers in this connection to *Epicoene*, *Westward Ho*, *A Mad World my Masters* and *Wit Without Money*. The emphasis in Shakespeare, and in the present scene, is on the unreliability of these, at that date, new-fangled instruments.

3. *St Mark's*] in Florence; previously mentioned at I. iii. 84 (see note).

St Anthony's] perhaps suggested by the famous church of St Anthony in Padua: the name might have a recognizably Italian flavour for Middleton's audience. Together with St Mark's at Venice (perhaps the real reference behind that name here, and not the church in Florence) this was possibly the best-known church in Italy. (For references, see Sugden under 'Padua').

8. *the sun*] Bianca implies that her sexual behaviour is above reproach, the sun never varying. Compare *The Honest Whore, Part Two* III. i. 113

I love to set by th' best; one shall not then
Be troubled to set often.
2 *Lady.* You do wisely in 't.
Bian. If I should set my watch as some girls do
By ev'ry clock i' th' town, 'twould ne'er go true;
And too much turning of the dial's point,
Or tamp'ring with the spring, might in small time
Spoil the whole work too. Here it wants of nine now.
1 *Lady.* It does indeed forsooth; mine's nearest truth yet.
2 *Lady.* Yet I have found her lying with an advocate, which showed
Like two false clocks together in one parish.
Bian. So now I thank you, ladies, I desire
A while to be alone.
1 *Lady.* And I am nobody,
Methinks, unless I have one or other with me.
'Faith my desire and hers will ne'er be sisters. *Exeunt* Ladies.
Bian. How strangely woman's fortune comes about;
This was the farthest way to come to me,
All would have judged, that knew me born in Venice
And there with many jealous eyes brought up,
That never thought they had me sure enough
But when they were upon me. Yet my hap
To meet it here, so far off from my birth-place,
My friends, or kindred; 'tis not good, in sadness,

(Dekker, *Wks*, II. 168); Infaelice, her virtue wrongly accused, protests: 'Mine [her watch] goes by heauen's Diall, (the Sunne) and it goes true.' 'Sun' refers also, as often, to the ruler: Bianca's relationship is with the Duke.

13–15. *And too . . . work too*] A bawdy reference to promiscuous sexuality. The 'dial's point' and the 'spring' refer to the male and female genitals. (Partridge s.v. 'Point', 'dial', 'peculiar river', 'turn'.)

18.] Presumably the clocks are the Advocate and the Lady. The former's falseness may be a gibe at legal dishonesty and self-interest; compare the proverb (Tilley C 425) 'The clock goes as it pleases the clerk.'

24. *This*] the experience she had been through.

30. *in sadness*] seriously.

30–4. *'tis not . . . strictly*] Richard Brathwaite (*Description of a Good Wife*, 1618) offers the same counsel: 'Restraint giues women greater

To keep a maid so strict in her young days;
Restraint breeds wand'ring thoughts, as many fasting days
A great desire to see flesh stirring again.
I'll ne'er use any girl of mine so strictly:
Howe'er they're kept, their fortunes find 'em out;
I see 't in me: if they be got in court,
I'll never forbid 'em the country, nor the court,
Though they be born i' th' country; they will come to 't
And fetch their falls a thousand mile about,
Where one would little think on 't.

Enter LEANTIO.

Lean. I long to see how my despiser looks,
Now she's come here to court. These are her lodgings;
She's simply now advanced. I took her out
Of no such window, I remember, first:
That was a great deal lower, and less carved.
Bian. How now? What silk-worm's this, i' th' name of pride?
What, is it he?
Lean. A bow i' th' ham to your greatness;
You must have now three legs, I take it, must you not?

---

appetite;/ . . . who knows not when *woman's* most withstood/Their wil's most froward & their wits most neare them,/And will be *frolike* thogh their husbands heare them?' And compare Webster, *White Devil* I. ii. 90–1 (Revels ed. pp. 16–17): 'women are more willingly and more gloriously chaste, when they are least restrained of their liberty.'

32–3.] James insisted that the legislation regarding Lenten fasts should be strictly enforced. Middleton's *A Chaste Maid in Cheapside*, II. ii. 53–174 (Revels ed. pp. 40–7) records the activities of 'promoters' (legal officials) arresting those breaking the fast by buying meat. Ostensibly 'flesh stirring' means 'meat going about', the reappearance of meat, but the phrase also has bawdy connotations.

36. *got*] begotten.

39. *falls*] into sin.

43. *simply*] greatly. The closest *O.E.D.* definition is 6d 'without exception, absolutely', but the context makes the meaning plain.

44. *first*] at the first; when we first met.

46. *silk-worm*] used contemptuously of a dandy, one who wore silk clothing.

48. *legs*] bows. With a bawdy quibble.

Bian. Then I must take another, I shall want else
The service I should have; you have but two there.
Lean. Y' are richly placed.
Bian. Methinks y' are wondrous brave, sir.
Lean. A sumptuous lodging.
Bian. Y' have an excellent suit there.
Lean. A chair of velvet.
Bian. Is your cloak lined through, sir?
Lean. Y' are very stately here.
Bian. Faith something proud, sir.
Lean. Stay, stay, let's see your cloth-of-silver slippers.
Bian. Who's your shoemaker? 'Has made you a neat boot.
Lean. Will you have a pair? The Duke will lend you spurs.
Bian. Yes, when I ride.
Lean. 'Tis a brave life you lead.
Bian. I could ne'er see you in such good clothes
In my time.
Lean. In your time?
Bian. Sure I think, sir,
We both thrive best asunder.
Lean. Y' are a whore.
Bian. Fear nothing, sir.
Lean. An impudent spiteful strumpet.
Bian. Oh sir, you give me thanks for your captainship;
I thought you had forgot all your good manners.
Lean. And to spite thee as much look there, [*Gives her a letter*] there read,
Vex, gnaw; thou shalt find there I am not love-starved.

---

49. *want*] lack.

50. *service*] (1) deference, ceremony (2) sexual satisfaction (the farmyard sense of 'service'). See Introduction pp. lviii–lix.

51. *wondrous brave*] very richly dressed.

53. *lined through*] with lining throughout: a mark of wealth. Gee (*Foote out of the Snare*, 1624, p. 50) describes a wealthy Jesuit as wearing 'a cloake lined thorow with velvet.'

54. *proud*] splendid.

57. *spurs*] as a mark of distinction; but also with a bawdy intention, which is not lost on Bianca.

The world was never yet so cold, or pitiless,
But there was ever still more charity found out
Than at one proud fool's door; and 'twere hard 'faith
If I could not pass that. Read to thy shame there;
A cheerful and a beauteous benefactor too,
As e'er erected the good works of love.

Bian. [*Aside*] Lady Livia!
Is 't possible? Her worship was my pandress.
She dote, and send and give, and all to him!
Why here's a bawd plagued home. [*To him*] Y' are simply happy, sir,
Yet I'll not envy you.

Lean. No court-saint, not thou!
You keep some friend of a new fashion;
There's no harm in your devil, he's a suckling;
But he will breed teeth shortly, will he not?

Bian. Take heed you play not then too long with him.

Lean. Yes, and the great one too. I shall find time
To play a hot religious bout with some of you,
And perhaps drive you and your course of sins
To their eternal kennels. I speak softly now,
'Tis manners in a noble woman's lodgings,

---

70. *that*] that door.

72.] 'as ever did homage to love by her behaviour.' (lit. 'Put up "monuments" to love'). Middleton's father was a builder or bricklayer, perhaps explaining the several metaphors from that trade in the play. A bawdy allusion is also intended.

76. *simply*] greatly, completely. See l. 43n. above.

78. *friend*] lover.

79–80.] 'friend' (l. 78) may have suggested 'devil', in the sense of a 'familiar spirit'; the movement of thought to 'suckling' is perhaps due to the popular belief that witches suckled their familiars with their own milk or blood (see e.g. K. M. Briggs, *Pale Hecate's Team*, 1962, p. 19). To 'breed teeth' is the usual expression for an infant cutting its first teeth. Leantio hints that the Duke, now apparently so tolerant towards him, will soon 'show his teeth'.

82. *the great one*] probably the devil.

83. *play . . . bout*] The incongruous sexual allusions catch very neatly Leantio's confused morality.

84–5. *drive . . . kennels*] The underlying metaphor is from the sport

And I well know all my degrees of duty.
But come I to your everlasting parting once,
Thunder shall seem soft music to that tempest.
Bian. 'Twas said last week there would be change of weather,
When the moon hung so, and belike you heard it.
Lean. Why, here's sin made, and ne'er a conscience put to 't;
A monster with all forehead, and no eyes.
Why do I talk to thee of sense or virtue,
That art as dark as death? And as much madness
To set light before thee, as to lead blind folks
To see the monuments, which they may smell as soon

87. know] *Dilke;* knew *O.*

---

of coursing (in which greyhounds pursue hares). 'Your course of sins' = simply, 'the sins you have run through'; by an association of ideas 'course' (in the sport properly the ground covered by the chase) was taken to mean 'animals engaged in coursing' (i.e. the greyhounds) thus suggesting the reference to 'kennels'.

87. *know*] Dilke's emendation is nearly certain. The error could arise in a number of ways, including foul case. It might be argued that 'and' = 'if' and that 'knew' is therefore correct; this seems to me strained and in conflict with the overt sense of the passage.

88–9.] Thunder, and bad weather ('tempest'), are frequent metaphors in this play for moral sanctions. (See esp. II. ii. 350–8 and note.).

90–1.] The cool impertinence (in both senses) of Bianca's remark is a brilliant touch. She affects to misunderstand Leantio's metaphorical use of 'thunder' and 'tempest' (l. 89; see previous note), and replies as if he were merely discussing the weather.

92. *put to 't*] troubled.

93. *all forehead, and no eyes*] all effrontery (L. *frons*, the forehead) with no scruples of conscience. The forehead's association with shamelessness may be classical (L. *salva fronte* without blushing, *frons urbana* impudence) or it may be biblical. For the latter compare Barnabe Rich, *My Ladies Looking-Glasse*, 1616, sig. B2v: 'Would they [women] now bethinke themselves, when they looke in their *Glasses*, that there is no *Forehead* heeld so gracefull (amongst many women) as that which the *Prophet Ieremie* tearmeth to be gracelesse, the *Forehead*, that is past shame and cannot blush.' The reference is to Jeremiah III. 3 (part): 'thou hadst a whore's forehead, thou refusedst to be ashamed.' Rich (sig. B3) also connects the eyes with conscience and moral discrimination: 'Eyes . . . that were first created to be the *Deemers* of my *Discretion*.'

97. *the monuments*] The definite article is difficult to explain; Middleton may simply mean *any* 'monuments' (memorials; see note at II. ii. 277). There may, however, be a lost contemporary allusion.

As they behold—marry, ofttimes their heads,
For want of light, may feel the hardness of 'em.
So shall thy blind pride my revenge and anger,
That canst not see it now; and it may fall
At such an hour, when thou least seest of all;
So to an ignorance darker than thy womb
I leave thy perjured soul: a plague will come. *Exit.*

Bian. Get you gone first, and then I fear no greater;
Nor thee will I fear long; I'll have this sauciness
Soon banished from these lodgings, and the rooms
Perfumed well after the corrupt air it leaves:
His breath has made me almost sick in troth.
A poor base start-up! Life! because 'has got
Fair clothes by foul means, comes to rail, and show 'em.

Enter the DUKE.

Duke. Who's that?
Bian. Cry you mercy, sir.
Duke. Prithee who's that?
Bian. The former thing, my lord, to whom you gave
The captainship; he eats his meat with grudging still.
Duke. Still!
Bian. He comes vaunting here of his new love,
And the new clothes she gave him. Lady Livia,
Who but she now his mistress?
Duke. Lady Livia?
Be sure of what you say.
Bian. He showed me her name, sir,
In perfumed paper, her vows, her letter,

110. 'has] *Dilke;* has *O.* 116. him. Lady Livia,] *This ed.;* him; Lady Livia. *O;* him; Lady Livia: *Dilke.*

---

102. *when . . . all*] when morality is farthest from your thoughts.

107–8. *rooms . . . leaves*] The Jacobeans were in the habit of 'smoking' or perfuming a room to sweeten the air and control the spread of infection (cf. 'corrupt').

110. *start-up*] one who has suddenly acquired social standing.

With an intent to spite me; so his heart said,
And his threats made it good; they were as spiteful
As ever malice uttered, and as dangerous,
Should his hand follow the copy.

Duke. But that must not;
Do not you vex your mind, prithee to bed, go,
All shall be well and quiet.

Bian. I love peace, sir.

Duke. And so do all that love; take you no care for 't,
It shall be still provided to your hand. *Exit* [BIANCA].
Who's near us there?

Enter Messenger.

Mess. My lord.

Duke. Seek out Hippolito,
Brother to Lady Livia, with all speed.

Mess. He was the last man I saw, my lord.

Duke. Make haste.
Exit [Messenger].
He is a blood soon stirred, and as he's quick
To apprehend a wrong, he's bold and sudden
In bringing forth a ruin. I know likewise
The reputation of his sister's honour's
As dear to him as life-blood to his heart.
Beside I'll flatter him with a goodness to her,
Which I now thought on, but ne'er meant to practise—

127.1.] *S.D. opposite line 125 in O.* 130.1.] *S.D. opposite* 'lord' *line 130 in O.* 130. haste.] *Dilke;* haste, *O.* 137. practise—] *This ed.;* practise. *O.*

---

123. *Should . . . copy*] referring to the 'copy-book' used to teach Jacobean and later schoolboys penmanship. Although ll. 100–4 do constitute a vague threat, the use of 'spiteful', 'malice', 'dangerous' (ll. 121–2) may derive from Middleton's source; in Malespini the Leantio-figure threatens to 'slit' Bianca's 'windpipe' (see Appendix 1, p. 174); the Duke orders (or connives at) his assassination partly because he fears for Bianca's life.

131. *a blood soon stirred*] a fiery young gallant.

136. *a goodness*] an advantage, benefit.

Because I know her base—and that wind drives him.
The ulcerous reputation feels the poise
Of lightest wrongs, as sores are vexed with flies:

Enter HIPPOLITO.

He comes; Hippolito, welcome.
Hip. My loved lord.
Duke. How does that lusty widow, thy kind sister?
Is she not sped yet of a second husband?
A bed-fellow she has, I ask not that,
I know she's sped of him.
Hip. Of him, my lord!
Duke. Yes, of a bed-fellow; is the news so strange to you?
Hip. I hope 'tis so to all.
Duke. I wish it were, sir,
But 'tis confessed too fast; her ignorant pleasures,
Only by lust instructed, have received
Into their services an impudent boaster:
One that does raise his glory from her shame,
And tells the midday sun what's done in darkness—
Yet blinded with her appetite, wastes her wealth,
Buys her disgraces at a dearer rate
Than bounteous house-keepers purchase their honour.

140.1.] *S.D. follows* 'welcome' *line 141 in O.*

---

138. *that wind drives him*] 'the thought of his sister's (potential) advantage will urge him on.' The metaphor is that of a sailing-ship.

139–40.] 'since his reputation is already unsound ('ulcerous'), he is the more sensitive to any hint of dishonour.' 'Poise' = weight, pressure.

143.] 'has she not succeeded yet in obtaining a husband?' 'To speed of' (compare 'God speed' = 'God make you prosper') means 'to be successful in acquiring (something)'.

143. *a second husband*] properly a *third*. Compare I. ii. 50: 'I have buried my two husbands in good fashion.'

148. *confessed too fast*] made manifest too plainly.

150. *services*] equivocal; see l. 50n.

151. *glory*] his grounds for boasting, or (more concretely) his newfound wealth and position. The suppressed metaphor in 'raise' is probably from gardening; cf. III. iii. 47–51.

154–5.] Cf. II. i. 12–14 and note.

Nothing sads me so much, as that in love
To thee, and to thy blood, I had picked out
A worthy match for her, the great Vincentio,
High in our favour, and in all men's thoughts.

Hip. Oh thou destruction of all happy fortunes,
Unsated blood! Know you the name, my lord,
Of her abuser?

Duke. One Leantio.

Hip. He's a factor.

Duke. He ne'er made so brave a voyage
By his own talk.

Hip. The poor old widow's son;
I humbly take my leave.

Duke. [*Aside*] I see 'tis done.
[*To him*] Give her good counsel, make her see her error,
I know she'll hearken to you.

Hip. Yes, my lord,
I make no doubt, as I shall take the course,
Which she shall never know till it be acted;
And when she wakes to honour, then she'll thank me for 't.
I'll imitate the pities of old surgeons
To this lost limb, who ere they show their art
Cast one asleep, then cut the diseased part.
So out of love to her I pity most,
She shall not feel him going till he's lost,

---

156. *sads*] saddens.

158.] The name 'L. *Vincentio*' occurs in *More Dissemblers* (I. ii.), the play printed with *WBW* (but dated by Bald *c.* 1615).

161. *blood*] desire.

163. *voyage*] quibbling on the secondary sense of 'voyage' = sexual adventure. Compare II. ii. 471–3 and note. For 'factor' see *Dramatis Personae* l. 9n.

171–3.] Though the efficient use of surgical anaesthetics dates only from the nineteenth century, rudimentary anaesthesia was practised in Western Europe at least as early as the thirteenth century, when a Dominican Friar, Theodoric of Lucca, was recommending the use of sponges soaked in a narcotic (mandragora or opium) to induce unconsciousness during surgery. This is no doubt the method of 'cast[ing] one asleep' of which Hippolito is thinking.

Then she'll commend the cure. *Exit.*

Duke. The great cure's past;
I count this done already. His wrath's sure,
And speaks an injury deep; farewell, Leantio,
This place will never hear thee murmur more.

Enter Lord CARDINAL *attended.*

Our noble brother, welcome!

Card. Set those lights down;
Depart till you be called. [*Exit* Attendants.]

Duke. [*Aside*] There's serious business
Fixed in his look; nay, it inclines a little
To the dark colour of a discontentment.
[*To him*] Brother, what is 't commands your eye so powerfully?
Speak, you seem lost.

Card. The thing I look on seems so,
To my eyes lost for ever.

Duke. You look on me.

Card. What a grief 'tis to a religious feeling
To think a man should have a friend so goodly,
So wise, so noble, nay, a duke, a brother,
And all this certainly damned?

Duke. How!

Card. 'Tis no wonder,

176. cure's] O; care's *conj. Dyce.* 179.1.] *S.D. follows* 'welcome' *line 180 in O.*

---

176. *cure's*] The Duke refers to Hippolito's surgical 'cure' of the preceding lines. The true reading might however be 'care's': 'a' and 'u' are often almost indistinguishable in Middleton's hand, and the compositor having set 'cure' immediately above, the word possibly lingered in his mind.

179.1 Lord *CARDINAL*] The Cardinal of history was Ferdinand de' Medici, Duke Francesco's brother and his successor. (See Introduction, p. xxxix).

180. *lights*] an obvious symbol of righteousness; compare lines 264–5.

185. *lost*] in thought.

If your great sin can do 't. Dare you look up
For thinking of a vengeance? Dare you sleep
For fear of never waking but to death,
And dedicate unto a strumpet's love
The strength of your affections, zeal and health?
Here you stand now; can you assure your pleasures
You shall once more enjoy her, but once more?
Alas you cannot; what a misery 'tis then
To be more certain of eternal death
Than of a next embrace! Nay, shall I show you
How more unfortunate you stand in sin
Than the low private man? All his offences,
Like enclosed grounds, keep but about himself
And seldom stretch beyond his own soul's bounds;
And when a man grows miserable, 'tis some comfort
When he's no further charged than with himself;
'Tis a sweet ease to wretchedness. But, great man,
Ev'ry sin thou commit'st shows like a flame
Upon a mountain, 'tis seen far about,

202. low] *Dilke;* love *O.*

---

195. *zeal*] energy (cf. *O.E.D.*, senses 2 and 3.).

202. *low*] Misreading may explain the octavo 'love'. Middleton spells 'lowe' (epilogue to the holograph *Game at Chess*); the malformation of his 'w' (see III. iii. 70n.) may lead to its being read as a 'v'.

203. *enclosed grounds*] land fenced off, in contrast to the common land and 'open field' system of medieval agriculture. The policy of Enclosure, a matter of hardship and strife under the Tudors, was still a subject of debate in early seventeenth-century England.

keep but about] only remain near.

206. *charged*] burdened.

207–14. *But . . . hill*] Though the image is not uncommon, Middleton may be half-remembering one of the contributions to the dispute over women, Patrick Hannay's *A Happy Husband* (1619): 'For *Vertue* (though aye clear) yet clearest shines/When she doth dart her lights from noble lines./A glorious flame blazing in valley low,/Is soon barr'd sight, nor doth it farre way show/Obscur'd with neighbour objects: but on hie,/A little Beacon to both far and nie/Shews like a bearded Comet in the Aire,/Admir'd of some, of most accounted rare.'

208–9. *a flame . . . mountain*] referring to the signal beacon, a large fire kindled on high ground to give warning of attack.

And with a big wind made of popular breath
The sparkles fly through cities—here one takes,
Another catches there, and in short time
Waste all to cinders. But remember still
What burnt the valleys first came from the hill.
Ev'ry offence draws his particular pain,
But 'tis example proves the great man's bane:
The sins of mean men lie like scattered parcels
Of an unperfect bill; but when such fall,
Then comes example, and that sums up all.
And this your reason grants. If men of good lives,
Who by their virtuous actions stir up others
To noble and religious imitation,
Receive the greater glory after death—
As sin must needs confess—what may they feel
In height of torments, and in weight of vengeance,
Not only they themselves not doing well,
But sets a light up to show men to hell?

Duke. If you have done, I have; no more, sweet brother.

Card. I know time spent in goodness is too tedious;
This had not been a moment's space in lust now.
How dare you venture on eternal pain
That cannot bear a minute's reprehension?
Methinks you should endure to hear that talked of
Which you so strive to suffer. Oh my brother!
What were you, if you were taken now!
My heart weeps blood to think on 't; 'tis a work

214. first] *Dilke;* first, *O.* 227. sets] *O;* set *Dilke.* 235. if you] *O;* if [that] you *Dyce.*

---

210. *popular*] of the (common) people. (L. *populus*).
216. *example*] being an example.
217–18. *scattered . . . bill*] the separate items of an incomplete bill (i.e. with the due amount not added up).
218. *such*] i.e. great men. The grammatical construction is loose.
232. *reprehension*] rebuke, censure.
235. *taken*] i.e. by death.
236–7. *a work . . . mercy*] According to medieval theology, there were

Of infinite mercy you can never merit,
That yet you are not death-struck, no, not yet—
I dare not stay you long, for fear you should not
Have time enough allowed you to repent in.
There's but this wall betwixt you and destruction,
When y' are at strongest, and but poor thin clay.
Think upon 't, brother; can you come so near it,
For a fair strumpet's love? And fall into
A torment that knows neither end nor bottom
For beauty but the deepness of a skin,
And that not of their own neither? Is she a thing
Whom sickness dare not visit, or age look on,
Or death resist? Does the worm shun her grave?
If not, as your soul knows it, why should lust
Bring man to lasting pain, for rotten dust?

Duke. Brother of spotless honour, let me weep
The first of my repentance in thy bosom,
And show the blest fruits of a thankful spirit;
And if I e'er keep woman more unlawfully,
May I want penitence at my greatest need—
And wise men know there is no barren place
Threatens more famine than a dearth in grace.

---

seven corporal and seven spiritual 'works of mercy' (*opera misericordiae*); Middleton's phrase may owe something to this doctrine. In 1621, Ralph Crane, scrivener and acquaintance of Middleton, published *The Works of Mercy*, a series of short poems celebrating each of the fourteen 'mercies' in turn.

239. *stay*] detain.

239–51.] The sentiment of these lines, familiar though it is, runs interestingly parallel to that of Vindice's address to the skull in *The Revenger's Tragedy*, III. v. 43 ff. (Revels ed. pp. 70–3).

241–2.] a common metaphor for the body. Compare *John*, III. iii. 20–1: 'within this wall of flesh/There is a soul counts thee her creditor.'

246.] The tendency to think of beauty as a matter of complexion rather than of form was common. Compare Overbury, *A Wife*, 1614: 'And all the carnall beauty of my wife,/Is but skin-deep, but to two senses known;/Short ev'n of pictures, shorter liv'd then life.'

247. *And . . . neither*] because produced by cosmetics. Less probably, the Cardinal may mean that beauty is God-given, and hence not a woman's 'own.'

Card. Why here's a conversion is at this time, brother,
Sung for a hymn in Heaven; and at this instant
The powers of darkness groan, makes all Hell sorry:
First, I praise Heaven, then in my work I glory.
Who's there attends without?

Enter Servants.

Serv. My lord!

Card. Take up those lights; there was a thicker darkness,
When they came first. The peace of a fair soul
Keep with my noble brother.

Duke. Joys be with you, sir.

Exit CARDINAL [*and* Servants.]

She lies alone tonight for 't, and must still,
Though it be hard to conquer; but I have vowed
Never to know her as a strumpet more,
And I must save my oath. If fury fail not
Her husband dies tonight, or at the most
Lives not to see the morning spent tomorrow;
Then will I make her lawfully mine own,
Without this sin and horror. Now I'm chidden,
For what I shall enjoy then unforbidden,
And I'll not freeze in stoves. 'Tis but a while,
Live like a hopeful bridegroom, chaste from flesh;
And pleasure then will seem new, fair and fresh. *Exit.*

[IV. ii]

Enter HIPPOLITO.

Hip. The morning so far wasted, yet his baseness so impudent?
See if the very sun do not blush at him!

266.1. *Exit Cardinal, &c. opposite line 266 in O.*

259–60. *Why . . . Heaven*] Cf. Luke XV. 7 (part): 'joy shall be in heaven over one sinner that repenteth.'

268. *it*] his desire for her.

270. *save my oath*] keep my word.

Dare he do thus much, and know me alive!
Put case one must be vicious, as I know myself
Monstrously guilty, there's a blind time made for 't;
He might use only that, 'twere conscionable—
Art, silence, closeness, subtlety, and darkness
Are fit for such a business; but there's no pity
To be bestowed on an apparent sinner,
An impudent daylight lecher. The great zeal
I bear to her advancement in this match
With Lord Vincentio, as the Duke has wrought it
To the perpetual honour of our house,
Puts fire into my blood, to purge the air
Of this corruption, fear it spread too far,
And poison the whole hopes of this fair fortune.
I love her good so dearly, that no brother
Shall venture farther for a sister's glory,
Than I for her preferment.

Enter LEANTIO.

Lean. Once again
I'll see that glist'ring whore, shines like a serpent
Now the court sun's upon her. Page!

Page. [*Within*] Anon, sir!

0.1. IV. ii] Scaen 2. *O.*

19.1.] *O. adds 'and a Page'.*

IV. ii. 2.] Cf. 'Beaumont and Fletcher', *The False One* I. i. (*Wks*, III. 306); 'A deed so dark, the Sun would blush to look on.'

5. *blind time*] the hours of darkness. Cf. *The Revenger's Tragedy* I. iii. 66–9 (Revels ed., p. 22): 'Well, if anything/Be damn'd it will be twelve o'clock at night,/That twelve will never 'scape;/It is the Judas of the hours, wherein/Honest salvation is betray'd to sin.'

7. *Art*] artifice, cunning. 'Closeness' = secrecy, furtiveness.

9. *apparent*] open, manifest (L. *apparere*).

15. *fear*] for fear.

21. *the court sun*] probably 'the court's favour', with an allusion to the sun/ruler equivalence.

Lean. I'll go in state too.

[*Enter* Page.]

See the coach be ready.
I'll hurry away presently. [*Exit* Page.]
Hip. Yes, you shall hurry,
And the devil after you; [*Strikes him*] take that at setting forth.
Now, and you'll draw, we are upon equal terms, sir:
Thou took'st advantage of my name in honour
Upon my sister—I ne'er saw the stroke
Come till I found my reputation bleeding;
And therefore count it I no sin to valour
To serve thy lust so. Now we are of even hand,
Take your best course against me. You must die.
Lean. How close sticks envy to man's happiness!
When I was poor, and little cared for life,
I had no such means offered me to die;
No man's wrath minded me. [*Draws his sword*] Slave, I turn this to thee,
To call thee to account for a wound lately
Of a base stamp upon me.
Hip. 'Twas most fit
For a base mettle. Come and fetch one now

22. *Lean.*] *S.H. before line 23 in O.* 38. mettle] *O;* metal *Dyce.*

---

22. Lean.] The single misassigned prefix in the play.

22–4.] Cf. *Revenger's Tragedy* II. i. 206–7 (Revels ed., p. 41): 'Nine coaches waiting,—hurry, hurry, hurry. / *Cast.* Ay, to the devil'.

24. *at setting forth*] to begin with.

24–31.] A passage in Moryson (p. 404) on the cowardice of the Italian avenger may have stuck in Middleton's mind: 'To conclude if an Italyan be wronged, he is very likely to take revenge, and that very deepe beyond the quality of the offence, but he will neuer fight vpon equall tearmes with his Adversarye.'

30. *of even hand*] on equal terms.

37. *a base stamp*] (1) a base nature, kind (2) an (uncurrent, false) impression embossed or engraved on the face of a coin.

38. *base mettle*] (1) a base temperament, disposition (2) a base metal.

More noble then, for I will use thee fairer
Than thou hast done thine own soul, or our honour.
[*They fight, and Leantio falls.*]
And there I think 'tis for thee.

Within. Help, help, oh part 'em.

Lean. False wife! I feel now th' hast prayed heartily for me.
Rise, strumpet, by my fall, thy lust may reign now;
My heart-string and the marriage-knot that tied thee
Breaks both together. [*Dies*]

Hip. There I heard the sound on 't,
And never liked string better.

Enter GUARDIANO, LIVIA, ISABELLA, WARD *and* SORDIDO.

Liv. 'Tis my brother;
Are you hurt, sir?

Hip. Not anything.

Liv. Blessed fortune;
Shift for thyself. What is he thou hast killed?

Hip. Our honour's enemy.

Guard. Know you this man, lady?

Liv. Leantio? My love's joy? [*To Hippolito*] Wounds stick upon thee
As deadly as thy sins; art thou not hurt?
The devil take that fortune. And he dead.

40. own] *Dyce; not in O.* 52. fortune. And he dead.] *This ed.;* fortune, and he dead, *O.*

This common quibble (ll. 37–8) may have been suggested by 'account' l. 36.

one] one *wound* (l. 36).

40. *thine own soul*] The compositor in setting 'thine' clearly intended a vowel to follow. Dyce's insertion of 'own' is almost indisputable.

44. *heart-string*] in Renaissance physiology thought to brace or sustain the heart.

46. *string*] the sound made by the vibrating string of a musical instrument. Compare *H8*, III. ii. 105–6 for a similar quibble: 'I would 'twere something that would fret the string,/The master-cord on's heart.'

Drop plagues into thy bowels without voice,
Secret and fearful. [*To the others*] Run for officers,
Let him be apprehended with all speed,
For fear he 'scape away; lay hands on him,
We cannot be too sure; 'tis wilful murder;
You do Heaven's vengeance and the law just service—
You know him not as I do, he's a villain,
As monstrous as a prodigy and as dreadful.

Hip. Will you but entertain a noble patience,
Till you but hear the reason, worthy sister!

Liv. The reason! That's a jest Hell falls a-laughing at:
Is there a reason found for the destruction
Of our more lawful loves? And was there none
To kill the black lust 'twixt thy niece and thee,
That has kept close so long?

Guard. How's that, good madam?

Liv. Too true, sir, there she stands, let her deny 't;
The deed cries shortly in the midwife's arms,
Unless the parents' sins strike it still-born—
And if you be not deaf and ignorant,
You'll hear strange notes ere long. [*To Isabella*] Look upon me, wench!
'Twas I betrayed thy honour subtly to him

57. sure;] *This ed.;* sure, *O.* 70. parents'] *Dyce;* parents *O;* parent's *Dilke.*

---

53. *without voice*] 'noiselessly', 'without warning.' For voice = noise, sound generally (as against the human voice) compare Isaiah LXVI. 6: 'A voice of noise from the city, a voice from the Temple.'

60. *prodigy*] portent. Livia may have in mind misshapen or unnatural ('monstrous') births, regarded by Jacobeans with horror, and widely reported among the credulous, finding their way into innumerable broadsheets.

67. *close*] hidden.

71. *ignorant*] wilfully closed to knowledge, disregardful (a rare use of L. *ignorare* = take no notice of.) Compare 'wilful forgetfulness', I. ii. 202 and note.

72. *strange notes*] the cries (see l. 69) of the new-born child. 'strange' = new, unfamiliar.

Under a false tale; it lights upon me now;
His arm has paid me home upon thy breast,
My sweet beloved Leantio!

Guard. [*Aside*] Was my judgment
And care in choice so dev'lishly abused,
So beyond shamefully—all the world will grin at me.

Ward. Oh Sordido, Sordido, I'm damned, I'm damned!

Sord. Damned, why, sir?

Ward. One of the wicked; dost not see 't, a cuckold, a plain reprobate cuckold.

Sord. Nay, and you be damned for that, be of good cheer, sir, y' have gallant company of all professions; I'll have a wife next Sunday too, because I'll along with you myself.

Ward. That will be some comfort yet.

Liv. [*To Guardiano*] You, sir, that bear your load of injuries,
As I of sorrows, lend me your grieved strength
To this sad burden, who in life wore actions,
Flames were not nimbler. We will talk of things
May have the luck to break our hearts together.

Guard. I'll list to nothing but revenge and anger,
Whose counsels I will follow.

Exeunt LIVIA *and* GUARDIANO
[*bearing Leantio's body*].

Sord. A wife, quoth 'a!

82. reprobate] *Dilke;* rebrobate *O.*

---

74. *it . . . now*] 'my treachery (implied in 'betrayed', l. 73) returns upon myself now.'

82. *reprobate.*] Octavo 'rebrobate' might be defended as representing the Ward's stumbling pronunciation. But a single use of mispronunciation is highly improbable; a compositor error (e.g. foul case) is far more likely.

84–5. *I'll . . . Sunday*] possibly in ironic reference to the saying (Tilley W378, first example 1659) 'Who will have a handsome wife let him choose her upon Saturday and not upon Sunday.'

90. *wore actions*] 'wear' = have as attribute, be characterized by.

Here's a sweet plum-tree of your guardiner's graffing!

Ward. Nay, there's a worse name belongs to this fruit yet, and you could hit on 't; a more open one. For he that marries a whore looks like a fellow bound all his lifetime to a medlar-tree; and that's good stuff, 'tis no sooner ripe, but it looks rotten—and so do some queans at nineteen. A pox on 't, I thought there was some knavery abroach, for something stirred in her belly, the first night I lay with her.

Sord. What, what, sir!

Ward. This is she brought up so courtly, can sing, and dance—and tumble too, methinks. I'll never marry wife again that has so many qualities.

Sord. Indeed they are seldom good, master; for likely when they are taught so many, they will have one trick more of their own finding out. Well, give me a wench but with one good quality, to lie with none but her husband, and that's bringing-up enough for any woman breathing.

95. guardiner's] *This ed.;* Gardiner's *O;* gardener's *Dilke;* guardianer's *Dyce.*

95.] 'the piece of grafting ("marrying" cf. III. ii. 194 and note) done at your guardian's instance has produced splendid fruit!' 'Plum-tree' carries an indecent allusion to the female genitals. (Partridge s.v. 'plum').

97–101. *For he . . . nineteen*] The medlar is a 'deciduous tree . . . found in hedges and woods in England' (*Encyclopedia Britannica*, 1881). Its fruit resembles a small brown-skinned apple, and is eaten when decayed to a soft, pulpy state ('rotten' l. 100). Compare Lyly, *Sapho and Phao*, II. i. 100–2 (*Wks*, II. 383): 'Bewtie is a slippery good, which decreaseth whilest it is encreasing, resembling the Medlar, which in the moment of his full ripenes is known to be in a rottennes.'

100. *rotten*] For the association of 'rotten' with venereal disease compare II. ii. 135 and note.

102. *something . . . belly*] equivocal: the Ward refers to the embryo, while Sordido takes him to refer to sexual intimacy (hence his insinuating response). 'Stir' has distinct sexual reference (see Partridge).

106. *tumble*] frequently alludes to copulation. Compare *Ham.* IV, v. 60–3: 'Young men will do 't, if they come to 't;/By cock, they are to blame./Quoth she, before you tumbled me,/You promised me to wed.'

108–13.] Roma Gill (New Mermaid ed., p. 95) quotes Middleton,

Ward. This was the fault, when she was tendered to me; you never looked to this.

Sord. Alas, how would you have me see through a great farthingale, sir? I cannot peep through a millstone, and in the going, to see what's done i' th' bottom.

Ward. Her father praised her breast, sh' had the voice forsooth; I marvelled she sung so small indeed, being no maid. Now I perceive there's a young chorister in her belly—this breeds a singing in my head I'm sure.

Sord. 'Tis but the tune of your wife's cinquepace, danced

118. and] *This ed.;* or *O.* 123. wife's] *Dilke;* wives *O.*

Father Hubbard's Tales, viii. 81, for a similar instance of distrust of the 'extras' in a girl's education; a 'delicate drab' kept at 'White-friar's nunnery' is described as 'some unthrifty gentleman's daughter . . . for so she seemed by her bringing up, though less by her casting down. Endued she was, as we heard, with some good qualities . . . she had likewise the gift of singing very deliciously.'

116–18.] For a similar complaint about the deceptiveness of the farthingale (see II. ii. 130n.) compare Webster, *Duchess of Malfi* II. i. 148–51 (Revels ed., p. 48): 'A whirlwind strike off these bawd farthingales,/ For, but for that, and the loose-body'd gown,/I should have discover'd apparently,/The young springal cutting a caper in her belly.'

117. *I cannot . . . millstone*] 'To peep (or see) through a millstone' is to be able to resolve difficulties. Compare Chamberlain to Carleton, 2 June 1621: 'Now what should be the true reason . . . is a matter of great discourse among them that take upon them to see far into a millstone (as they say).' (*Letters*, ed. N. E. McClure, Philadelphia, 1939, I. 378.)

118. *and*] I can make no sense of the octavo 'or'. A misreading ('an' misread as 'or') is possible, and immediately provides good sense.

and in the going] 'while moving too!', referring both to the circling of the millstone, and to Isabella's walking (see III. iv. 119–21; 'going' = walking).

i' th' bottom] probably, below the millstone; also perhaps an indecent reference to the female genitals.

120–1. *I . . . maid*] If the Ward is referring to Isabella's song before the Duke (see his references to 'little kitlings' III. iii. 153–6) he prevaricates, for he did not then know that she was pregnant. Perhaps 'sung so small' (= sang so quietly), should be taken not only literally but as = 'behaved so modestly'; the first *O.E.D.* record of this sense is, however, eighteenth century.

122. *singing . . . head*] he now wears the cuckold's horns.

123. *wife's*] Octavo 'wives' *might* be a generalization, but the context here is so specific to Isabella that I think this improbable.

cinquepace] see note at III. iii. 215.

in a feather-bed. 'Faith, go lie down, master—but take heed your horns do not make holes in the pillowbeers. [*Aside*] I would not batter brows with him for a hogshead of angels, he would prick my skull as full of holes as a scrivener's sand-box.

Exeunt WARD *and* SORDIDO.

Isab. [*Aside*] Was ever maid so cruelly beguiled
To the confusion of life, soul, and honour,
All of one woman's murd'ring! I'd fain bring
Her name no nearer to my blood than woman,
And 'tis too much of that. Oh shame and horror!
In that small distance from yon man to me
Lies sin enough to make a whole world perish.
[*To Hippolito*] 'Tis time we parted, sir, and left the sight
Of one another; nothing can be worse
To hurt repentance; for our very eyes
Are far more poisonous to religion
Than basilisks to them. If any goodness
Rest in you, hope of comforts, fear of judgments,
My request is I ne'er may see you more;
And so I turn me from you everlastingly,
So is my hope to miss you. [*Aside*] But for her
That durst so dally with a sin so dangerous,

---

125. *horns . . . pillowbeers.*] The 'horns' are those of the cuckold; 'pillowbeers' are pillowcases.

127. *angels*] gold coins. 'The Angel-Noble, first coined by Edward IV, was so-called from having on it . . . a design of St Michael killing the dragon.' (F. L. Lucas, note to *The Duchess of Malfi* I. i. 286). A 'hogshead' is a large barrel, properly with a capacity of 52½ imperial gallons.

128. *scrivener's sand-box*] a box with a perforated top, used for sprinkling fine sand on to the wet ink of a manuscript, and thus acting like blotting paper.

132. *blood*] family, kinship.

133. *'tis . . . of that*] 'even that is too near' (for 'of' compare *O.E.D.* sense 62b); or just possibly, 'she's too much a woman.'

138. *hurt*] hinder.

140. *basilisks*] fabulous reptiles (sometimes called 'cockatrices') said to have been hatched by a serpent from a cock's egg. The name derives from the crownlike crest imagined on the animal's head (Gr. βασιλεύς a king). Its glance was held to be fatal.

And lay a snare so spitefully for my youth,
If the least means but favour my revenge,
That I may practise the like cruel cunning
Upon her life, as she has on mine honour,
I'll act it without pity.

Hip. Here's a care
Of reputation, and a sister's fortune
Sweetly rewarded by her. Would a silence,
As great as that which keeps among the graves,
Had everlastingly chained up her tongue;
My love to her has made mine miserable.

Enter GUARDIANO *and* LIVIA [*and talk aside*].

Guard. If you can but dissemble your heart's griefs now,
Be but a woman so far.

Liv. Peace! I'll strive, sir.

Guard. As I can wear my injuries in a smile,
Here's an occasion offered that gives anger
Both liberty and safety to perform
Things worth the fire it holds, without the fear
Of danger, or of law; for mischiefs acted
Under the privilege of a marriage-triumph
At the Duke's hasty nuptials, will be thought

---

158. *As I can*] 'in so far as I can', 'if I can'; less probably 'since I can.'

161–2. *without . . . law*] Parker notes that in Florence during the time of Carnival, and on other occasions of public rejoicing, the law was suspended (see 'privilege' l. 163 and note). (And see Moryson p. 457.)

163. *privilege*] legal immunity (compare 'privilege of Parliament', the immunities enjoyed by members of both Houses). Or, more generally, protection, shelter. Compare *R3*, III. i. 40–2: 'God in heaven forbid/We should infringe the holy privilege/Of blessed sanctuary!'

triumph] a lavish spectacle. Compare Dekker's definition, *Troia Nova Triumphans* ll. 1–10 (*Wks*, III. 230): '*Tryumphes*, are the most choice and daintiest fruit that spring from *Peace* and *Abundance;* . . . *Princes* themselves take pleasure to behold them . . . They are now and then the *Rich* and *Glorious Fires* of *Bounty*, *State* and *Magnificence*, giuing light and beauty to the *Courts* of *Kings:* and now and then, it is but a debt payd to *Time* and *Custome*.'

Things merely accidental—all 's by chance,
Not got of their own natures.
Liv. I conceive you, sir,
Even to a longing for performance on 't;
And here behold some fruits. [*Kneels. To Hippolito and Isabella*] Forgive me both;
What I am now returned to, sense and judgement,
Is not the same rage and distraction
Presented lately to you; that rude form
Is gone for ever. I am now myself,
That speaks all peace and friendship; and these tears
Are the true springs of hearty penitent sorrow.
For those foul wrongs, which my forgetful fury
Slandered your virtues with, this gentleman
Is well resolved now.
Guard. I was never otherways;
I knew, alas, 'twas but your anger spake it,
And I ne'er thought on 't more.
Hip. Pray rise, good sister.
Isab. [*Aside*] Here's e'en as sweet amends made for a wrong now,
As one that gives a wound, and pays the surgeon;
All the smart's nothing, the great loss of blood,
Or time of hindrance. Well, I had a mother,
I can dissemble too. [*To Livia*] What wrongs have slipped
Through anger's ignorance, aunt, my heart forgives.
Guard. Why, this is tuneful now!

165. all 's] *O;* all *Dilke, White.* 168. both;] *This ed.;* both, *O.* 169. judgement,] *Dyce;* Judgment. *O.* 171. you;] *Dilke;* you? *O.* 176. with,] *This ed.;* with: *O.* 186. this is] *This ed.;* thus *O;* that's *Dilke.*

---

165. *all 's*] all *as* (if).

166. *Not . . . natures*] not as evil in conception ('got') as in effect.

166–8. *conceive . . . longing . . . fruits*] The train of allusions to pregnancy and birth is suggested by 'got' (l. 166; see previous note).

177. *resolved*] informed, satisfied.

183. *time of hindrance*] the time during which the wound impeded activity.

186. *this is*] Octavo 'thus' may be an attempt to make sense of a total elision of 'is' in the copy; compare III. ii. 30n.

Hip. And what I did, sister,
Was all for honour's cause, which time to come
Will approve to you.
Liv. Being awaked to goodness,
I understand so much, sir, and praise now
The fortune of your arm, and of your safety;
For by his death y' have rid me of a sin
As costly as e'er woman doted on.
'T has pleased the Duke so well too, that behold, sir,
'Has sent you here your pardon [*Gives him a letter*] which I kissed
With most affectionate comfort; when 'twas brought
Then was my fit just past; it came so well methought
To glad my heart.
Hip. I see his Grace thinks on me.
Liv. There's no talk now but of the preparation
For the great marriage.
Hip. Does he marry her, then?
Liv. With all speed, suddenly, as fast as cost
Can be laid on with many thousand hands.
This gentleman and I had once a purpose
To have honoured the first marriage of the Duke
With an invention of his own; 'twas ready,
The pains well past, most of the charge bestowed on 't,
Then came the death of your good mother, niece,
And turned the glory of it all to black.
'Tis a device would fit these times so well too,
Art's treasury not better; if you'll join
It shall be done, the cost shall all be mine.

194. 'Has] *Dilke;* Has *O.*

---

188. *approve*] show, prove.
204. *invention*] composition, piece of writing.
his own] probably Guardiano's; the Duke's, possibly, making for an even more ironic outcome.
205. *pains*] effort.
charge bestowed] money paid out.

Hip. Y' have my voice first, 'twill well approve my thankfulness
For the Duke's love and favour.
Liv. What say you, niece?
Isab. I am content to make one.
Guard. The plot's full then;
Your pages, madam, will make shift for Cupids.
Liv. That will they, sir.
Guard. You'll play your old part still.
Liv. What is 't? Good troth, I have e'en forgot it.
Guard. Why, Juno Pronuba, the marriage-goddess.
Liv. 'Tis right indeed.
Guard. [*To Isabella*] And you shall play the nymph
That offers sacrifice to appease her wrath.
Isab. Sacrifice, good sir?
Liv. Must I be appeased then?
Guard. That's as you list yourself, as you see cause.
Liv. Methinks 'twould show the more state in her deity
To be incensed.

216. What is't? Good] *Dilke;* What, is't good? *O.*

---

211. *voice*] consent, support.

213. *make one*] play a part.

The plot's full] Our cast is complete. A rather unusual use of 'plot'. W. W. Greg, *Dramatic Documents*, p. ix describes 'plots' as 'skeleton outlines of plays scene by scene, written on large boards for the use of actors and others in the playhouse.' The word could also (see Greg, *op. cit.*, p. 1 n.2) refer to a more detailed outline sketch of the play. The first sense is probably that in Middleton's mind.

214. *make shift for*] improvise as.

217. *Juno Pronuba, the marriage-goddess*] Ben Jonson (note to *Masque of Hymen*, *Wks*, VII. 217) quotes Virgil (*Aeneid*, bk. 4) as his authority for giving Juno this office: 'Dant signum prima et Tellus, et Pronuba *Juno*.' The irony of having Livia, the marriage-wrecker, play this part is exceptionally sharp.

219. *sacrifice*] the word frequently used by Jonson to refer to the symbolic marriage before Juno's altar in his *Masque of Hymen:* e.g. at ll. 103–6 (*Wks*, VII. 213): 'Sit now propitious *Aides*,/To *Rites*, so duely priz'd;/ And view two noble *Maides*,/Of different sexe, to VNION sacrific'd.'

222. *state*] dignity.

223. *incensed*] enraged. A weak pun (on the poisoned incense that kills Livia) is probably intended. The octavo's initial capital (extremely rare

Isab. 'Twould, but my sacrifice
Shall take a course to appease you, or I'll fail in 't—
[*Aside*] And teach a sinful bawd to play a goddess.
Guard. For our parts, we'll not be ambitious, sir;
Please you walk in, and see the project drawn,
Then take your choice.
Hip. I weigh not, so I have one.

Exeunt [ISABELLA, GUARDIANO *and* HIPPOLITO].

Liv. How much ado have I to restrain fury
From breaking into curses! Oh how painful 'tis
To keep great sorrow smothered! Sure I think
'Tis harder to dissemble grief than love.
Leantio, here the weight of thy loss lies,
Which nothing but destruction can suffice. *Exit.*

[IV. iii]

Hoboys. Enter in great state the DUKE *and* BIANCA, *richly attired, with* Lords, Cardinals, Ladies, *and other* Attendants; *they pass solemnly over. Enter Lord* CARDINAL *in a rage, seeming to break off the ceremony.*

228.1. *and* 234.1.] *O. reverses these S.D.'s.*

0.1. IV. iii] Scaen 3. *O.*

---

in this text except in nouns) may be authorial, and intended to underline the pun.

227. *project*] a table or plan. Guardiano is presumably referring to the masque's 'plot' (see l. 213 and note).

drawn] drawn up, written out.

228. *I weigh not*] I am indifferent.

IV. iii. 0.1. Hoboys] oboes; often used for musical effects on the Elizabethan stage.

0.3. they pass . . . over] Allardyce Nicoll ('Passing Over the Stage', *Shakespeare Survey*, XII, 1959, 47–55) shows that to 'pass over' meant to enter the playhouse yard, ascend and cross the stage, and then return to, and exit from, the yard. For other instances of this quite frequent stage-practice see *Revenger's Tragedy*, I. i. 0.2 (Revels ed., p. 3); *Atheist's*

Card. Cease, cease; religious honours done to sin
Disparage virtue's reverence, and will pull
Heaven's thunder upon Florence—holy ceremonies
Were made for sacred uses, not for sinful.
Are these the fruits of your repentance, brother?
Better it had been you had never sorrowed
Than to abuse the benefit, and return
To worse than where sin left you.
Vowed you then never to keep strumpet more,
And are you now so swift in your desires,
To knit your honours and your life fast to her?
Is not sin sure enough to wretched man,
But he must bind himself in chains to 't. Worse!
Must marriage, that immaculate robe of honour,
That renders virtue glorious, fair, and fruitful
To her great master, be now made the garment
Of leprosy and foulness? Is this penitence
To sanctify hot lust? What is it otherways
Than worship done to devils? Is this the best
Amends that sin can make after her riots?
As if a drunkard, to appease Heaven's wrath,
Should offer up his surfeit for a sacrifice:
If that be comely, then lust's offerings are
On wedlock's sacred altar.

Duke. Here y' are bitter
Without cause, brother. What I vowed, I keep,
As safe as you your conscience, and this needs not—
I taste more wrath in 't, than I do religion,

11. honours] *O;* honour *Dilke.*

Tragedy, II. iv. 0.1–2 (Revels ed., p. 40); and *White Devil*, III. i. 64.1 (Revels ed., p. 63).

11. *knit*] Compare III. ii. 194 and note.
16. *her great master*] God.
17. *leprosy and foulness*] Compare II. ii. 424–5 and note.
22. *surfeit*] over-indulgence, and the nausea that may go with it.
26. *this needs not*] this reproach is unnecessary.

And envy more than goodness. The path now
I tread is honest, leads to lawful love,
Which virtue in her strictness would not check.
I vowed no more to keep a sensual woman:
'Tis done, I mean to make a lawful wife of her.

Card. He that taught you that craft,
Call him not master long, he will undo you.
Grow not too cunning for your soul, good brother;
Is it enough to use adulterous thefts,
And then take sanctuary in marriage?
I grant, so long as an offender keeps
Close in a privileged temple, his life's safe;
But if he ever venture to come out,
And so be taken, then he surely dies for 't.
So now y' are safe; but when you leave this body,
Man's only privileged temple upon earth,
In which the guilty soul takes sanctuary,
Then you'll perceive what wrongs chaste vows endure,
When lust usurps the bed that should be pure.

Bian. Sir, I have read you over all this while
In silence, and I find great knowledge in you,
And severe learning; yet 'mongst all your virtues
I see not charity written, which some call

---

28. *envy*] ill-will, enmity.

33. *He*] the devil.

39. *privileged*] compare IV. ii. 163 and note.

42–3. *this body . . . temple*] the very common (biblical) metaphor. Compare *The Peace Maker: or Great Brittaines Blessing*, attributed in large part to Middleton (1619) sig. D4: 'And as the bodie of euery true Christian is said to the Temple of the holy Ghost, 1 Cor. 3.16. What does the accursed man-slayer but in the blood of his Brother destroyes the Temple, as the Blasphemer wounds the Lord of the Temple?' In *WBW* the soul, commonly thought of as the body's *prisoner*, becomes a suppliant protected by the body and afraid to venture out to judgement.

47. *read you over*] observed you closely. (Compare L. *legere* = (1) to survey, scan (2) to read.)

49. *severe*] probably combining *O.E.D.* senses 3c 'unsparing in censure' and 5a 'grave, serious, not light or recreative.'

49–50. *'mongst . . . written*] Evil characters in the drama of this period often take this line. Compare e.g. *The White Devil* III. ii. 70–1 (Revels ed.,

The first-born of religion, and I wonder
I cannot see 't in yours. Believe it, sir,
There is no virtue can be sooner missed,
Or later welcomed; it begins the rest,
And sets 'em all in order. Heaven and angels
Take great delight in a converted sinner;
Why should you then, a servant and professor,
Differ so much from them? If ev'ry woman
That commits evil should be therefore kept
Back in desires of goodness, how should virtue
Be known and honoured? From a man that's blind
To take a burning taper, 'tis no wrong,
He never misses it; but to take light
From one that sees, that's injury and spite.
Pray, whether is religion better served,
When lives that are licentious are made honest,
Than when they still run through a sinful blood?
'Tis nothing virtue's temples to deface,
But build the ruins, there's a work of grace.

Duke. I kiss thee for that spirit; thou hast praised thy wit
A modest way. On, on there.

Hoboys. [*Exeunt* DUKE, BIANCA *and* Attendants.]

---

pp. 68–9): '*Vit.* O poor charity!/Thou art seldom found in scarlet.', and *R3*, I. ii. 68–9: '*Gloucester.* Lady, you know no rules of charity,/Which renders good for bad, blessings for curses.'

53–4. *can be . . . welcomed*] 'whose absence is sooner noted or whose appearance, however belated, is more welcome.' Bianca, as a crowning piece of impudence, offers moral advice to the Cardinal.

54–5. *it begins . . . order*] alluding to I Corinthians XIII. 13: 'And now abideth faith, hope, and charity, these three; but the greatest of these is charity.'

55–6. *Heaven . . . sinner*] compare IV. i. 259–60 and note.

57. *professor*] one of those who profess Christianity. Compare the title of John Knox's *A Faythfull Admonition . . . vnto the professours of God's truthe in England*. Perhaps more specifically, 'one who has made profession; a professed member of a religious order' (*O.E.D.*).

67. *Than*] or.

blood] desire.

69. *build the ruins*] i.e. restore Bianca's reputation by marrying her.

Card. Lust is bold,
And will have vengeance speak, ere 't be controlled. *Exit.*

72.1. *Exit.*] *Dyce; Exeunt. O.*

---

72. *controlled*] brought to book, checked. Compare Skelton, *Quix* I Pref. 9: 'To be controaled for the Evil, or rewarded for the Good.' (*O.E.D.*).

Act V

[Act V. Scene I.]

Enter GUARDIANO *and* WARD.

Guard. Speak, hast thou any sense of thy abuse?
Dost thou know what wrong's done thee?
Ward. I were an ass else—
I cannot wash my face, but I am feeling on 't.
Guard. Here take this galtrop then; convey it secretly
Into the place I showed you; look you, sir,
This is the trap-door to 't.
Ward. I know 't of old, uncle, since the last triumph; here rose up a devil with one eye, I remember, with a company of fireworks at 's tail.

4. galtrop then;] *This ed.;* Galtrop, then *O.*

V. i. 3. *feeling on 't*] i.e. feeling his forehead for any sign of the cuckold's horns.

4. *galtrop*] 'a caltrop; or iron engine of warre, made with foure pricks, or sharp points, whereof one, howsoever it is cast, ever stands upward' (Dyce, quoting Cotgrave's *Dictionary* s.v. *Chaussetrape*). The caltrop or 'galtrop' was used mainly against cavalry.

6. *trap-door*] Guardiano would probably indicate one of the practical traps usual on Elizabethan stages. If we are to take the dialogue literally, the trap would be hand-operated, not mechanical (as some traps almost certainly were): Guardiano's victim has to fall suddenly through an opened trap-door, not be gradually lowered on one by some mechanism.

7. *triumph*] See IV. ii. 163n.

7–9. *here . . . at 's tail*] The comic devil, for long a familiar stage-figure, was often accompanied by exploding fireworks. (See C. R. Baskerville, *The Elizabethan Jig*, Chicago, 1929, pp. 315–16). So much so that *The Two Merry Milkmaids*, written *c.* 1619, printed 1620, and therefore roughly contemporary with *WBW*, fears ill-success for lack of these expected trimmings: ''Tis a fine play/For we have in't a Coniurer, a Deuill,/And a Clowne too; but I feare the euill,/In which perhaps vnwisely we may

Guard. Prithee leave squibbing now, mark me, and fail not;
But when thou hear'st me give a stamp, down with 't—
The villain's caught then.

Ward. If I miss you, hang me; I love to catch a villain, and your stamp shall go current I warrant you. But how shall I rise up and let him down too, all at one hole? That will be a horrible puzzle. You know I have a part in 't, I play Slander.

Guard. True, but never make you ready for 't.

Ward. No? My clothes are bought and all, and a foul fiend's head with a long contumelious tongue i' th' chaps on 't, a very fit shape for Slander i' th' out-parishes.

Guard. It shall not come so far, thou understand'st it not.

Ward. Oh, oh!

---

faile,/Of wanting Squibs and Crackers at their taile.' (*Prologue*). The unusual 'Devil with one eye', though it looks like a particular reference, has not been traced. Fleay tries unsuccessfully to date the play by associating this devil with Envy in Dekker's *London Triumphing*, a pageant of October 1612 (see Introduction, pp. xxxii–xxxiii).

10. *squibbing*] punning on 'squib' = a slight or foolish piece of talk. Compare Vilvain *Theorem. Theolog*. iii. 87 (1654): ''Tis a silly Sophisters squib to say, Bishops are called Elders, and contrarily.' (*O.E.D.* gives this quotation under sense 3, but does not formally note the appropriate meaning).

13. *miss you*] fail to hear the 'stamp'. With an irony typical of Middleton: in the event the Ward does *not* 'miss' Guardiano, who falls to his death on the galtrop. (The phrase is repeated at line 27.)

14. *stamp . . . current*] punning on 'stamp' = the design impressed upon the face of a coin, and then the coin itself.

20. *contumelious*] insolent, offensive.

21–2. *out-parishes*] defined by John Stowe (*A Survey of London*, 1633 ed., pp. 889 ff.) as areas other than those covered by the plague-bills. When Middleton claims that the Ward's 'foul fiend' is peculiarly suited to the out-parishes, he may be thinking of the boisterous and popular dramatic activity that was carried on there, exempt from the jurisdiction of the City. Both the Red Bull in St James', Clerkenwell, and the Fortune, in St Giles' without Cripplegate, were situated in outparishes and were well-known for material of this kind. (See G. Fulmer Reynolds, *The Staging of Elizabethan Plays at the Red Bull Theater*, New York, 1940, pp. 7–8). The phrase may, however, simply be a gibe at the expense of scandal-mongering in the suburbs.

Guard. He shall lie deep enough ere that time,
And stick first upon those.
Ward. Now I conceive you, guardiner.
Guard. Away, list to the privy stamp, that's all thy part.
Ward. Stamp my horns in a mortar if I miss you, and give the powder in white wine to sick cuckolds; a very present remedy for the headache. *Exit* WARD.
Guard. If this should any way miscarry now,
As, if the fool be nimble enough, 'tis certain,
The pages that present the swift-winged Cupids
Are taught to hit him with their shafts of love
(Fitting his part) which I have cunningly poisoned.
He cannot 'scape my fury; and those ills
Will be laid all on fortune, not our wills.
That's all the sport on 't; for who will imagine,
That at the celebration of this night
Any mischance that haps can flow from spite? *Exit.*

[V. ii]

Flourish. Enter above DUKE, BIANCA, *Lord* CARDINAL, FABRITIO, *and other* Cardinals, Lords *and* Ladies *in state.*

Duke. Now our fair duchess, your delight shall witness
How y' are beloved and honoured; all the glories

25. guardiner] *This ed.;* Gardiner *O;* guardianer *Dyce.*

0.1. V. ii] Scaen 2. *O.*

---

25. *those*] the points of the galtrop.
26. *privy*] secret.
27–9.] Parker notes that in Renaissance pharmacology horn was considered an antidote to poison, and white wine was often used as a base for mixing medicines.
32. *present*] the technical term for acting a part on the stage.
34. *Fitting his part*] since Hippolito is to play one of the lovesick shepherds.

Bestowed upon the gladness of this night
Are done for your bright sake.

Bian. I am the more
In debt, my lord, to loves and courtesies
That offer up themselves so bounteously
To do me honoured grace, without my merit.

Duke. A goodness set in greatness; how it sparkles
Afar off, like pure diamonds set in gold!
How perfect my desires were, might I witness
But a fair noble peace 'twixt your two spirits!
The reconcilement would be more sweet to me
Than longer life to him that fears to die.
[*To Lord Cardinal*] Good sir!

Card. I profess peace, and am content.

Duke. I'll see the seal upon 't, and then 'tis firm.

Card. You shall have all you wish. [*Kisses Bianca*]

Duke. I have all indeed now.

Bian. [*Aside*] But I have made surer work; this shall not blind me;
He that begins so early to reprove,
Quickly rid him or look for little love.
Beware a brother's envy; he's next heir too.

V. ii. 7. *grace . . . merit*] a phrase suggested by Church controversy: Protestant apologists lay heavy stress upon Divine Grace being obtained because of 'faith', not 'works' ('merit'). See Romans, III. xx and xxiv: 'Therefore by the deeds of the law there shall no flesh be justified in his sight . . Being justified by his grace.'

11. *your two spirits*] the Cardinal's and Bianca's.

15. *seal . . . 'tis firm*] from the practice of sealing documents with wax impressed with a coat of arms or other device; when the seal had been affixed the papers were secure ('firm'). The Duke is half-alluding to the common phrase 'to seal with a kiss.'

19. *rid*] get rid of.

20. *envy*] compare IV. iii. 28 and note.

he's next heir] probably the main reason for the Cardinal's hatred for Bianca: he feared she would produce a male child to take precedence in line of succession. The manuscripts assign other causes of discontent; see Appendix I section B, p. 176. Bianca, like Hamlet, seeks to kill an enemy when he is least 'fit and season'd for his passage.' (See *Ham.* III. iii. 73–95).

Cardinal, you die this night, the plot's laid surely—
In time of sports death may steal in securely,
Then 'tis least thought on.
For he that's most religious, holy friend,
Does not at all hours think upon his end;
He has his times of frailty, and his thoughts
Their transportations too through flesh and blood
(For all his zeal, his learning, and his light)
As well as we, poor soul, that sin by night.
[*Fabritio gives the Duke a paper.*]

Duke. What's this, Fabritio?

Fab. Marry, my lord, the model
Of what's presented.

Duke. Oh we thank their loves;
Sweet Duchess, take your seat, list to the argument.
[*Reads*] *There is a nymph that haunts the woods and springs,*
In love with two at once, and they with her.
Equal it runs; but to decide these things,
The cause to mighty Juno they refer,
She being the marriage-goddess. The two lovers
They offer sighs, the nymph a sacrifice,
All to please Juno, who by signs discovers
How the event shall be; so that strife dies.
Then springs a second; for the man refused
Grows discontent, and out of love abused,

29. soul] *O;* soul[s] *Oliphant.* 33.1.] *S.D. above at left-hand margin in O.*

26–7.] probably 'his thoughts, like ours, sometimes occupy themselves with the things of the flesh.' 'Transportation' may have been suggested by its meaning of 'rapture', 'ecstasy' (compare the modern cliché 'a transport of delight').

29. *we, poor soul,*] Oliphant's 'we poor souls' is attractive, especially in view of the compositor's habit of dropping final letters. But Bianca is here speaking in soliloquy, and the octavo reading may well be correct.

30. *model*] abstract, 'plot' (compare IV. ii. 213 and 227 and notes).

40. event] outcome.

42. love abused] love frustrated.

He raises Slander up, like a black fiend,
To disgrace th' other, which pays him i' th' end.

Bian. In troth, my lord, a pretty pleasing argument,
And fits th' occasion well; envy and slander
Are things soon raised against two faithful lovers;
But comfort is, they are not long unrewarded. *Music*

Duke. This music shows they're upon entrance now.

Bian. [*Aside*] Then enter all my wishes.

Enter HYMEN *in yellow,* GANYMEDE *in a blue robe powdered with stars, and* HEBE *in a white robe with golden stars, with covered cups in their hands. They dance a short dance, then bowing to the Duke, &c. Hymen speaks.*

Hym. [*Giving Bianca a cup*] To thee, fair bride, Hymen offers up
Of nuptial joys this the celestial cup.
Taste it, and thou shalt ever find
Love in thy bed, peace in thy mind.

Bian. We'll taste you sure, 'twere pity to disgrace
So pretty a beginning.

Duke. 'Twas spoke nobly.

Gan. Two cups of nectar have we begged from Jove;

---

44. which pays him] The antecedent of 'which' may be either 'this course of action' (understood) or 'th' other'. 'Pays him' = gives him his due, punishes him fittingly.

50.1. *HYMEN* in yellow] The colour usually associated with the god. Compare e.g. Jonson, *Masque of Hymen* (*Wks*, VII. 210): 'On the other hand, entred HYMEN (the god of *marriage*) in a saffron-coloured robe.' The origin of the Hymen/yellow association is not certain. The late Mr F. L. Lucas (privately) suggested a link between the colour of the god's clothing and the yellow bride's veil (*flammeum*) of Roman antiquity, itself perhaps adopted 'for good luck, because it was regularly worn by the *flaminica* (*flamen's* or priest's wife) who was not allowed divorce.' Mr Lucas thought it likelier, however, that yellow was worn simply as an auspicious colour, by both *flaminica* and bride, and hence considered appropriate to Hymen.

GANYMEDE] page and cup-bearer to Zeus (Jove).

powdered] sprinkled.

50.2. *HEBE*] daughter of Zeus.

50.3. covered cups] cups with lids (covers) attached.

Hebe, give that to innocence, I this to love.
[*To the Duke the wrong cup by mistake*]
Take heed of stumbling more, look to your way;
Remember still the Via Lactea.

Hebe. Well, Ganymede, you have more faults, though not so known;
I spilled one cup, but you have filched many a one.

Hym. No more, forbear for Hymen's sake;
In love we met, and so let's parting take.
Exeunt [*Masquers*].

Duke. But soft! here's no such persons in the argument
As these three, Hymen, Hebe, Ganymede.
The actors that this model here discovers
Are only four, Juno, a nymph, two lovers.

Bian. This is some antemasque belike, my lord,

58.1. S.D.] *so MS note in Yale copy of O.* 64. parting take] *This ed.;* part: *O.*

---

58. *innocence . . . love*] The Cardinal and the Duke respectively.

59–60.] alluding to a little-known myth concerning the formation of the Milky Way. An Elizabethan account of it occurs in William Fulke's *A goodly gallerye with a most pleasaunt prospect into the garden of natural contemplation*, 1563, sig. E6v: 'The thirde [myth] that *Hebe*, one which was *Iupiters* Cupbearer, on a tyme stombled at a starre, and shedde the wyne or mylke, that was in the cuppe [compare l. 62] which colloured that part of heauen to this daye, wherfore she was pout [*sic*] out of her office.' The same myth is referred to in 'E. K.'s' gloss on l. 195 of the November Eclogue in Spenser's *Shepherd's Calendar*; a measure of its unfamiliarity is W. L. Renwick's blunt note: 'This tale of Hebe I cannot find elsewhere' (*Works of Edmund Spenser* ed. Edwin Greenlaw *et al*, Baltimore, Md., 1932–57, *Minor Poems*, I. 416.).

64. *parting take*] a bold emendation of the octavo 'part', but justified by the obvious necessity to rhyme. Bullen suggests 'leave take', but this reads awkwardly (though it keeps to eight syllables); my own reading has ten syllables, but is rhythmically more plausible, and represents understandable compositor practice: the compositor might easily substitute in his memory the perfectly sensible 'let's part' for the required 'let's parting take.'

67. *model*] see line 30 and note.

69. *antemasque*] Enid Welsford (*The Court Masque*, Cambridge, 1927, p. 186) thinks it likely that Jonson invented the term 'antimasque' about 1608 to denote matter contrasted to that of the main masque. The earlier

To entertain time. Now my peace is perfect,
Let sports come on apace. Now is their time, my lord: *Music*
Hark you, you hear from 'em!

Duke. The nymph indeed.

Enter two dressed like Nymphs, bearing two tapers lighted; then ISABELLA *dressed with flowers and garlands, bearing a censer with fire in it; they set the censer and tapers on Juno's altar with much reverence; this ditty being sung in parts.*

DITTY.

Juno, nuptial-goddess,
Thou that rul'st o'er coupled bodies,
Tiest man to woman, never to forsake her,
Thou only powerful marriage-maker,
Pity this amazed affection;
I love both, and both love me,
Nor know I wherè to give rejection,
My heart likes so equally,

70. perfect] *Dilke;* perfect. *O.* 71. apace.] *Dyce;* a pace, *O.* 73. *Juno*] *O;* [Io] Juno *Dilke.*

---

term 'anticmasque' referred only to some kind of comic-grotesque performance. The octavo's 'Antemask' (even if the spelling is the compositor's) is a correct third variation, since it refers to material preceding the main performance, but not necessarily contrasted with it. Bianca uses the term, of course, merely as a hastily-contrived cover for her treachery.

70. *entertain*] occupy, while away (*O.E.D.* sense 9b).

my peace is perfect] Bianca may simply mean that now she will be perfectly happy and contented, since the Cardinal is, she believes, poisoned. But 'perfect' had a special relevance to marriage; as Jonson, quoting and translating the Greek scholiast on Pindar, indicates (note to *Masque of Hymen*, l. 295, *Wks*, VII. 220): '*Nuptialls are therefore calld* τέλειοι ['perfect'], *because they effect Perfection of life*, and do note that maturity which should be in Matrimony.' Bianca may be saying that she is now successfully and fully married.

72.5. in parts] referring to the practice of each singer taking a different 'part' in the melody, not singing in unison.

77. amazed] bewildered.

Till thou set'st right my peace of life,
And with thy power conclude this strife.

Isab. [*To the Nymphs*] Now with my thanks depart you to the springs,
I to these wells of love. [*Exeunt Nymphs.*]
Thou sacred goddess,
And queen of nuptials, daughter to great Saturn,
Sister and wife to Jove, imperial Juno,
Pity this passionate conflict in my breast,
This tedious war 'twixt two affections;
Crown one with victory, and my heart's at peace.

Enter HIPPOLITO *and* GUARDIANO, *like shepherds.*

Hip. Make me that happy man, thou mighty goddess.
Guard. But I live most in hope, if truest love
Merit the greatest comfort.
Isab. I love both
With such an even and fair affection
I know not which to speak for, which to wish for,
Till thou, great arbitress 'twixt lovers' hearts,
By thy auspicious grace, design the man;
Which pity I implore.
Both. We all implore it.

LIVIA *descends like Juno.*

89. one] *This ed.;* me *O.*

---

83. *the springs*] the Nymphs' dwelling-place. See line 33.

84. *these wells of love*] Wells were an old-fashioned stage-property. Feuillerat (*Documents Relating to the Office of the Revels*, Louvain, 1908, pp. 277 and 365) records two payments for 'y[e] well counterfeit' and 'canvas for a well'. Prof. M. C. Bradbrook remarks (privately) that the whole masque seems in many ways 'an old-fashioned affair.'

89. *one*] Though plainly wrong, the octavo 'me' is accepted in all previous editions. Isabella is asking Juno to pick out *one* suitor. A one/me misreading is a simple matter in most early hands.

96. *design*] indicate, point out (L. *designare*).

97.1.] Jonson describes in the *Masque of Hymen* (ll. 212–26 *Wks*, VII.

Isab. And after sighs, contrition's truest odours,
I offer to thy powerful deity
This precious incense; may it ascend peacefully—
[*The incense sends up a poisoned smoke.*]
[*Aside*] And if it keep true touch, my good aunt Juno,
'Twill try your immortality ere 't be long,
I fear you'll never get so nigh heaven again,
When you're once down.

Liv. Though you and your affections
Seem all as dark to our illustrious brightness
As night's inheritance hell, we pity you,
And your requests are granted. You ask signs;
They shall be given you, we'll be gracious to you.
He of those twain which we determine for you
Love's arrows shall wound twice; the later wound
Betokens love in age, for so are all
Whose love continues firmly all their life-time
Twice wounded at their marriage; else affection
Dies when youth ends. [*Aside*] This savour overcomes me.

98. contrition's] *Dyce;* contritions, *O.* 102. be long] *Dilke;* belong *O.* 114. savour] *Dilke;* favor *O.*

216–17) the descent of Juno; we may take it Middleton's Juno would have been similar, though the staging may have been less elaborate: '*Here the vpper part of the* Scene, . . . *began to open; and the ayre clearing, in the top thereof was discouered* Iuno, *sitting in a Throne, supported by two beautifull Peacockes; her attyre rich, and like a Queene; . . . in her right hand she held a Scepter, in the other a trimbrell, at her golden feete the hide of a lyon was placed . . . Aboue her the* region of fire, *with a continuall motion, was seene to whirle circularly, and* Ivpiter *standing in the toppe (figuring the* heauen) *brandishing his thunder.*'

98. *contrition's*] The compositor clearly thought that 'contritions' stood in apposition to 'sighs' and 'truest odors'; compare II. ii. 159n. Neither Middleton nor the octavo uses the apostrophe for possessives.

101. *keep true touch*] 'fulfil the expectations I have of it', 'prove trustworthy.' The underlying metaphor is from the 'trying' or testing of gold and precious metals with a 'touchstone', a sense carried on in 'try your immortality' (l. 102).

105. *to*] compared to, set beside.

114. *savour*] the odour from Isabella's 'incense.' The poison lore of the

[*As Juno*] Now for a sign of wealth and golden days,
Bright-eyed prosperity which all couples love,
Ay, and makes love, take that— [*Throws flaming gold upon Isabella, who falls dead*]
Our brother Jove
Never denies us of his burning treasure,
T' express bounty.

Duke. She falls down upon 't,
What's the conceit of that?

Fab. As over-joyed belike.
Too much prosperity overjoys us all,
And she has her lapful it seems, my lord.

Duke. This swerves a little from the argument though:
Look you, my lords.

117. love,] *This ed.;* love *O.* 117.1–2. S.D.] *MS note in Yale copy of O*

Renaissance included the possibility of poisoning by smell. Pedro Mexia (*The Treasure of Ancient Times*, English tr., 1613, II. xvii) considers whether 'a man may be impoysoned by Pomanders of sweete smell, fumes of Torches, Tapers, Candles; by Letters, Garments, and other such like things.' The above is quoted in a note on *Every Man in His Humour* that goes on to refer to 'a plot to take away the Queen's life by poisoned perfumes, for which purpose Geraldi, a Bergamasco, was employed by the Pope.' (Jonson, *Wks*, IX. 385). Compare also the poisoned vapour which rises from the 'fum'd picture' in *The White Devil* II. ii. The octavo's 'favor' represents the very frequent s/f confusion.

117. *makes*] creates.

117.1–2.] The suggested action in the Yale copy fits well with Jonson's description of Juno, quoted at l. 97.1n. The 'flaming gold', however represented, would come from the '*region of fire*' which Jonson describes as 'whirling' above Juno. This inference is strengthened by Livia's mention of Jove's 'burning treasure' (l. 118): Jonson speaks of 'IUPITER' or Jove 'standing in the toppe' above Juno. It also fits Fabritio's quibbling 'she has her lapful' in l. 122; he is thinking of the shower of gold in which Jove violated Danae.

117. *Our brother Jove*] As Jonson (*Wks*, VII. 216) explains, Juno 'was call'd *Regina Iuno* with the *Latines*, because she was *Soror & Coniu*[*n*]*x Iouis, Deorum & hominum Regis*.'

118. *burning treasure*] presumably 'flaming gold.' See l. 117.1–2n.

120. *conceit*] meaning, significance (*O.E.D.* sense I. i. d).

Guard. [*Aside*] All's fast; now comes my part to tole him hither;
Then with a stamp given, he's dispatched as cunningly.

Hip. Stark dead. Oh treachery, cruelly made away!

[*Guardiano falls through the trap door.*]

How's that?

Fab. Look, there's one of the lovers dropped away too.

Duke. Why, sure this plot's drawn false, here's no such thing.

Liv. Oh I am sick to th' death, let me down quickly;
This fume is deadly. Oh 't has poisoned me!
My subtlety is sped, her art has quitted me;
My own ambition pulls me down to ruin. [*Dies*]

Hip. Nay, then I kiss thy cold lips, and applaud
This thy revenge in death.

Fab. Look, Juno's down too.
What makes she there? Her pride should keep aloft;
She was wont to scorn the earth in other shows—
Methinks her peacocks' feathers are much pulled.

Cupids shoot [*at Hippolito.*]

138.1.] *S.D. in left-hand margin opposite lines 135–6 in O.*

---

125. *fast*] fixed, as arranged.
tole] lure.
hither] to the trap-door.
127. *How's that?*] how did it happen?
132. *is sped*] an ironic inversion of the usual sense; 'has succeeded'. But it is possible that 'sped' here is used in the less common sense cited by *O.E.D.* (*speed*, v. 7b) 'in contexts implying an evil plight or awkward situation', with, among the examples, Holland's tr. of Pliny (1601), II. 49: 'Like as those that be sped with the yellow jaunise'.
quitted me] requited me, paid me in my own coin.
133. *ambition*] presumably in aspiring to the part of the goddess Juno; but perhaps with a hint of the old sense of 'vain-glory', 'pomp' (*O.E.D.* sense 2).
136. *makes she*] is she doing.
138. *peacocks' feathers*] See l. 97.1n for the '*two beautiful Peacockes*' which '*supported*' Juno's throne. Jonson's note (*Wks*, VII. 216), quoting Ovid, explains that these birds 'were sacred to *Iuno*, in respect of their colours, and temper, so like the *Aire*.'

Hip. Oh death runs through my blood; in a wild flame too.
Plague of those Cupids, some lay hold on 'em;
Let 'em not 'scape, they have spoiled me; the shaft's deadly.

Duke. I have lost myself in this quite.

Hip. My great lords, we are all confounded.

Duke. How?

Hip. [*Pointing to Isabella's body*] Dead; and I worse.

Fab. Dead? My girl dead? I hope
My sister Juno has not served me so.

Hip. Lust and forgetfulness has been amongst us,
And we are brought to nothing. Some blest charity
Lend me the speeding pity of his sword
To quench this fire in blood. Leantio's death
Has brought all this upon us—now I taste it—
And made us lay plots to confound each other.
The event so proves it, and man's understanding
Is riper at his fall than all his life-time.
She in a madness for her lover's death
Revealed a fearful lust in our near bloods,
For which I am punished dreadfully and unlooked for;
Proved her own ruin too: vengeance met vengeance
Like a set match, as if the plagues of sin

158. plagues] *Dilke;* plague *O.*

---

139. *in . . . too*] The usual effect of Elizabethan stage-poisons is, as Macleod Yearsley (*Doctors in Elizabethan Drama*, 1933, p. 47) notes, this sense of 'burning inside.'

141. *spoiled*] destroyed.

144. *and I worse*] Hippolito may mean that he is not only dying but damned: Isabella at least entered unknowingly into the incestuous relationship with himself.

146. *forgetfulness*] Compare I. ii. 202 and note; no involuntary lapse of memory is in question, but a willed disregard for moral values.

148. *speeding*] helpful.

152. *event*] outcome.

154. *She*] Livia.

157. *Proved*] it proved.

158. *a set match*] 'an agreement, conspiracy, an appointment made for a highway robbery' (*O.E.D.*). *Not* 'match' in the sense of 'contest': the several 'vengeances' reinforce each other.

Had been agreed to meet here altogether.
But how her fawning partner fell I reach not,
Unless caught by some springe of his own setting;
For, on my pain, he never dreamed of dying,
The plot was all his own, and he had cunning
Enough to save himself—but 'tis the property
Of guilty deeds to draw your wise men downward.
Therefore the wonder ceases. Oh this torment!
Duke. Our guard below there!

Enter a Lord *with a* Guard.

Lord. My lord.
Hip. Run and meet death then,
And cut off time and pain. [*Runs on a guard's halbert; dies*]
Lord. Behold, my lord,
'Has run his breast upon a weapon's point.
Duke. Upon the first night of our nuptial honours

159. here] *O;* her *Dilke.* 168.1.] *MS note in Yale copy of O.*

---

plagues] The context seems to require a plural subject. The compositor rather frequently omitted a word's final letter.

160. *her fawning partner*] Guardiano. 'Fawning' is not an easy adjective to associate with Guardiano, though he does of course behave deferentially towards the Duke. Just possibly the quality of his voice is being described: compare Edward Topsell, *The historie of foure-footed beastes* (1607, ed. 1658, p. 109) 'The lower and stiller (voice of a dog) is called 'whining' or 'fawning.' (*O.E.D.*)

reach] understand, grasp.

161. *springe*] a snare for catching small game, especially birds. Compare *Ham.* V. ii. 317–18 (a similar context): '*Laertes.* Why, as a woodcock to mine own springe, Osric;/I am justly kill'd with mine own treachery.'

162. *on my pain*] on my suffering in hell.

164. *property*] tendency, effect.

168.1.] A halbert is a weapon combining spear and battle-axe. Previous editors have given a sword as the instrument of Hippolito's death. But the Yale note has about it the vividness of stage-practice, and Hippolito's impaling himself on this weapon, perhaps lowered in self-defence by a guard, is more plausible than his dying on a sword. Parker is of course correct when he points out that Dilke's direction 'Falls on his sword' is mistaken (see l. 169).

Destruction plays her triumph, and great mischiefs
Mask in expected pleasures, 'tis prodigious!
They're things most fearfully ominous, I like 'em not.
[*To Guard*] Remove these ruined bodies from our eyes.
Bian. [*Aside*] Not yet, no change? When falls he to the earth?
Lord. Please but your Excellence to peruse that paper,
Which is a brief confession from the heart
Of him that fell first, ere his soul departed;
And there the darkness of these deeds speaks plainly.
'Tis the full scope, the manner, and intent;
His ward, that ignorantly let him down,
Fear put to present flight at the voice of him.
Bian. [*Aside*] Nor yet?
Duke. [*To Lord Cardinal*] Read, read; for I am lost in sight
and strength.
Card. My noble brother!
Bian. Oh the curse of wretchedness!
My deadly hand is fallen upon my lord.
Destruction take me to thee; give me way;
The pains and plagues of a lost soul upon him
That hinders me a moment.
Duke. My heart swells bigger yet; help here, break 't ope,
My breast flies open next. [*Dies*]
Bian. Oh with the poison

171. plays] *White;* play *O.*

---

171. *plays*] A singular subject with a plural verb is a possible seventeenth-century agreement. But 'play' (the octavo reading) comes very awkwardly here. Omission of a final 's' would be entirely in line with the compositor's practice elsewhere.

triumph] see note at IV. ii. 163.

172. *Mask in*] referring to the masks or disguises held by revellers before their faces at a Ball.

prodigious] ill-omened, menacing. For 'prodigy' compare IV. ii. 60 and note.

178. *him that fell first*] Guardiano.

181. *let him down*] through the trap door.

189–90.] At death, the body's blood-supply was thought to rush to the heart, causing it to swell.

That was prepared for thee, thee, Cardinal!
'Twas meant for thee.

Card. Poor Prince!

Bian. Accursed error!
Give me thy last breath, thou infected bosom,
And wrap two spirits in one poisoned vapour.
[*Kisses the Duke's body*]
Thus, thus, reward thy murderer, and turn death
Into a parting kiss. My soul stands ready at my lips,
E'en vexed to stay one minute after thee.

Card. The greatest sorrow and astonishment
That ever struck the general peace of Florence
Dwells in this hour.

Bian. So my desires are satisfied,
I feel death's power within me.
Thou hast prevailed in something, cursed poison,
Though thy chief force was spent in my lord's bosom;
But my deformity in spirit's more foul—
A blemished face best fits a leprous soul.
What make I here? These are all strangers to me,
Not known but by their malice, now th' art gone;
Nor do I seek their pities. [*Drinks from the poisoned cup*]

Card. Oh restrain
Her ignorant wilful hand!

Bian. Now do; 'tis done.
Leantio, now I feel the breach of marriage
At my heart-breaking. Oh the deadly snares
That women set for women, without pity
Either to soul or honour! Learn by me
To know your foes; in this belief I die:

207. malice,] *This ed.;* malice; *O.* 210. Leantio,] *Dilke; Leantio. O.*

205.] perhaps referring to the twisted features caused by poison; more likely, Bianca tears at her face with her nails. For 'leprous' compare II. ii. 424–5 and note.

Like our own sex, we have no enemy, no enemy!
Lord. See my lord
What shift sh' has made to be her own destruction.
Bian. Pride, greatness, honours, beauty, youth, ambition,
You must all down together, there's no help for 't.
Yet this my gladness is, that I remove,
Tasting the same death in a cup of love. [*Dies*]
Card. Sin, what thou art these ruins show too piteously.
Two kings on one throne cannot sit together,
But one must needs down, for his title's wrong;
So where lust reigns, that prince cannot reign long.
Exeunt.

FINIS.

215. no enemy, no enemy] *O;* no enemy *White.*

---

215. *no enemy, no enemy*] perhaps intended to imitate Bianca's voice trailing away as she dies. White and later editors delete the repetition, presumably for metrical reasons, or because they believe the compositor inadvertently repeated himself. Neither argument is convincing. Nor should the words be explained away as an actor's elaboration of his part; the copy, in all probability, was not theatrical in origin. The repetition is quite effective, and is easily contained within Middleton's generous prosody.

221.] Reginald Scot's *Discoverie of Witchcraft* (Bk VI. ch. 7) a book Middleton certainly knew (it is the basis of much in *The Witch*), examines the proposition 'that love cups ingender rather death through venome, then love by art.'

225.] a stock moral. Compare e.g. *Philaster* V. i., (Beaumont & Fletcher, *Wks*, I. 148): 'Let Princes learn/By this to rule the passions of their blood,/For what Heaven wills, can never be withstood.' and *The White Devil*, V. vi. 240–1 (Revels ed., p. 183) '*Vit.* O my greatest sin lay in my blood./Now my blood pays for it.'

APPENDIX I

Sources and Analogues

A. THE SOURCE OF THE MAIN PLOT

The following is a translation from Celio Malespini's *Ducento Novelle* (Venice, 1609), novelle 84 and 85 of Part Two (pp. 275 ff.). I have translated Malespini (rather than a manuscript) since his account is, if not the source of, certainly the highest common factor in, all the narratives I have seen, both manuscript and printed. And his book was, conceivably, available to Middleton in the 1620's. Only so much of the novelle as is directly relevant to *Women Beware Women* has been included. Where the omitted sections are material to the narrative they are summarized; otherwise their omission is indicated by dots.

My translation aims to be literal rather than graceful, and so to convey something of the 'feel' of Malespini's jaded, marginally-articulate prose. I have however, in the interests of readability, almost wholly disregarded his endlessly-contorted sentence and paragraph structure. I have also sometimes, for clarity's sake, translated a simple *giovane* or *gentildonna* as 'Pietro' or 'Bianca'.

The figures to the left of the text refer to passages of *Women Beware Women* parallel to those translated or summarized. Summaries are enclosed in square brackets, as are the necessary brief additions and explanations.

[*Malespini tells first how Bianca Cappello and Pietro Buonaventura became acquainted, he a young and penniless Florentine employed by a banking-house in Venice, she the daughter of a rich patrician family of that city. Bianca, Malespini relates, was attracted by the young man's poise and fine manners, and in the belief that he was at least part-owner of the banking-business, she returned the love he already felt for her. Arriving home one night after one of their clandestine meetings, Bianca found her intended entrance locked against her; terrified of the consequences of discovery she and Pietro eloped to Florence.*]

I. i. There they took refuge in the house of Pietro's father, on the Piazza di San Marco not very far from the Chiesa della Nonciata. Old Buonaventura [the father], though a citizen, lived in very poor circumstances, and when he was burdened with two new mouths to feed, was compelled to dismiss his servant-girl, and to put in her place the unfortunate Bianca—whom Pietro spoke of as his wife. As Pietro's mother was old and decrepit, Bianca had to occupy herself with household tasks, and these she performed cheerfully and patiently for many months.

[*On discovering her elopement, Bianca's relatives used their influence with the* Consiglio dei Dieci *to have the fugitives proclaimed outlaws, and a price put on their heads. Hearing of this, Bianca never ventured out of doors.*]

While [Pietro and Bianca] lived in this miserable and
I. iii. 72 ff. unhappy condition, it came about that one day by good fortune the Grand Duke Francesco passed in his carriage beneath their windows. Bianca, since she had never seen him before, raised the Venetian blind a little for a better view, and their eyes met. Perceiving this she lowered the blind immediately, and drew back from the window. The Grand Duke, on the contrary, kept on craning his head out of the carriage, gazing up at the window in hope of seeing her again—but all to no purpose.

II. ii. 8–23 This most sudden and unexpected glimpse engendered in the Grand Duke's breast an emotion I cannot describe, and he became very eager to find out who Bianca was, and all about her circumstances. When he heard about her unhappy condition, unwonted pity wrung his heart, and he felt deeply moved by her misfortune. . . . Wishing to see her close at hand, he had to share his thoughts with a Spanish gentleman, whom the Grand Duke Cosimo had appointed as his tutor and guardian from his earliest years. The Duke imparted his wishes, and the other, who desired the gratifying of [Francesco's] every taste and whim, took up the assignment gladly, and ordered his wife to strike up a friendship with Bianca's mother-in-law, a matter very easy to accomplish.

II. ii. 137–228 Since it is customary for ladies to gossip intimately about their affairs, the gentlewoman, when she knew what she had to do, came straight to the point in conversation with [Pietro's mother], and asked her if Pietro were her son. 'Yes indeed, Signora,' she answered, 'but unhappily.' And there and then she recounted what had happened in Venice. The gentlewoman feigned much compassion at this, and besought her insistently to bring Bianca with her one day, as she herself very much wished to know her, and to offer her every favour and service.

When the old woman heard this, she answered, 'That, Signora, would be very difficult, since she never goes out of doors, and has no clothes other than those she is wearing. Because of our poverty we have been unable till now to do anything for her, and indeed she would be ashamed to appear before you in such a mean guise, particularly as she is so much a gentlewoman and of such noble stock.'

'We shall easily remedy that; I shall send her some clothes of mine. And so I shall be able to see her and get to know her.' 'I don't know,' replied the good old woman, 'whether she will be willing without her husband's permission. Still, I shall make every possible effort to have her come to you. Yet I fear I may not be able to induce her to do it, since she is happy to live so retired, not caring that anyone should see her. And although my son has many times told her that she should come with me to Mass in St Mark's, she has all the same never been willing to come there. Ever since that happy hour when she entered our house, she has never been anywhere outside.'

'Use, I beg you, your best means and authority to bring her. I shall send you my carriage, in which, unseen by anyone, she may come in safety. And tell her that my friendship will not harm her at all, but will perhaps be productive of not a little profit and advantage.' 'I shall not fail,' answered the good woman, 'to do all I can to oblige you.'

[*Pietro's mother talked the matter over with Bianca, laying stress on the advantages she and Pietro might hope to gain from friendly relations with the Signora's husband. Bianca, with Pietro's permission, agreed to visit the Signora's palazzo, hoping to gain from the Duke, through the good offices of his favourite, an 'official permission to remain' in Florence, under Florentine protection.*]

The gentlewoman [sent] her carriage at a convenient moment. [Bianca and her mother-in-law] entered it
II. ii. 242 ff. alone, and drove to the gentlewoman's palazzo, where she received them with looks of joy, and treated them with great ceremony. They then withdrew into some very beautiful and ornate apartments, and discussed many

topics, the gentlewoman offering them every assistance, and her influence with her husband in the matter of the official permission that Bianca desired, and for which alone she had left her house. While they were still making plans, there suddenly arrived Mondragone, as the gentlewoman's husband was called, and he, after making them his bow, feigning not to know the two ladies, asked his wife who they were.

'They are,' she replied, 'people in need of your favour, and of the influence you possess with the Grand Duke.' Then in a few words she told him all the events of Bianca's history (which he knew better than she), begging him to speak in her favour to His Highness—who from a place of concealment saw and heard everything.

While the gentlewoman was talking like this, Bianca stood with lowered eyes in such a way that anyone could have gathered, without her speaking at all, how very great was her desire to have the 'official permission'. Mondragone answered his wife's narration by saying to Bianca, 'Signora, what you desire is a very small service in comparison with the much greater I would gladly do for you. There is no need for me to exercise myself greatly to obtain your request, for the Grand Duke is a most courteous and magnanimous Prince, and always grants every legitimate boon to anyone who asks him—to gentlewomen in particular, as the requirements of chivalry constrain him. So take comfort, and rest assured that you will be satisfied in your every desire.'

'I want to show you, Signora, this palazzo of ours' [interposed Signora Mondragone], 'so that you may tell me whether it resembles in any part the very great and proud buildings of your own city. And meanwhile your mother-in-law, who is advanced in years and weak-legged, will stay and rest till we return to her.' 'Go by all means,' said the old woman, 'I haven't enough breath to go up and down so many stairs.'

Then smiling and arm in arm they traversed almost the whole palazzo, which Mondragone had had rebuilt (though the work was as yet incomplete) in the Via di Carnesecchi, near the church of Santa Maria Novella. Bianca was full of praise for the palazzo, marvelling beyond measure at the very ornate furnishings that had been arranged in such abundance in every room. They returned at length to a very beautiful little room, in which stood a lavishly-appointed bed. Nearby was a study of marvellous beauty, with windows overlooking a very beautiful garden. Unlocking this, Signora Mondragone brought out many beautiful jewels, at which Bianca gazed in stupefaction one by one. While she was still marvelling Signora Mondragone said to her, 'I want to show you some clothes, which I believe have been made in the fashion you Venetian gentlewomen are accustomed to wear. So please be so good as to wait for me a little, while I go for the keys to those goods that are there within; amuse yourself with as many of my few jewels as are about you until I return to you in a few moments.'

No sooner had she departed than on a sudden entered the Grand Duke. At his august and unexpected presence, Bianca trembled all over and her heart contracted within her; like a prudent woman she guessed at once the reason for his coming. She immediately went down on her knees, and in a humble and piteous fashion said to him, 'Since, Signore, you have looked kindly on my hard fortune in being parted from my relatives, wealth and native place, and since nothing now remains to me in the world except my honour, I humbly beg that you will respect it.'

When the Grand Duke heard that, he at once took her beneath the arms and assisted her to rise, saying to her, 'Have no fear, Signora, since you may be certain that I have not come to stain your honour, but, full of pity for the unhappy situation in which you find yourself, to console you, and to assist you in your every need (as you shall daily discover) to real and true effect. Be cheered then at having found such a protector, and be absolutely sure that you will always receive from me every favour and courtesy.'

Making his bow to her, he went off, leaving her very pale and shaken, until Signora Mondragone returned and said smiling, 'Do not be amazed, my dear Signora, at the Grand Duke's unexpected arrival; as he is so very familiar with the whole palazzo he often appears at moments when he is least in our thoughts: he delights in playing similar tricks on me and on my maids. But I am persuaded that you have excellently reproved him, and that he has gone off because he has been made to blush with shame. How incomparably glad I feel, for he will not be so bold in future, having found at last an adversary who has given him such a thorough scolding.'

'I have said nothing to him,' replied Bianca, 'save that, fearing for my honour, I asked him to respect it and begged him to be its guardian and defender.' 'I assure you truly,' said Signora Mondragone, 'that he will do so. And as I need not waste time in fruitless conversation with a gentlewoman as wise and prudent as yourself, I shall therefore come down to the hard facts of the business, and say this to you. Heaven is taking pity on your great sufferings and hardships, in that the Grand Duke is now offering you so generously his most potent arm to raise you up out of all your miseries. If you know how to grasp it firmly, you will with its help become happy and blessed. These, Signora, are privileges and favours granted to very few women—that so mighty a Prince should burn and consume away in the fires of love for your sake. You may therefore be certain of securing from him the fullness of joy and happiness.'

Many similar conversations and discussions were engaged in and repeated on both parts, and because of them Bianca at length consented to bestow her love on the enamoured Grand Duke. Her indulgence of this passion, and her most happy familiarity [with the Duke], she increased from day to day. Mutual love grew between them, from which the Grand Duke did not waver till he took her for his wife, and had her crowned Grand Duchess of Tuscany. The two of them afterwards ended their days in a common and untimely death.

Novella 85. Pietro's death, and events leading to it.

Pietro, owing to the amazing love which the Grand Duke felt for Bianca, had reached such a pitch of felicity and good fortune, that not only had the Duke made him his
III. iii. 37–43 chamberlain [*guardarobbiere*], but there was nothing else besides that he asked for that was not granted him.

The Duke loved Pietro for his wife's sake; Bianca he loved better than his own eyes, and had given her a very
III. iii. 237–9 beautiful palazzo in the Via Maggiore, where she and Pietro lived happily, with such an abundance of worldly possessions that more could not be desired.

Pietro, being somewhat puffed up with his good

fortune, and full of arrogance because of the very great authority he had, became inflamed (apart from many other mistresses) with an immoderate passion for a

III. iii. 251–376 widowed gentlewoman called Cassandra Buongiani, a woman of the most marvellous beauty. He was so skilled in successfully initiating and furthering these affairs, that in a short time he gained her love and her good grace; and they enjoyed each other freely, without taking into consideration the very noble stock from which the lady sprang, a family held and considered one of the first in the whole city.

[*Pietro, relying on the Grand Duke's favour for protection, infuriated the widow's family by his insolence and shamelessness. The Buongiani threatened him repeatedly, but this 'did not dismay the enamoured Pietro for one moment; on the contrary he talked in public about his enjoyment of the widow'. His taunts were directed in particular against a nephew of Signora Buongiani, a certain Roberto de' Ricci. More than once, complaints were made to the Grand Duke, who, finding his own cautions ineffectual, persuaded Bianca to talk with her husband.*]

IV. i. 41–111 She considered whether she would be able with sweet prayers and warnings to persuade him to give up so dangerous an escapade. And as he was not accustomed to return home till late, when she heard him in his room she descended the stairs, went to find him, and said, 'The immeasurable love I feel for you, my husband, certainly could not be greater. Still, I beg you by a love as much again as any I can encompass to bear with me and to hear me patiently to the end. I will talk of nothing save matters very useful and necessary to your well-being and your safety.' Then in brief summary she told him all that the Grand Duke had said, and about the plans that he was making to shelter him [Pietro] from the great danger that hung over him.

Pietro, infuriated, could not wait till she had finished her discourse, but bounded up instantly right beside her and said, 'Let him hang himself by the neck, and babble as much as he will, for I shall do as I please. And you, you filthy cow,' he went on, 'let me have no more of your talk. But do not doubt that I shall cut off those horns of gold that you have set on my crest, and as your deserved punishment, I shall slit your windpipe.'

IV. i. 112–27 By good fortune the Grand Duke had entered the house, and when he knew that Bianca was with her husband, he went down the steps very quietly and approached the door. Stealthily he listened to their whole quarrel which disturbed him not a little. [At that moment] Pietro in a rage flung out of the door. Seeing this Bianca burst into a flood of tears and called after him; but he despising her would listen to her no more.

When the unhappy lady had shut the door without noticing the Grand Duke, she withdrew to her own rooms, weeping beyond measure and bewailing her hard lot. She poured out such an abundance of tears that her whole breast and bosom were damp with them, cursing the day and hour when she came into the world. And she would have lamented still longer if the Grand Duke had not come in, feigning to know nothing of the matter. He stopped her crying and asked, 'What do these tears mean and this sobbing? What misfortune has come upon you, my dear one?' 'Nothing else, Signore, save that when I reproved my husband, as you bade me, and he took little heed of my words, I began, because of the great sorrow I felt, to cry and weep at his hard indifference.' 'There is nothing more you can do,' said the Duke. 'Let him alone to act as he will and have his fling, for in the end it will be he who suffers.'

[*After a particularly outrageous insult from Pietro, de' Ricci went to the Grand Duke and described his enemy's latest piece of recklessness.*]

When he heard of it, the Grand Duke was finally convinced of Buonaventura's boundless insolence. As he had heard with his own ears that Pietro intended to cut off his golden horns and to kill his wife, he said to himself, 'There is no more time to be lost before giving him the punishment fitted to his deserts. He
IV. i. 141–79 therefore led de' Ricci aside, and they conversed together, walking for some time in the garden. Then he dismissed him, and, mounting his horse early the next morning, went to Pratolino; there he remained a whole day and night.

IV. ii. 1–46 [*De' Ricci mustered a formidable band of ruffians, and with them ambushed Pietro as he returned home at an early hour, after a night spent with Cassandra Buongiani, the widow. Despite stout resistance, Pietro was hacked to pieces. Bianca was overwhelmed with grief; no-one could comfort her except the Duke himself.*]

B. A MANUSCRIPT ACCOUNT OF BIANCA'S DEATH

MS Moreni 49 of the Biblioteca Riccardiana e Moreniana, Florence, adds to the 'Malespini' narrative a section describing Bianca's death. Though quite obviously written many years after the event, and many years after some manuscripts I have examined, this 'final section' may be regarded as typical of these manuscripts. Malespini perhaps thought it prudent to omit it from his *novelle* because of the dangerous material it contains; Bianca had, after all, been created a Daughter of the Venetian Republic, and Venice was Malespini's home. As in the previous appendix, my translation is literal.

The Marriage and Death of Signora Bianca Cappello, and of his Highness the Grand Duke Francesco.

After some time had passed by, there passed away also the lady Bianca's grief at the loss of her much-loved husband. The Grand Duke, to prevent Bianca getting to know that he had connived at her husband's death, raged against the killers with apparent fury. But at length, with the passage of time, the whole business was taken as settled, and the Grand Duke and de' Ricci and all his relatives became wholly at one with regard to what had happened.

The Grand Duke's fervent love for the lady Bianca went on increasing from day to day. He reflected that he had been living constantly in the sin of adultery for a long time now; he reflected too on the very great deserts of the lady Bianca, and on her faithfulness (in that, apart from her husband and himself, her body was most chaste); he knew also that she was of high birth; and so at length, overwhelmed by the depth of his love for her, he determined to marry her. So it came about, and she was made Grand Duchess of Tuscany.

This altogether unforeseen decision of the Grand Duke's became known to the Cardinal Ferdinand his brother, at that time living in Rome. [He received the news] with a feeling of aversion such as anyone can imagine, since Francesco was almost pledged to another marriage-arrangement, and that with a Crowned Head. The Cardinal was beside himself at this extraordinary blunder of his brother's (who had told him nothing whatever about the affair). With that vigour conferred on him by nature, as accounts of him show, he devised a thousand ways of meeting the situation, and among the rest sought with poisoned gifts, or even by bribing her servants, to have the lady Bianca poisoned. But she was wary of him, or to speak more accurately had been forewarned about him, and so remained on her guard. The Cardinal too lived after the same manner, and so each of them entertained a mortal hatred for the other—though not openly, out of respect for the Grand Duke.

It happened on one of the Cardinal's visits to Florence that they had occasion to talk and to eat together. The wicked, shrewd and crafty Bianca one morning made a tart with her own hands, and put into it a very strong poison. The Cardinal—he was already on his guard—wore on his finger a ring whose stone had the property of changing its colour when any poisoned food appeared on the table. And so he directed the stone of this ring at every dish that was brought to table. At the close of the meal there came some sweetmeats, and among the rest the lady Bianca's poisoned tart. The Cardinal watched the stone, and seeing it troubled, recognized the villainy prepared against him. He surmised that his brother knew of it also, and so he became watchful, while still discoursing as was his wont with all affability, seeming not to be aware of any treachery.

The Grand Duke eventually told his brother several times that he ought to show himself sensible of the Signora Bianca's kindness by taking a piece of the tart that she had made with her own hands. The Cardinal, however, contented himself with proffering compliments, and with promising to take a piece. In the end the Grand Duke himself took a portion and said, 'No-one wants to be the first, so I shall.' He took the piece and ate it.

The helpless Signora, being unwilling to reveal the treacherous design in front of the Cardinal and her husband, and seeing the Duke poisoned, also without hesitation took a piece of the tart and ate it. She preferred to share in the fateful tragedy of her husband's death rather than outlive him and so make known the treachery aimed at the Cardinal her brother-in-law.

The Grand Duke, innocent of this underhand practice, went on with what he was saying; until a few minutes later he began to feel very severe pains in his belly, as the lady Bianca did too. Because of them, they both had to retire to their rooms. There they went to bed, and kept expecting the doctors and the remedies which the Cardinal had given them to understand were in preparation. But no-one ever appeared. On the contrary, there was an express command from this same Cardinal that anyone—let him be who he might—who approached the rooms of the unfortunate pair should be put to death. He himself with his loyal servants kept diligent watch and guard. The wretched pair might therefore beg for mercy and assistance as much as they wished; the one who could allow and give it them was he who with every cruelty kept it from them. And so it came about that the ill-fated pair most unhappily ended their lives in this most barbaric fashion.

The Cardinal saw to it that honourable burial was given the dead, and noised it abroad that there had been no remedy for the poison, as it was very strong and in great quantity. He then resigned his Cardinal's hat, and was crowned Grand Duke of Tuscany. He lived and died with a magnificence that is known universally throughout the world, and especially to the Turk, who feared him greatly.

The Grand Duke Francesco died in the year 1588* on . . . [*sic*].

C. A CONTEMPORARY ENGLISH ACCOUNT OF BIANCA FROM FYNES MORYSON'S 'ITINERARY'

The extract below is from the originally unpublished chapters of Moryson's *Itinerary*, as transcribed by Charles Hughes from a manuscript now in the Bodleian Library. The section referring to Bianca appears on pp. 94–5 of *Shakespeare's Europe*, ed. Charles Hughes (1903).

Fraunces the last deceased Duke before my being at Florence, had to wife Joane of the house of Austria, and by her had a sonne who dyed yong, and two daughters Leonora then maryed to the Duke of Mantua, and Maria then a Virgin and a most fayre lady, of whose marryage I shall hereafter speake. His wife Joane being dead, he liued long vnmaryed, and it was vulgarly spoken aswell among his subiects as strangers, and a thing sowell knowne in Italy as I thincke it fitt for good vses to be here mentioned, that during the tyme of his single life a Floryntine marchant intangled in his loue a Venetian gentlewoman called la Signora Bianca di Capelli, so as shee stole from her frendes, and being his Concubyne came with him to Florence, where he hauing wasted his estate in shorte tyme, shee was thought a fitt pray for a better man. Wherevpon Duke Fraunces, after the manner of Italy, in the tyme of Carnovall or shrouetyde going masked through the streetes with a little basked [*sic*] of egges filled with Rose water, passed by her windowe and threwe vp an egge, which shee caught and retorned it broken into his bosome, and so modestly played the wanton with gracefullnes, as the Duke inamored brought her to his Palice, where shee being his Concubyne, first brought him a sonne called Antonio, then seeming to make conscience to liue a Concubyne, at last shee had the power to make him to take her to wife, which donne shee bent all her witts to haue her sonne legitimate, and admitted to succeede in the Dukedome, and while Cardinall Ferdinand brother to Duke Fraunces opposed this her desseigne, it happened that he came to Florence to passe some dayes merrily with the Duke, and they being to goe out hunting earely in a morning, the Duchesse sent the Cardinall a March payne for his breakfast, which he retorned with

* In error for 1587 (October).

due ceremony saying that he did eate nothing but that was dressed by his owne Cooke, but the Duke by ill happ meeting the messenger, did eate a peece thereof, and when the Duchesse sawe it broken, shee smiled and spake some wordes of Joy, but the messenger telling her the Cardinalls Answer, and that the Duke had eaten that peece, shee with an vnchanged Countenance tooke another peece, and having eaten it, locked herselfe in a clossett, and herevpon the Duke and shee dyed in one hower, and the Cardinall Ferdinand succeeded in the Dukedome, who lived at the tyme when I was at Florence.

D. EXTRACTS FROM THE SUB-PLOT SOURCE

Act II scene i is that part of the play in which Middleton worked most closely with an identified source, *The True History* (see Introduction, pp. xliv–xlvii). Space does not allow me to transcribe all the many parallels even from this part of the source; those that do appear will however show how the skilled playwright customarily handled his working material, selecting from it, shaping and compressing it with extraordinary sureness of touch. Relevant line-references from II. i. are provided in the margin to assist comparison between source and play.

My Introduction argues that Middleton used the French original, rather than the translation attributed to Alexander Hart. But the seventeenth-century English is faithful to the French in its near-literalness, and in conveying the original's brisk and informal vigour, so that I have not thought it necessary to offer a new translation.

I have, very infrequently, altered the pointing and spelling of my source when these were obviously in error. The spellings 'Hipolito' and 'Fabricio' are those used throughout *The True History*. The Livia of *Women Beware Women* is here a Nun.

> [Hipolito was in despair at the rejection by Isabella of his suit, and at the non-committal replies he received to his letters. So] hee went to visit a sister of his, a Nunne, betweene whom and him, by reason of the simpathie of their natures, there was an extraordinarie loue and amity.
>
> This Nun understood but too much for her profession, and was then of the age of thirtie fiue yeeres, hauing more exercised her wit about honest affaires of the world (as farre as the restraint of a Cloister might suffer her) then in the strict obseruance of the duties of her order. . . .

1–2 [She said to Hipolito] Certainly Brother, either it is
your sicknesse hath so strangely altered you, that I may
say, I scarce know you, or you haue somewhat in your
minde, that you will keepe to your selfe, that makes you
so melancholy, as may hazard the casting of you downe
againe, if you take not heede. You know there is no
disease more dangerous then that of the minde, the
Physitians haue no Receipt, nor Apothecaries any
Drugge, that may auaile to heale it: the best thing for it,
is the aduice of a faithfull friend, and where can you
18–27 expect it more faithfull, then from me, who you know
and have not onely loved you above my other Brothers, but
70–4 even before my selfe: I beseech you by that inviolable,
and more than sisterly love, make mee a partner of your
30–2 sufferings; upon this assurance that you shall finde me
secret, serviceable, and assisting you to all you can
desire; despise not a vailed head, as an unprofitable thing
that cannot give you comfort equall with others more
conversant in the world. Deere sister (answered *Hipolito*)
my affection to you is built vpon too sure a foundation to
49,53 bee shaken, or indangered by any earthly accident, nor
and haue I euer doubted of the abilitie of your vnderstanding,
55–6 but my despaire of remedy to my affliction, takes from
me all will to giue it you; forgiue me good Sister and
since you can in nothing helpe, let me alone endure the
34–44 Penance of my idle thoughts. How? (answered she)
where is the resolution you men attribute to your selues
aboue the courage of women? Certainely, your part of
it is very little, that you dispaire of executing, before you
attempt the means; if your owne inuention doe not
presently giue you a smoothe way to your desires, you
must not therefore thinke that others cannot finde it out
for you; the fullest vnderstandings, in their owne
affaires are distrustfull, and for feare of loosing themselves, doe often repaire to the faith of a friend for their
19–20 resolution: If I can serue in nothing else but to keepe
your griefes from you, it is no litle lightning to a heauy
and oppressed heart, to leaue his vexations with those he
knowes, wil affectionately imbrace all, to take but a
part from him. . . .

Deere Sister (answered hee) out of the meere dutie
of my loue, and no hope at all of any allay to my griefes;
4–16 I will tell you their subiect, which shame ought still as
much to conceale, as reuerence to the lawes of Nature,

should haue at first forbidden. Know (deere Sister) I
haue beene so long engaged, that now in despight of
my best oppositions, I am constrained to giue my selfe
vp to the loue of our Neece *Isabella*. This hath beene,
and is the occasion of my anguish and must so remaine
as long as my vnhappy fate shall allow mee life: behold
the laborinth of my paines, and the little meanes I haue
to get out, since I am already gone on so farre. With this
he told her the discourse of all had past betweene them,
shewing her the letters hee had writ, and her answers to
them. To which his Sister said, . . . Vpon the first
difficulty that affronts you in your designe, [you]
remaine astonished and confounded. You love a Lady
92–3 that is upon the point of marriage with another. There
are many marriages intended, yet so crost, as they never
arrive to their consummation: & though that must bee,
160–2 yet were not that the worst that might happen you;
marriage often bringing convenience to love. Next, you
love one that you cannot marry. Well, and hath love no
other ends for his contentment, then marriage? since it
as often dissevers affections as it joynes them, while
being subjected to the lawes of an obligation and dutie,
you disarme him of his chiefest forces. A wife (though
never so faire) is like a guest, or the raine that becomes a
trouble in three dayes.

But you will say, I love one whom the lawes do forbid
me both all desire & all hope to enjoy, which so distracts
me in this thornie way, as I am there ruined with the
46–7 impossibilitie of getting out. You are not the first that
haue vndertaken things as much forbidden, which haue
yet attained to a happie end. Thinke vertue consists in
55–7 great and difficult things, and is pleased in a resistance,
and the more paine and difficultie there is in an affaire,
the more glorie followes the enterprize, and pleasure the
execution: the attempt may content you, whether you
gather the desired fruits of your paines, or fall vnder an
impossible enterprize, and where your fortune failes you,
not your courage. In summe, you stand not in ill tearmes.
. . . Be you of good cheere, goe see your Mistresse, and
procure her repaire hither vpon our *Ladies* day to heare
the Vespers, and faile not to bee here your selfe.

61–2 All these faire promises of the Nunne wrought little
in her Brothers beleefe. . . .

[Isabella] being arriued at the Nunnerie [on ‘our

Ladies day'], she found her Vncle and her Aunt walking
together in a Garden, there attending her comming,
74 who assoone as they had perceiued her, and seeing her
paler then shee vsed to bee, her Aunt said to her; Certainly Neece you haue not brought your best lookes
hither, me thinks you are afraid of shaming my Brother,
and therefore will partake with his sickly lookes.

[The Nun steers the conversation to the subject of
love, and remarks,] There is nothing that his brand
99–100 cannot fire, or his arrowes pierce; and I had ill spent my
time in the house of your dead Mother, who was the
woman I loued best in this world, and whose memory
I doe most honour, if I had learned nothing of this.

My Mother Aunt (answered *Isabella*) what can you say of her? I was not so blest as to see her in an age fit to iudge of her condition, but sure she died with a more faire and vnquestioned reputation, then (if her life and manners had not thoroughly deserued it) this age would haue given her. . . .

163–4 Neece (answered the Nunne) nothing vndoth vs but
149–53 indiscretion: your Mother was happie in placing her
fauours vpon a wise and respectfull Gentleman, and
shee of her part was in nothing vnwarie. This preserued
her, and will keepe vp the honour and happinesse of
all that ioyne it with their loue. I will giue you the whole
truth, for I saw it.

The yeare I was profest Nunne (it is some eighteene
143–9 yeares since) the Marquesse of *Coria* was sent to this
Towne in businesse of his Maiesties; hee stayd here
some seuen or eight moneths, bestowing the time his
great employments left him in the noblest exercises,
and most worthy his qualitie; hee was some fiue and
thirty yeares old, and the most accomplished man that
I euer saw. The Lords and Gentry to doe him honour,
made him many feasts, and there alwayes followed Balls,
Masques, Comedies, and other pleasurable pastimes, in
which he would againe returne his thanks to them. He
tooke much pleasure in Masques, for the priuiledge it
gaue him of discoursing with Ladies. My eldest Brother
was the man of this Towne he most affied in, and to
whom he did most freely impart his negotiation; my
Sister the woman that pleased him best, finding her
excellently faire, well graced, of a pleasing discourse,
and an vnderstanding aboue the rest. This inclination

grew to a loue, in which hee gouerned himselfe so well,
and so well disguised it, that hee escaped all suspition.
He resolued to impart it to my Sister, but with such
fitnesse as none but shee, or some most trusted woman
should know it. . . .

149–51 To be short, his discretion so managed his affaire
for him, as that helpt with the force of his vertue and
noblenesse, (and the seruice of my Sisters Nurce, whom
hee found meanes to gaine, and make the messenger
of his letters) hee led my Sister to such composition,
as that (conuenience and safetie permitting) shee gaue
him promise of sight, and speech with her in more
priuacy. Such as are practised in *Italy* and *Spaine*,
vnderstand well enough, what such permissions doe
promise to those that women haue a will to fauour. To
bring this to passe, there happened a very fit meane;
which was the necessity of an affaire of import for the
138–9 Kings seruice, wherein hee was to send to *Rome* out of
hand to his Holinesse. The Marquesse (and the Councell
by his aduice) iudged my Brother [-in-law] fitter than
any other for this purpose; whereupon, soone as the
Carneuall was ended, my brother [-in-law] made that
voyage where hee was fiue or six weekes; in which time,
the Marquesse taking the occasion, found meanes to
visit my Sister by night, following her permission, which
stretcht at length euen to the point, whither they say
loue pretends. . . .

My Brother being returned, this practise betweene them ceased, not their loues; but vertue was of both sides so reciprocally obeyed, as their pleasure, nor desire, had not the power to carry them beyond the limits of respect, nor had they other commerce then by letters, and those but seldome. Not long after Easter, the Marquesse hauing dispatcht the affaires hee had in charge, was called home by the King his Master, which summons, honour, and duty both commanded him to obey. . . .

He being gone, and my Sister big with child, and
98–9 drawing neere her time, she came hither to see me, and
tooke of me the greatest assurances she could deuise of
97–105 secresie, of what I should receiue from her. Which I haue
hitherto most inuiolably kept; and should still, had not
this occasion pluckt it from me, besides that, yee and I
owe an equall respect vnto her memory, and all other
danger is long since past. . . .

[The Nun then tells how the Marquis was informed of Isabella's birth.] Behold the truth of the History, to which, I sweare to you, I haue added nothing of my owne, but deliuered the simple truth of all as it past; being one of the seldomest seene, and rarest passages carried in this kinde, that I thinke hath beene lightly
167–71 heard, or reade of; and by relation wherof, I hope I shall not haue diuerted, or slackt either of you in the offices of that amity, which the mutuall opinions of your nere alliance each to other hath ingendered betweene you: and wherein (though yee may in truth discouer the mistaking of your beleefes hitherto) yet your vertues I know will smoothe ouer greater errours, for the honour of your house, and the memory of so worthy a woman as she was. . . .

229–30 I would not Sister (said *Hipolito*) for the better halfe of my life but you had brought me this vnexpected quiet, and drawne me out of the conflict my soule was in, and rebellion against mee, and my destinies, against all my dearest desires, nay, against Heauen it selfe, for hauing plunged mee into a gulfe of miseries so deepe, as no other thing but the remedie this your discourse may prepare for me, can deliuer me out of. . . .

Isabella, though she made shew that these discourses displeased her, and that she beleeued the tale of her Mothers loues to be but a cunning imposture of her Aunts, to draw her to her Brothers desires, neuerthelesse this serued for the first excuse of their loues, and to cleare them of those difficulties which till now had diuided them; for in the end, led by her destinies, woone by her Aunts perswasions, with the oaths and assurances shee gaue her of the truth of her relation, and by the teares and coniurations of *Hipolito*, but chiefly by the force of loue, shee yielded her selfe wholly to his power: for alas, how can a silly Maid maintaine her libertie against him who subdues all whom he will, and euen when he will to his yoke and subiection.

APPENDIX II

Lineation

For a discussion of the problems presented by lineation in this and other Middleton texts, see Introduction, pp. xxx–xxxii. The following list records all departures from the octavo, together with a few emendations proposed by other editors but not accepted in the present text.

I. i. 155–6. must/Leave her still] *This ed.;* must leave her/Still *O;* must leave/Her still *Dilke.*

159–60. night. Marry/It] *Dyce;* night:/Marry it *O.*

I. ii. 21–2. 'Twas . . . seemed] *Dyce;* 'Twas . . . that/Being . . . seem'd *O.*

93–104. Now . . . safe] *O; prose in Dilke;* Now . . . 'em,/There . . . complaint/Of . . . struck/A . . .egg. /An . . . time/The . . . am/In . . . eyes/In . . . No,/Were . . . head,/I . . . that./I . . . play,/I . . . Guardianer!/Prithee . . . safe *Dyce.*

137–8. cacklings of geese/In] *Bullen;* cacklings/Of Geese *O.*

141–2. staff; you were/Up] *Parker;* staff;/You were up *O;* staff; you were up/ *Dyce.*

152–3. would; but/'Twas] *O;* would;/But 'twas *Oliphant.*

174–5. look sometimes./By'r] *Dyce;* look/Sometimes by'r *O.*

218. that? Methought] *Oliphant;* that?/Methought *O.*

I. iii. 78–9. then,/Away, sir] *Dyce;* then, away Sir./ *O.*

II. i. 1–2. A . . . by 't] *O; prose in Ellis.*

II. ii. 33–4. ware./Within there!] *Dilke;* ware. Within there!/ *O.*

42–3. dish./Signor] *Dilke; O has* 'Seignior Fabritio' *on next line but as if continuing a single verse-line.*

44. sir, I] *O;* Sir,/I *Dyce.*

95. Sordido. I] *This ed.; two lines in O.*

86–92. That's . . . pottage] *This ed.;* That's . . . list./A . . . hope;/I'll . . . Pottage (*prose*) *O; prose throughout in Dilke;* That's . . . list./A . . . pottage (*prose*) *White;*

That's . . . list./A . . . hope;/I'll . . . congregation/ If . . . licence:/My . . . herb-woman,/That . . . nose-gays/And . . . pottage *Dyce.*

124–5. How . . . skin] *This ed.;* How . . . too;/I . . . skin *O.*

130–1. 'Faith . . . penthouse] *This ed.;* 'Faith . . . Farthingale,/Is . . . Pent-house *O.*

159–60 account ourselves/] *Dilke;* accompt/Our selves *O.*

258–9. one,/And] *Dyce; one line in O.*

259–60. intentions/Are] *Dyce; one line in O.*

415–16. Yes . . . game] *Dyce; one line (run on) in O.*

III. i. 2–3. Or . . . since] *Dilke; one line in O.*

8–12. I'd . . . Lady (*prose*)] *This ed.;* I'll . . . me/Again . . . any/That . . . mother/Fell . . . sometime/A . . . Lady/ *O.*

III. ii. 44–5. Unless . . . pride] *Dyce; one line in O.*

99–102. A . . . too] *This ed.;* A . . . Gentlewoman ?/I . . . Sir ?/At . . . Sir./There's . . . too *O.*

179–80. You . . . hope] *Dyce;* You . . . me./But . . . hope *O.*

III. iii. 59–60. Yes . . . now] *Dyce; one line in O.*

102. indeed; where] *O;* indeed/Where *Oliphant.*

148–52. *But . . . me] This ed.; But . . . fresh/In . . . be/ Mother . . . me O; But . . . blood/Force . . . cheek,/ She . . . be/Mother . . . me Dilke.*

153–6. Here's . . . kitlings (*prose*)] *in O printed in a column parallel to that of the song, ll. 143–52;* Here's . . . Pish/I . . . now,/Of . . . Oxen,/Then . . . Catsguts,/And . . . Kitlings *Dyce.*

190–1. sir ?/He . . . command] *O;* Sir ? He shall/Command *Dyce.*

219–20. Here's . . . minstrels (*prose*)] *Dilke;* Here's . . . him/Pay . . . Minstrels *O;* Here's . . . finds/The . . . minstrels *Dyce.*

250–1. Whose . . . oil] *Dilke; one line in O.*

365. Why . . . dream] *O;* Why sure/This . . . dream *Dyce.*

III. iv. 36. Thus . . . alas] *O;* Thus . . . into;/When alas/*Dyce.*

72–4. They . . . last (*prose*)] *Dilke;* They . . . better/Then . . . them ?/And . . . last *O.*

96-7. 'Twill . . . enough (*prose*)] *O;* 'Twill . . . Sordido,/ We . . . enough *Dyce.*

107–8. They'll . . . so] *This ed.;* They'll . . . Gamesters/ Never . . . so *O;* They'll . . . matter:/Wise gamesters/Never . . . so *Dyce.*

130–1. 'Faith . . . sweetheart] *Dilke; one line in O.*

	134–6.	Nay . . . bagpipes] *Dyce; prose in O.*
IV. i.	3–4.	St Anthony's . . . truer] *Dyce; one line in O.*
	32.	Restraint . . . days] *O;* Restraint/Breeds . . . days *Dyce.*
	57.	Will . . . spurs] *Bullen;* Will . . . pair ?/The . . . Spurs *O.*
	59–60.	I . . . time] *Bullen;* I . . . you/In . . . time./In . . . time *O.*
	127–8.	It . . . there] *Dyce; one line in O.*
	163–4.	He . . . talk] *Dyce; one line in O.*
IV. ii.	1–2.	The . . . him] *This ed.;* The . . . baseness/So . . . him *O;* The . . . baseness/So . . . Sun/Do . . . him *Dilke.*
	83–6.	Nay . . . myself (*prose*)] *Dyce;* Nay . . . Sir,/Y'have . . . wife/Next . . . self *O.*
	119–22.	Her . . . sure (*prose*)] *Dyce;* Her . . . forsooth;/I . . . Maid./Now . . . Belly:/This . . . sure *O.*
V. i.	10–12.	Prithee . . . then] *Dyce; prose in O.*
	26.	Away . . . part] *O;* Away,/List . . . part *Dyce.*
V. ii.	22–3.	In . . . on] *Dilke; one line in O.*
	73–80.	*Juno . . . equally*] *Dilke;* Iuno . . . *bodies,/Ty'st . . . marriage-maker,/Pitty . . . me,/Nor . . . equally O.*
	123–4.	This . . . lords] *Dilke; one line in O.*
	127.	Stark . . . that ?] *O;* Stark . . . away!/How's that ?/ *Dyce.*
	142–3.	I . . . How] *O;* I . . . lords,/We . . . How *Dyce.*
	168–9.	Behold . . . point] *Dyce; one line in O.*

APPENDIX III

Press Variants

A list of the copies collated and the abbreviations used will be found in the Introduction, p. xx.

The reading before the bracket is that of the corrected state of the forme.

SHEET H (inner forme)

Corrected: BM1, BM2, D1, D2, Bod1, Bod2, W, C, Tr, Br, F, Hunt, H, Y, Pr, T, N, Ch, B.

Uncorrected: Con.

Sig. H1v.
I. ii. 117 exercife] exercife,
124 Sir ?] Sir,

Sig. H2r.
I. ii. 162 it.] it,

Sig. H5v.
pagination 106] 306

Sig. H8r.
II. i. 119 Fathers] Fathers,

SHEET I (inner forme)

Corrected: BM1, BM2, D1, D2, Bod1, W, Tr, Br, Con, F, Hunt, H, Y, T, Ch, B.

Uncorrected: Bod2, C, Pr, N.

Sig. I1v.
II. i. 211 now;] now,
213 either;] either,
226 Love] love
226 Sir;] Sir,
231 her] her,
233 Art] art

Sig. I2r.
II. ii. 8 window;] window,
16 folly;] folly,
21 heart!] heart;

Sig. I3v.
II. ii. 74 vein] vain
79 heir!] heir.

Sig. I3v.
II. ii. 85 Ward,] Ward
87 anywhere] any where
90 Herb-woman] Herb-woman,

Sig. I5v.
II. ii. 179 evening!] evening,
187 hearts-eafe ?] hearts-eafe.
201 requeft ?] requeft

Sig. I6r.
II. ii. 205 now] now,
211 truth;] truth,

Sig. I8r.
II. ii. 309 Simplicitie] Simplicities

SHEET M (*inner forme*)
Corrected: BM1, BM2, D1, D2, Bod1, Bod2, W, Br, Con, F, H, Y, Pr, B.
Uncorrected: Tr, C, Hunt, N, T, Ch.

Sig. M1v.
III. iv. 62 by,] by;
71 well ?] well.
79 bottom ?] bottom:

Sig. M2r.
III. iv. 83 th] th'
87 dancing ?] dancing,
100 Handkercheif;] Handkercheif,

Sig. M3v.
IV. i. 22.1 *Exeunt*] *Exit*
27 enough,] enough;
28 me;] me,
30 kinred;] kinred,
31 days;] days,
36 me;] me,

Sig. M4r.
IV. i. 53 Sir ?] Sir.
55 Slippers;] Slippers ?
56 Shoomaker ?] Shoomaker,
57 pair ?] pair,

Sig. M5v.
IV. i. 124 go,] go
128 there ?] there.

Sig. M6r.
IV. i. 134 honor's] honor:
139 poyſe] poyſe,
140 Of] If
142 Siſter ?] Siſter;
145 Lord!] Lord:
148 faſt;] faſt,

Sig. M7v.
IV. i. 228 done] done,
232 minutes] minuts
235 now!] now,
236 on't;] on't,

Sig. M8r.
IV. i. 243 Brother;] Brother,
246 beauty] beauty;
247 neither ?] neither:
249 reſiſt ?] reſiſt,
257 place] place,
259 converſion] converſion,
260 Hymn] Himn
263 Lord!] Lord:

A reading on Sig. G5v may be either a press- or inking-variant:
SHEET G (*inner forme*)
Corrected: BM2, Bod1, Bod2, W, Tr, Br, C, Con, F, Hunt, H, Y, Pr, T, N, Ch, B.
Uncorrected: BM1, D1, D2.

Sig. G5v.
I. i. 77 year,] year;

A number of apparent variants are not recorded in the above list. On G4v (I. i. 42) nine copies (BM1, D1, D2, Bod1, Tr, Hunt, T, Ch, B) read 'mine,' while the rest lack the comma. Since no adjustment was made in spacing, this variant was probably due, not to press-correction, but to the stop falling out during the machining of outer G. Three probable inking-variants are: H1v (I. ii. 111) do't:] do't.; H5r (I. iii. 101.2) *Cardinal,*] *Cardinal*; N5v (IV. iii. 44) sanctuary;] sanctuary,. The apparent reading 'gois' (for 'goes') on M3r (IV. i. 1) in the Huntington copy is probably due to a distortion of the 'e' impression due to dirt on the type-surface. Two apparent colons in the Folger copy, after 'perfect' (N8r, V. ii. 70) and 'me' (O1r, V. ii. 114) are due to a spot of printer's ink on the copy, immediately above the full-stop of other copies (information given privately by Dr James G. McManaway). The reading given in Jacobs as that of the Texas and Harvard copies (I7r, II. ii. 243) 'refpect' in place of the other copies' 'refpect' is again probably due to inking: there is no other evidence of press-correction of the outer forme of I.

A copy of *Two New Playes* in the library of Massey College, University of Toronto, shows the corrected states of H inner, I inner and M inner; it also has the 'correction' 'year,' on G5v. I am indebted for this information to Mr Thomas A. Lytle of Bishop's University, Lennoxville, Quebec.

Glossarial Index to the Commentary

This index lists words and phrases which have been explained in the Commentary. Words are normally listed in their uninflected form, but phrases are given the form in which they appear in the text, and are normally cross-indexed under each key word. Where the Commentary lemma is a simple line-reference, the annotation has been indexed under a key word or words from the appropriate passage in the text. An asterisk before a word indicates that the meaning given in the Commentary is not covered, or only partly covered, in the *O.E.D.*, or that the dates given in the *O.E.D.* for this meaning are significantly modified.